P9-BZT-627

MY FIRST COUP D'ETAT

MY FIRST COUP D'ETAT

*And Other True Stories from the
Lost Decades of Africa*

John Dramani Mahama

B L O O M S B U R Y
NEW YORK · LONDON · NEW DELHI · SYDNEY

Published by Bloomsbury USA, New York

All papers used by Bloomsbury USA are natural, recyclable products made
from wood grown in well-managed forests. The manufacturing processes
conform to the environmental regulations of the country of origin.

LIBRARY OF CONGRESS CATALOGING-IN-PUBLICATION DATA

Mahama, John Dramani, 1958–
My first coup d'etat and other true stories from the lost decades of Africa /
John Dramani Mahama.—1st U.S. ed.
p.   cm.
ISBN 978-1-60819-859-7
1. Mahama, John Dramani, 1958– 2. Ghana—History—1957–
3. Ghana—History—Coup d'etat, 1966. 4. Vice-presidents—Ghana—
Biography. 5. Ghana—Biography. I. Title.
DT512.3.M35A3 2012
966.705'4092—dc23
[B]
2011053052

First U.S. edition 2012

3 5 7 9 10 8 6 4 2

Typeset by Westchester Book Group
Printed in the U.S.A. by Quad/Graphics, Fairfield, Pennsylvania

To the memory of my father, Mr. E. A. Mahama,
a man of humility and integrity, who lived
in service to his family, his people, and his nation

We plan our lives according to a dream that came to us in
our childhood, and we find that life alters our plans.
And yet, at the end, from a rare height, we also see that
our dream was our fate. It's just that providence had
other ideas as to how we would get there. Destiny
plans a different route, or turns the dream around,
as if it were a riddle, and fulfils the dream in
ways we couldn't have expected.

—BEN OKRI

CONTENTS

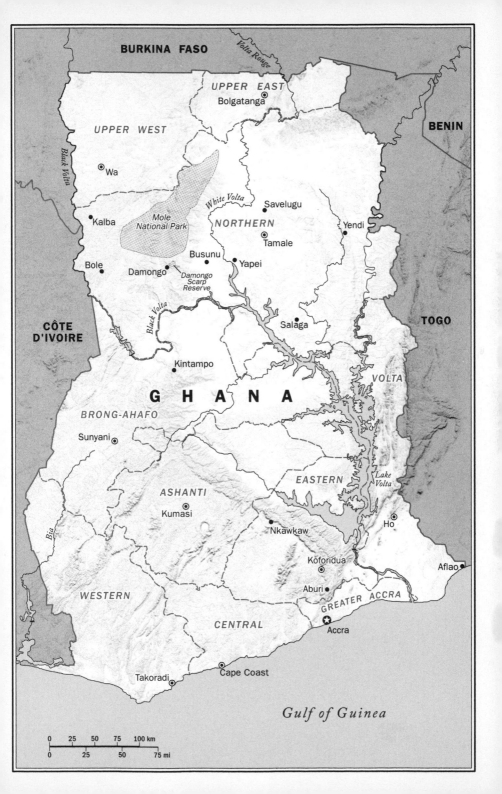

AUTHOR'S NOTE

This is a work of nonfiction. I have changed the names of some individuals and modified identifying features, including physical descriptions and occupations, in order to preserve their anonymity. Occasionally, timelines have been compressed in order to further preserve privacy and to maintain narrative flow. The goal in all cases was to protect people's privacy without damaging the integrity of the story.

INTRODUCTION:
THE "LOST DECADES"

THERE IS A period of time often referred to as the "lost decades" of Africa. That description speaks to the dismal post-independence performance of African countries during the 1970s and 1980s into the early part of the 1990s. The median per capita growth of developing African countries during those "lost decades" was 0.0 percent. It was a period of crippling stagnation, especially when compared with the era of liberation that preceded it, within which is also included the initial post-colonial period that began in the late 1950s and continued throughout the 1960s and the early 1970s.

The description "lost decades" is used primarily to address matters of economy and development, but during those years, other aspects of life in Africa were undergoing an equally marked period of stagnation, particularly the arts. During the era of liberation, an entire generation of visual art, literature, music, and international cultural exchange was empowered by the electricity of a continent shaking off its oppression. The Western world (and by that I mean the United States of America, Canada, Australia, and the countries in Europe, collectively) was introduced to dashikis, *geles*, *fufu*, and *jollof* rice; it learned the rhythms of highlife from Osibisa and of *makossa* from Manu Dibango. Miriam Makeba's hit single "Pata Pata" had us all, in every country and on every continent, singing in Xhosa; and Fela Anikulapo Kuti's new musical alchemy that he called Afrobeat—which has recently made a ferocious comeback—was already turning heads and moving feet.

An entire canon of literature was created with books like *Things Fall Apart* by Chinua Achebe, *Weep Not, Child* by Ngũgĩ wa Thiong'o, *The Beautyful Ones Are Not Yet Born* by Ayi Kwei Armah, and *So Long a Letter* by Mariama Ba. Yet this period of productivity, excitement, and unbounded creativity was short-lived as, during the 1960s, the continent ever so slowly devolved into what would ultimately become a lengthy cycle of political unrest and then, by the mid-1970s, made a rapid plunge into poverty.

During the "lost decades," Ghana—and in fact all of Africa—experienced a "brain drain," a mass exodus that found many of our artists, intellectuals, professionals, and politicians living abroad in either a forced or a self-imposed exile. As a result, that period of time and the direct impact it had on the cultural, educational, and political lives of those who remained has not been heavily documented, especially not from a personal perspective. They are years that are rarely discussed, years of untold difficulty and hardship, of ever-present hunger and fear. They are years that many have, understandably, tried to forget, to erase entirely from memory.

But rarely is anything all bad. There are always pockets of light, however small, to be found during periods of darkness. A number of us who stayed during the "lost decades" and lived through the difficulties, whether by choice or by force, discovered that it was, ironically, during this time that we found ourselves, our voices.

For many individuals, there is a moment that stands out as pivotal to the awakening of their consciousness. Often that moment can feel like a harbinger of disaster: the first tremors of an earthquake or rains of a hurricane, the eruption of civil war or riots, an assassination or a coup d'etat. It is a moment that serves as the line of demarcation, separating the certainty of what was from the uncertainty of what lies ahead. It is a moment in which you suddenly become aware of who you are; you become aware of the fragility and unpredictability of the world in which you live. Ghana's descent into the "lost decades" began with such a moment, with the coup d'etat that unseated our first president, Dr. Kwame Nkrumah. When I look back on my life, it's clear to me that this moment marked the awakening of my consciousness. It changed my life and influenced all the moments that followed.

The "lost decades," from that first coup d'etat to the final reintroduction of constitutional rule, were the years that defined my life, and as a result, they are the years that I have wanted most to write about, to commit not only to memory, but to paper. It was my desire, through the stories in this book, to document the effects that the events that occurred during those years had on the country and, more personally and specifically, on my family and me.

Each of the stories in this book is a memory of a specific incident or set of incidents, and true to the zigzag way in which memory works during the piecing together of a narrative, they are more fluidly circular than strictly linear, pulling in whatever is relevant and necessary—such as historical facts and background—to complete the picture and help the experience make sense. Throughout the book, from one story to another, there are instances of what, on the surface, might seem to be repetition or overlap of the narration of events. However, the details of each event described are specific to the story being told and the contextual understanding of it. Because Africa is often thought of in monolithic terms, I also made every effort to be as specific as possible in the descriptions and details that I provided of the lifestyle and general atmosphere of the various towns, villages, and cities in Ghana and Nigeria. I wanted, in these stories, to explore the diversity that exists in Ghana, which is but one of the continent's fifty-four countries.

Furthermore, I wanted to display the differences between life in the northern part of the country, which remains the most underserved, and life in the southern part. I also wanted to highlight the vibrant life in the urban centres that are becoming more and more modernised and show the contrast between it and the rapidly vanishing traditional life in the villages.

The world I try to capture in this book, through these stories, does not exist anymore. There are times when I stop and wonder if it ever did exist or if I merely dreamed it into being. Some of the experiences I either had or heard about were that incomprehensible. The places have changed and the customs have died out. Even some of the vernacular has become extinct. In these stories there are words, expressions, and phrases I use that are specific to the time and place and experience I am describing but are no longer part of our everyday vocabulary.

In Ghana, as in most African countries that were part of the Commonwealth, we have inherited words and terminology that are part of the so-called Queen's English. We have also bastardised words and terminology and made them our own. Since language is a primary element of civilisation, of culture, I have chosen to be representative and authentic, in both the narrative and the dialogue, of who we were and how we were in those days.

Nowadays so much of the information about Africa that reaches the rest of the world is negative, and it places our continent in an unflattering and almost irredeemable light. As a resident African, and a political leader of an African nation, I am saddened by this, because however "factual" the information, it's never the entire truth. Headlines are made of isolated, often aberrational, events. Statistical data are usually presented without context or explanation. There are a million stories that can fill all the blank spaces of what has been left unspoken and unwritten, stories that will shift your perceptions and challenge your prejudices.

Though my intention in writing the stories in this collection was merely to present the life that I led and the Ghana and Africa that I knew during a specific period of time, not to alter any preconceived notions, I do hope that in reading them, you will suspend all previous opinions or judgements and allow the reality of these recollections to occupy its own canvas.

I suspect that Africa, as the motherland of humankind, has always been and will always be something of an enigma. How and why, as civilisations on other continents perished, the African continent and its people have survived throughout the centuries, despite countless wars, diseases, and natural disasters, may very well remain an ongoing mystery. If, however, my own experiences during the "lost decades" can serve as a guide, I would have to say the key to that mystery must be somewhere in our stories, in the seeming minutiae of the day-in and day-out, the customs and the rituals, the adaptations and requisite improvisations, the mistakes and the miracles. The key to Africa's survival has always been, and will most likely always be, in the story of its people, the paradoxical simplicity and complexity of our lives.

MY FIRST COUP D'ETAT

IT HAPPENED ON February 24, 1966. I was seven years old, a class 2 pupil in the primary division of Achimota, an elite boarding school in Accra, Ghana's capital. That day there was a lot of commotion; teachers rushed about in a noticeably scattered fashion and huddled in corners whispering. It did not take long for the news to spread, first through the upper school's student body, then down to the younger pupils.

The words I heard people speaking that day seemed to hold a certain air of mystery and urgency, especially the phrase *coup d'etat*, which was being repeated like a mantra. I had never heard it before. Yet I knew, without having to be told, that it did not belong to any of the six languages I spoke: not Gonja, not Twi, not Hausa, Dagbani, or Ga; not even English. To my child's ear, the phrase sounded exciting, like a game that all the upper-form students would soon be playing; and from the moment I first heard it—coup d'etat—I wished I could learn how to play this new game as well.

The day after the coup, once the initial flurry of fear and excitement had passed, our teachers explained that it wasn't a game after all; the phrase *coup d'etat* apparently meant the government had been overthrown. Even in plain English the concept seemed nonsensical to me. How can you overthrow an entire government? And what exactly are you throwing it over?

Days passed. The news became more precise and I began to piece bits of information together. While our president, Osagyefo Dr. Kwame Nkrumah, was on an official visit to North Vietnam, the military had seized control of Ghana.

Dr. Nkrumah was Ghana's first president, and he was a true visionary. At the time it was fairly commonplace for Ghanaian intellectuals to travel to Europe to complete their education and receive their advanced degrees. Dr. Nkrumah opted instead to attend institutions in the United States, receiving his undergraduate degree at Lincoln University and graduate degrees at the University of Pennsylvania.

Dr. Nkrumah's return to Ghana upon the completion of his studies added more steam to the struggle for independence. He, along with Dr. J. B. Danquah, Dr. Ebenezer Ako-Adjei, Mr. Edward Akufo-Addo, Mr. William Ofori-Atta, and Mr. Emmanuel Obetsebi-Lamptey, became affectionately known as "the Big Six" for their frontline role in the fight against British colonialism. They were victorious in that fight, and on March 6, 1957, the British colony called Gold Coast became Ghana, an independent self-ruled nation. As a result, Ghana was and still is the country heralded as the trailblazer of the African liberation movement.

Ghana's freedom sparked a chain reaction in sub-Saharan Africa, with at least sixteen nations becoming independent in 1960 alone. Dr. Nkrumah, who was a leading Pan-Africanist and also one of the founding fathers of the Organisation of

African Unity, which in 2002 became the African Union, was a dynamic and controversial figure with a far-reaching vision for Ghana and for Africa. He was revered by many, but there were some who either did not share that vision or did not approve of his methods for making it a reality. The transition from having been a colony to becoming a country had been relatively smooth for Ghana, especially when compared with other fledgling nations that were rife with rebellion. Conditions did not seem at all ripe for a coup, not in Ghana. Three years prior, there had been a coup in the neighbouring country of Togo, during which the president, Sylvanus Olympio, was assassinated. That was the first major coup of its sort in contemporary Africa, and it left the continent shaken. Still, the political climate in Ghana was not as hostile as it had been in Togo, and Ghanaian citizens seemed less inclined toward violence; this is why our first coup d'etat was such a shock to everyone.

At Achimota we heard that all the ministers of state had been arrested. This particular titbit of information gave me pause because my father was a minister of state. Even so, I don't think I was able to fully absorb all the implications. Not then. Perhaps it was because I had not received word from my family that anything was wrong. Or it might have been because I felt, as children so often do, that my family and I were somehow shielded, automatically exempt from anything tragic.

The coup d'etat became real to me, an event that constituted more than just words, in early April when my school vacated for the Easter holidays and nobody came to pick me up. I watched as all the other children left with their relations. Room after room of each dormitory was emptied of its occupants until mine were the only footsteps in the halls. And still, no one came.

At Achimota, there was an adult, a maternal figure of sorts, assigned to each dormitory in the primary school. We called them aunties. Each auntie generally had about ten small boys in her charge. The aunties looked after us. They made sure we woke up on time, had our baths, ate our breakfasts, and were not late to our studies. They saw to our overall well-being.

That night I slept at school by myself, the only child. My auntie, a stereotypical schoolmarm, was also in the dormitory. The next morning, my auntie took me to the headmistress and sought permission to leave the school grounds with me. She wanted to try to locate my house so that she could take me to my family or, more accurately, to my father and siblings. When my father took his first government post, as a member of Parliament and then as a minister of state, my mother did not relocate south to the capital with him. She remained in his family home in the town of Bole, which is in the northern region of Ghana, roughly six hundred kilometres from Accra. The arrangement whereby they were separated for the purposes of his employment was not uncommon then, nor is it now.

My auntie was granted permission for us to leave. We took a taxi from the Achimota campus to Kanda, the section of Accra in which my father's house was located. Back then, Kanda was a solidly upper-middle-class enclave, populated primarily with ministers of state and members of Parliament.

Almost immediately after we left Achimota, I began noticing plenty of military vehicles, each packed full of men. Never had I seen that many soldiers in town, and all of them were armed. It was simply unheard of. In those days, a "soldier sight-ing" right in the middle of town was so rare that it made you stop in your tracks. Soldiers generally stayed in the barracks, their self-contained city within a city.

I'd been to the barracks before. They were located in Burma Camp, the main military base in Accra. My elder sister Rose lived there with her husband, a captain in the army. Our father would occasionally take some of us children to Burma Camp to spend time with our big sister. Rose, who was statu-esque and as pretty as a cinema star, worked as a stewardess for Ghana Airways. She travelled often, so being able to see her was always a treat.

Somehow, driving through Accra with my auntie felt like driving through the barracks, which reminded me of those visits to Rose with our father, which in turn made me all the more homesick. As the taxi approached my home, I noticed that the house and the area immediately surrounding it was filled with police officers and soldiers. They had even erected tents in which they seemed to have taken up residence. The taxi stopped and my auntie got out. I followed sheepishly, my tiny fingers barely resting in the palm of the hand that she held out to me.

My auntie greeted the soldier who appeared to be in charge. Her tone was official and respectful. Not warm, but also not stern. It was the sort of voice she would use to speak with the parents of a badly behaved student.

"We are in search of Honourable E. A. Mahama," she said, using the honorific associated with my father's political posi-tion.

The soldier looked at us through bloodshot eyes. His presence was imposing, a tad threatening. He sucked his teeth and then hesitated, as though he was contemplating whether or not we were even worthy of a response. When he finally did speak, his tone was gruff, especially in contrast with my auntie's.

"He no longer lives here."

My auntie did not need to hear any more. She knew the information would not be good. She closed her fingers around my hand, tightening her grip, then turned on her heels and rushed away. We marched hastily to the taxi, which had been waiting for us, and we got in. The driver, who had witnessed my auntie's interaction with the soldier and sensed the possibility of danger, quickly spun the vehicle around. As he did that, I too spun around so my body was no longer facing forward. I knelt on the seat, leaned my chin and elbows against the top of its backrest, and stared out the rear window, wondering if I would ever see our home again, if I would ever see my father again.

I did not cry that day; but in the days, weeks, and months that followed there were numerous times when I would remember it all—the makeshift tents, the soldier's bloodshot eyes, his weapon, the dirt and dust rising from the tyres and filling the air as the taxi drove me away into a cloud of uncertainty. I would remember, and I would weep.

"Where do you think your family might be?" my auntie and the headmistress asked me the morning after our fruitless attempt to find my father. It was a harrowing question, one that I was ill prepared, at seven years old, to contemplate, let alone answer.

"Do you have any aunties or sisters who might come for you?" I suppose because my mother was so far away, they never stopped to consider the possibility of her coming to collect me. At that time, the northern region of Ghana seemed like an entirely different country. It was the hinterland. Even I could not envision my mother making her way to Accra to find me, not without my father sending his driver, Mallam, for her.

For a moment, my mind went blank and all I could do was panic. What if there was no one left to come for me? What would I do? Where would I go? I'd barely had an opportunity to entertain the fear that had begun to slowly engulf me when all the details of what, before the coup d'etat, had once been my life suddenly came rushing back to me.

"Oh," I said, my eyes widening with the renewed sense of self. It was the first time since the day of the coup that I'd displayed anything resembling confidence or certainty. "I have a sister!" I went on to tell my auntie and the headmistress about Rose in Burma Camp. Using the telephone directory, they were able to track down Rose, who thankfully was in town and immediately came to pick me up.

Even as I waited for Rose to come for me, despite the frantic efforts of my auntie and the headmistress to find my father, we still had not received any word of his whereabouts. My auntie and the headmistress tried as best they could, with smiles and toffee, to shield me from their rising anxiety, but I could feel it bouncing off the quick sideways glances they shot each other and taking flight like some dark, winged creature on the breath of their long, exhausted exhales. It was rumoured that people had been executed. I knew the headmistress and my auntie were worried my father might have been among them. I was worried, too.

It was at Rose's that I discovered our father was not dead; he had been detained the day after the coup. My other siblings had been picked up by their mothers and various other relatives and were now scattered all throughout the country. It would be quite a while before I would see them again, but when I did, they told me what happened on the day of the coup and immediately after.

The military had taken over the Flagstaff House, which was the official residence of Dr. Nkrumah, and then they had gone on to take over the broadcasting station. It was announced over the airwaves that there had been a coup d'etat. All the ministers of state, members of Parliament, district commissioners, chairmen, and secretaries of the ruling political party, as well as a long list of other people of interest, were requested to report to the nearest police station for "their own safety."

Dad gathered a few things, got in his car, and drove to the police station, where he was sent into interrogation and then, much to everyone's surprise, placed into custody. After a night in custody at the police station, he was transported to Ussher Fort, one of the various slave forts that were built in the mid-1600s by the Dutch colonists, which was now being used as a prison.

The National Liberation Council, the name of the governing body that was instituted by the military officials who'd staged the coup, had set up a Commission of Inquiry to investigate members of Dr. Nkrumah's government, ostensibly for the purpose of uncovering activities, acquisitions, and alliances that could be deemed inappropriate and therefore punishable. My father and his political colleagues who had also been detained were made to report to the commission repeatedly for questioning. Once the commission had obtained all the information it needed to conclude its investigations and present a report, those individuals were either released or recommended for legal action.

As coup d'etats go, that first one which took place in Ghana was swift and unexpected. It is sometimes incorrectly referred to in texts as a bloodless coup, yet it was anything but. The night after the coup while my eldest brother, Peter, was being taken to his mother's house, the taxi in which he was riding was made to stop at the Flagstaff House. Once there, the military officer posted at the entrance ordered Peter and the other children in the taxi to close their eyes while he interrogated the driver. They did as they were told, but not before Peter had caught a glimpse of the courtyard in front of the Flagstaff House, which, he later told me, was filled with rows and rows of dead bodies. It is an image that Peter, who was only ten years old at the time, has never been able to forget.

My father remained in detention, a prisoner of politics, for well over a year. Dr. Kwame Nkrumah, who'd never been able to return home after what was intended to be a brief official visit abroad, remained in exile until his death in 1972. When I was not in school at Achimota, I lived with Rose and her husband at Burma Camp.

Though I loved my sister and did not associate either her or her husband with what had happened to my father, the irony of my having nowhere else to live except the military barracks because of my father's detention after a military coup was not at all lost on me. But what could I do? What could any of us do?

By the time my father was released from prison, Ghana was a much different country. Not surprisingly, I was a much different boy, the course of my future having already been irreversibly impacted by that unspeakable period of violence.

THE DISTRICT
COMMISSIONER'S HAT

THIS IS WHAT I remember: riding in the car with my mother. Mallam, my father's favourite driver, was behind the wheel. My mother and I were in the back, she sitting straight and stiff, intently studying the passing scenery as though she might at some undetermined time in the future be asked to recall it: the rough roads that turned from mud brown to clay red the farther south we travelled, the trees bending and whistling in the wind, their branches swaying back and forth as though waving "hello" or "good-bye" to each passing vehicle.

I sat beside my mother, my three-year-old body tucked tightly in the space between her rib cage and the slender but sturdy arm she was using to hold me in a half embrace. I don't remember being nervous, but surely I must have been. I clung to my mother, studying her face as intently as she was studying the scenery. She was sloe-eyed and her pupils shone brightly with a flame that seemed to be rekindled after each blink. Her skin was dark and liquid-smooth, like chocolate after it has been placed on the fire and allowed to melt for one full minute.

Not knowing when I might see her again, I etched the details of her face into memory.

She was taking me to live with my father, just as she had taken my brother Alfred two years before. Alfred loved living with our father, but for me, the prospect was like venturing into the unknown, and at that age I found tremendous comfort in the familiar. Though I enjoyed the time I spent with my father whenever he would come and visit my mother and me, he was not a constant presence in my life, which for all intents and purposes made him a virtual stranger. And now I was being taken to live with him.

Damongo is my mother's hometown, a respectable-sized village in the northern region of Ghana, at the edge of Mole, the country's most popular game reserve. It was where I was born and spent the better part of my first year. My mother, Alfred, and I then moved to Bole, my father's hometown, which is about one hundred kilometres away. Bole was also a village, but Damongo, because of its location near the reserve, saw a bit more activity.

My father's house was on the outskirts of Bole. It was sizable, with six bedrooms and a large living room. Bole was not on the national grid, but we had a little diesel generator, which meant ours was the only house in the town with lights. Every night our generator would switch on at six and switch off at ten. Everybody else in town resorted to little paraffin lamps, and most nights, once the darkness had fully settled in, they would leave their homes, walk to our house, and stand by the roadside to stare. They would stare for what felt like hours, mesmerised by the brightness of the electric lights. Once the spell was broken, they would nonchalantly turn and walk away, with soft echoes of their conversation trailing behind them.

At the time, my father was a member of Parliament and a minister of state, so he didn't live with us. He was based in Accra, which was and still is the seat of government. That was where Mum and I were headed. Besides Alfred, I had two other brothers, Peter and Adam, who were already living with my dad. They were going to school, which was why my father had sent for me. He also wanted me to begin attending. Most children in Ghana start school at the age of six, but Dad wanted me to have an early advantage. He valued education with an unshakable passion. He saw it as one of the few risk-free endeavours in life. There was nothing to be lost from it and everything to be gained. In fact, if it hadn't been for the education he'd received by way of a chance encounter in his childhood with a cocky and annoyingly insistent Englishman, my father may well have ended up as some underemployed illiterate bemoaning the difficulties of his existence.

The first school I attended was a little day nursery in the Ringway Estates neighbourhood of Accra. I fared well at the school and quickly made friends with the other students. I was an observant child with an active imagination and an unbounded curiosity. This must have placed me directly in the path of my teacher's attention, because one afternoon when my father came to fetch me, the headmistress of the nursery asked to speak with him.

Since it was not a meeting for disciplinary purposes, I walked into the headmistress's office with my father, unafraid.

"Honourable Mahama," she said, motioning to the two seats positioned in front of her desk. My father sat down and I followed his lead. My feet did not reach the floor, so I slid myself to the very edge of the seat until I could tap my toes without lifting my heels. "This your little boy Dramani," the headmistress continued, calling me by what has now so many decades later evolved into my middle name. "I think he has the potential to make you really proud."

The instant she said this, I could feel the power of her prediction take root. I straightened my spine so that my bony little chest was puffed out. Until then I'd been listening only halfheartedly, but suddenly I cared to know how the headmistress had come to this conclusion and, more important, what I had to do to make my father always look at me with the sort of emotion I was seeing in his eyes. Already, my father had become the most important person in my life. Dad was a mild-mannered man. He was deeply committed to the job of fatherhood, and that dedication was evident in his warm and openly affectionate interactions with us, his children. Within days of my arrival in Accra, despite my sadness at my mother's return to Bole, I saw why Alfred loved living with Dad and I quickly began to feel right at home, as if I'd always been there. As if I belonged nowhere else. There was nothing I wanted more than to make my father proud of me.

The headmistress explained that she had an arrangement with Achimota College and School whereby they allowed her to send a few of the pupils from her nursery whom she felt were capable of excelling. She told my father that with his permission she would complete the forms for my admission and make arrangements for an interview. My father readily agreed and thanked her. We walked out of her office, his hand resting gently below my neck, as though he were patting me on the back for a job well done.

As far as schools were concerned, Achimota was considered the best of the best. It was founded by the colonial government with a great deal of assistance from several local chiefs. Construction on the school began in the mid-1920s. In 1925, the Prince of Wales paid an official visit and agreed to allow the school to use his name, so it was known for many years afterward as the Prince of Wales College. In 1926, the school admitted its first group of kindergartners. By the time I started attending Achimota in the mid-1960s, the school—including the primary and secondary divisions, which had been fully functioning for decades—was highly selective and had graduated some of the most intelligent and successful individuals not only in Ghana, but in all of Africa.

That history and prestige did not stop me from hating it. I wasn't aware that day in the headmistress's office that Achimota was a boarding school. Even at the interview, once I'd learned that boarding meant being away from home, how could I have been aware of the depth of loneliness that would accompany the experience? I was homesick all the time. It had been difficult to leave my mother, but at least I'd had family to buffer the pain. At Achimota, there was no one. I missed my brothers and I especially missed my father.

Though it was not unusual in Ghana for a student to attend a residential school at the secondary level, it was highly unusual for a six-year-old to be packed up and sent away, and that is exactly what I felt was being done to me. To add insult to injury, I was the only one in the family who had to go away to school. The others attended public school near our home. They would leave at the start of the day and return in the late afternoon, when they'd completed their studies. I didn't understand why I had been singled out like that by our father. It felt like punishment.

In Ghana, when you go to boarding school, you take with you a chopbox and a trunk. A chopbox is an unfinished wooden box with dimensions similar to those of a bedside chest of drawers. Chopboxes are where students keep their provisions, foodstuffs used to supplement whatever meals they are given, items like sugar; tin milk; Milo, a brand of chocolate and malt powder used to make hot cocoa drinks; *shitto*, which is a black pepper sauce; canned sardines; and *gari*, which is made from fresh cassava that has been grated, dried, and then fried over an open fire until it has a consistency similar to that of uncooked couscous or *atcheke*.

The trunks that boarding school pupils use are essentially steel boxes in which they can place their clothes and other belongings. In Ghana there is a particular pattern displayed on these sorts of steel trunks. They are painted a shiny black and then stamped all over with red half-moon designs.

When I began schooling at Achimota, I was outfitted with these necessities. My brothers gathered round as Mallam loaded my chopbox and trunk into the boot of the car, and they would tease me. It pained me to sit in the car with Mallam and be driven away. When I turned and looked through the rear windscreen, I could see my brothers talking and then doubling over into side-splitting laughter. I knew it was probably because Alfred was telling the others one of his jokes. He was known for his wit and sense of humour. There was never a dull moment if Alfred was close to you. I wondered how my brothers could be having so much fun while I was feeling so miserable, and how they could forget about me so quickly.

Of course, I made the best of my situation at school, and there were definitely moments of laughter and joy with the new friends I met. Nevertheless, it wasn't until one of the first Speech and Prize-giving Days held at Achimota that I began to fully comprehend the need for my presence there. I was ten years old and had just entered class 4. I received two prizes: one was for my performance in history and the other was for my performance in English. For my award, I was given two Charles Dickens novels, *Oliver Twist* and *David Copperfield*. I cherished those books more than anything else. I still remember one of my favourite quotes from *Oliver Twist*: "Surprises, like misfortunes, seldom come alone."

The best part of the entire experience was that the prizes were announced and the awards were given at an event that was attended by our parents. I was one of the youngest awardees. To this day, even considering all the accolades I have been blessed to receive thus far in my life, nothing can ever top those few precious moments of having my name called, of climbing up on that stage and having all the parents clap for me. And the best moment of all was when I looked into the audience and saw my father, his straight, pointed nose and calmly pensive expression. I noticed that my father was looking at me the way he had that day we'd sat in the headmistress's office.

Being chosen for those two awards was indeed a surprise. And, true to Dickens's words, it was a surprise that did not come alone. That was also the day my father explained to me why it was he had sent me to Achimota and how it was that he, too, had been chosen among all of his brothers to go away to school.

IT IS DIFFICULT, STILL, TO imagine that the fate of my entire family rested on the brim of a district commissioner's hat, but it did. During colonial times, the district commissioners were the most powerful people in the land, answering only to the governor, who oversaw the entire Gold Coast colony; and he in turn answered only to the queen or king of England.

On a more local and immediate level—but only in matters that were domestic and day-to-day—chiefs had the authority to legislate and adjudicate. It was an impressively effective system, known as "indirect rule," devised by the colonials to appease the chiefs and feign respect for the indigenous power structure while at the same time instituting a way to manage the larger population.

Interestingly, there is no word in any of the native Ghanaian languages for "chief." The proper translation is "king." This is the weight of power that the so-called chiefs and subchiefs had with the populace in their villages and kingdoms. With the colonial powers, however, there could be only one king or queen, the one who ruled the British Empire, and every person in every colony was but a subject. Period.

The chiefs were given a toothless-bulldog type of power. They were able to autonomously make decisions that affected the lives of individual people, but the more significant decisions, the ones that could potentially determine the future of the land and its entire populace, had to be approved, if not entirely instigated, by the colonial government.

My great-grandfather was a chief, the Soma Wura. He lived in a palace. It was not at all the Western world's version of a palace that has come to dominate the popular imagination. Nonetheless, it was a palace. During that era in Bole, the houses were made primarily of mud and roofed with thatch. The chief's palace consisted of one big round hut, which was where the chief sat in state with his court or council of elders, as they are called, and then a series of other huts behind it, set in an oval. A wall extended behind each of the huts to create an enclosure so the main access to the palace was through that stateroom. In that enclosure was a courtyard in which all the family activities, including cooking, took place.

Once you actually entered the compound you would be surrounded by the other huts, each of which had its specific purpose and resident. In all but one of these huts, the chief kept a wife. All of the wives lived with their children. The one hut that was not occupied by a wife was for the chief alone, a room of his own for work, peace, and quiet. Throughout the course of a week, the chief slept rotationally in the huts of his various wives. On the night when he did not have to fulfil any chiefly or husbandly duties, he would retire to his own hut and sleep all by himself.

In the round room, the stateroom, there was a slightly elevated platform covered with animal skins and soft pillows and cushions. It's where the chief, my great-grandfather, would sit. He would be flanked by the elders, who would sit along the walls, their backs pressed against the skins behind them. That is where my great-grandfather would hear cases and complaints ranging anywhere from theft and petty fraud to divorce. The person or people involved in the case would be seated in the centre, in the direct view of the chief and elders.

My father's mother was the Soma Wura's daughter, and the two of them lived in his palace. Often, after a woman has given birth, she returns to her family with the baby and resides there. Her family cares for both mother and child until such time as the child is deemed old enough to accompany his or her mother back to her marital home.

On this particular day, the day when my father met the Englishman, he was outside playing with his friends and various relations, cousins and uncles, some of whom were his age or even younger. His grandfather was in the stateroom with the elders, tending to chiefly matters. My father, like his young cousins and uncles, was dressed only in a pair of shorts. No shirt, no shoes, only the warm golden brown of his skin like just-baked bread. They heard a car approaching, and right away they abandoned whatever game they were playing and ran to the roadside to watch as it passed by. This was in the 1930s. Cars were a rarity. People travelled either by walking or by riding horses, and it was only the royals and the aristocrats who could afford horses. It was mostly the English people who owned cars, especially in that part of the country.

The children who had gathered by the dusty roadside to catch a glimpse of the car grew alarmed when it slowed down and then came to a complete stop right in front of the chief's palace. They stood watching in anticipation as the driver's-side door opened. Out stepped an Englishman who, despite the heat, was dressed in a safari-style suit and tie, blindingly shiny shoes, and the dashing, wide-brimmed khaki hat that was almost requisite among district commissioners.

When my father was young he had a herniated umbilicus, otherwise known as a big, protruding navel. As the district commissioner got out of the car and walked toward the palace, the throng of children moved in closer and surrounded him. He paved a path through them and walked steadily toward the chief's stateroom. One of the last children he passed was my father. For some reason, the district commissioner was enticed by my father's navel; he bent down and reached out, thumb and forefinger poised, and pinched it. This caused my father a great deal of pain, and his first instinct was to strike back. He raised his hand and swatted at the air, not thinking about or caring what he hit, whether it was the district commissioner's face, his body, or nothing at all.

The heel of my father's palm met the district commissioner's temple, just above his left eye, in a dirty, full-forced slap. The rest of my father's hand, the upper palm and its outstretched fingers, landed on the brim of the district commissioner's hat. The force of the blow caused the hat to tip over and fall off his head. Clearly bemused, the Englishman bent down and picked it up. He looked at my father, patted him forgivingly on the head, and said a few things in English that my father did not understand; he then continued on his way to the chief's stateroom.

The reason for the district commissioner's chance visit to the Soma Wura's palace was that the colonial government had decided to finally introduce formal education to the northern territories of the colony. Because there were only one or two schools for the entire region, the children who attended had to board. As a result, people in the north resisted the education that was being offered. They were apprehensive about turning their children over to be taken away by white men to God knows where. Because of this, the district commissioners went about the task of personalised recruitment, so determined were they to right the wrong that had been done to the northerners by the colonial government.

The Asante kingdom and the northern portion of what is now known as Ghana were the last parcels of land to be added by the British to the Gold Coast colony in the early 1900s. Believing that the inhabitants of the northern territories were better suited for labour than for intellectual endeavours, the colonials deliberately withheld formal education from them. While the inhabitants of the southern portion of the colony were sending their children off to reside and be educated at the newly established Prince of Wales College, the northerners were toiling in the gold mines and cocoa farms and fighting on the battlefields during the world wars.

The district commissioner had come to ask the Soma Wura to volunteer at least one of his many children to be educated. I imagine that while he was in the stateroom, the district commissioner sat on a bench or chair situated in the same spot as the cushions of the complainants whose cases my great-grandfather heard.

My great-grandfather, accustomed to being the decision maker, politely told the district commissioner that he did not have any children who were of school-going age. This was not entirely true, as the majority of the children who had gath-

ered round to greet the district commissioner's vehicle were
clearly old enough to attend school.

"What about the boy with the big navel?" the district commissioner asked. My great-grandfather frowned and refused
right away.

"No," the Soma Wura declared. "You said to give you one
of my children. He is not my child. He is my grandson. He cannot be sent away." The district commissioner insisted. It appeared that the small boy's fearlessness had stirred something
in him.

"I see something in that boy," he explained to the Soma
Wura. In this case, he told my great-grandfather, an exception
would be made. Instead of one of the Soma Wura's sons, the
district commissioner would take his grandson, because he
wanted that boy and none other. And he would not take no
for an answer.

The Soma Wura was also not accustomed to being refused
his desire. The two had reached an impasse, but it was clear
that the district commissioner held the ultimate power. He was
going to get what he came for; he would not allow his authority to be undermined. He reminded my great-grandfather that
sanctions could—and would—be applied if the Soma Wura did
not agree to send the boy to school.

The sanction that was routinely applied to chiefs who did
not, for whatever reason, conform to the requests and desires
of the district commissioners was a permanent removal from
power. So in actual fact, this process of recruitment for education was not at all voluntary; it was by force.

Naturally, my great-grandfather wanted to avoid having

sanctions applied and being removed from his position, but the situation was much more complex than it appeared on the surface. Even if my great-grandfather had wanted to acquiesce and allow the district commissioner to take his grandson, he could not do so without first seeking permission from the boy's father, who was also a chief, the Gbemfu Wura.

Within the hierarchy of chiefs, the Gbemfu Wura, my father's father, was at a level that was senior to the Soma Wura. So my great-grandfather found himself in the rather untenable position of having to go to the Gbemfu Wura, who, though married to his daughter, was also his senior in the chieftancy, and tell him of the district commissioner's request.

"The white man will not take any of my sons," the Soma Wura explained. "He says it is only your small boy he will take." The Gbemfu Wura knew full well the sanction that would be applied to the Soma Wura, and possibly even to him, if the boy was not handed over to the district commissioner, so he reluctantly agreed.

It was, rather, my father's mother who begged and pleaded with both her father and her husband to find some other solution, anything at all except giving her son away to the colonials. But what other solution was there? They sent my father, a boy of no more than five or six years old, away with the district commissioner as his mother screamed and wailed in the compound, believing with all her heart that she would never see her son again.

My father, along with the sons of chiefs from neighbouring towns and villages, went first to a school in Salaga, which was about two hundred kilometres from Bole. They made the journey by foot, all except my father, who, being too small to walk such a distance, was carried. Because the children were too young to travel alone, they were provided with escorts— colonial policemen, officers of the Gold Coast Constabulary. The sight of these men was not at all one that was taken lightly. They wore crisp khaki shirts with khaki knickerbockers that fell just below the knees. Around their waist was a red cummerbund-style wrap; around their lower legs, from the knees to the ankles, were stark white puttees. They did not wear shoes or boots; their feet were bare, always. And atop their heads was a red tarboosh, the ends of its tassel just grazing their left eyebrow.

Colonial policemen induced tremendous fear. They were a symbol of the British Empire's absolute authority. If the governor asked an officer of the Gold Coast Constabulary to bring you to him, then that is precisely what would happen. There was nothing you could do to prevent it; there was nowhere you could hide. You could climb to the sky, swim to the bottom of the river, or run deep into the forest, but that colonial policeman would find you and he would deliver you. "Massa say make I bring you," he would announce; then he would take you, hold you by the midriff, and with your feet half scraping the floor, he would drag you all the way to the station.

They were disciplined and single-minded; they had to be. Being a colonial policeman was a potentially dangerous job, especially in the early days of colonisation. They were considered traitors and were often subjected to vicious verbal and physical assaults. There are even documented incidents of colonial policemen being stoned. Consequently, it was a job that did not allow for any wavering of loyalty or commitment.

When the British first entered the territory in 1845, they brought with them their own police and military, made up of officers from various Crown colonies. Within two decades, the first official police force was organised. It was called the Gold Coast Armed Police, though people unofficially and derisively referred to it as the Hausa Constabulary because, aside from the British officers, that particular tribe made up the majority of the force. The colonial government felt that the Hausa people, much more than any other ethnic group within the territory, were ideally martial. By the time the colony was officially established in 1874, though it was still overwhelmingly Hausa, men from other ethnic groups were also allowed to join the police force, which was now known as the Gold Coast Constabulary.

Prior to the proclamation of the colony, the constabulary had been used for military duties, civil duties, and day-to-day policing as well. After the Gold Coast became an official Crown colony, a separate military was formed, the Gold Coast Regiment. Additionally, a subdivision was created within the constabulary called the Native Authority Forces, and their function was to enforce customary laws. Officers of the main constabulary were outfitted with single-shot rifles, but the officers of the Native Authority Forces were not armed; they only carried truncheons.

I imagine that the two colonial policemen who showed up to escort the group of primary school students from Bole to Salaga were from the Native Authority Forces. Each of the boys was allowed to bring a small bag with clothing and other necessities. The colonial policemen carried these bags for the children. One day during my father's primary school years, as he and his schoolmates were making the journey, there were several lions in the middle of the road on which they were travelling.

They had not yet come upon the lions but could see them in the distance. They stopped and wondered what to do. The road they were on was dusty and barely formed. On either side were trees and shrubs and grasses that stood taller the farther away they grew from the road. There were only two directions the group could travel—backward or forward. They couldn't very well turn around; already they'd been walking for more than a day. "Even if we had wanted to go back," my father told me, "the colonial policemen would not allow it. They had been directed to deliver us to the school, and that is what they were going to do."

What the colonial policemen did instead was help the boys climb the trees by the side of the road. They divided the group, with each colonial policeman taking half of the number of boys. They found the tallest, fullest trees with solid branches, ones that were not easily accessible from the ground. One at a time, the colonial policemen hoisted the boys up onto their shoulders. The boys stood on the tips of their toes, their arms stretched skyward, reaching for the nearest branch. Once the children were perched securely in the trees, the colonial policemen joined them. They stayed like that throughout the night, feasting on the trees' fruit and whatever little provisions were in the boys' bags, until the lions left the area and it was safe for them to get down the next morning and continue their journey.

After completing primary school, my father attended middle school in Wa, which is 120 kilometres from Bole. Later, he went to school in Tamale, which was the seat of the colonial administration in the northern territories. When my father completed his education, he was certified as a trained teacher and sent to start a school in his hometown, Bole. Now that there was a school in town and the children did not have to be sent away, parents in Bole and the surrounding areas were more eager and willing to let their children be formally educated.

My father took this opportunity to recruit his younger siblings. He also recruited his nephews and cousins and the children of friends. He wished, more than anything, that his mother could have lived to witness not only his success but also the spread of education in the north. While he was away at school she had died, it was said, of a broken heart, grieving the absence of the son who had been taken from her. I believe this loss shaped my father in some very fundamental ways and made him all the more vigilant about what ultimately became his quest to improve the conditions of his people, the long-overlooked citizens of the north, who had already paid too high a price for their survival under the colonial administration.

Whenever possible, my father would encourage whomever he could to attain an education. He understood the tremendous difference it could make in an individual's life, what it would mean to that person's future. If any of his employees wanted to complete or further their studies, he would readily agree to personally finance the courses.

Teachers were also brought from the southern part of the

country to train and then work at the schools that had been established in the north. It was while he was at the teachers' training facility in Tamale that my father noticed firsthand the institutionalised discrimination that northerners still routinely faced. Whereas people from the southern part of the colony could travel freely, northerners were required to carry a pass to gain entry into the southern part of the colony.

At the training college in Tamale, the teachers were made to abide by a dress code. The ones from the south were allowed to wear trousers and white shirts, but the ones from the north were required to wear shorts and white shirts with a *batakari*, a traditional loose, pullover smock-like tunic that is made from coarse, hand-spun cotton. Though my father was a quiet man by nature, he had a strong sense of justice, one that often led him to act in the interest of what he felt was right and true. He gathered the northern teachers and encouraged them to lead a successful revolt against the colonial administration, to demand that they be treated equitably.

After my father had been teaching for some time, he decided that he wanted to further his own education. He applied to the former Prince of Wales College, which was now known as Achimota College. Dad was more than qualified for admission, but his application was denied. Though no official reason was given for the rejection, he knew right away that it was a result of the confrontation he'd led against the colonial government over the teachers' dress codes. Be that as it may, there was nothing he could do.

Years later, when it came to pass that one of his children was granted admission to Achimota, he saw it not only as a victory for me, his son, but as a vindication of his own aspirations as a northerner who wanted to advance beyond the limitations that had been set in place for him and those like him, aspirations that had been purposely blocked.

AFTER THAT SPEECH AND PRIZE-GIVING DAY, I no longer questioned my father's intentions, not when it came to my enrolment in Achimota.

My entire educational career, from kindergarten to college, was spent as a residential pupil. Those pain-filled early years at Achimota provided me with the foundation, the support, and the motivation that saw me through the remainder of my education. And in time, I learned to thank my father for insisting upon it.

Looking back now, I see that it is no coincidence that in class 4 I was recognised for my aptitude and achievement in history and English, and that years later, in university, I graduated with a degree in history and then later pursued a graduate diploma in communication studies to satiate my love of reading and my desire to write. I can see how direct the line is from the burgeoning interests of the boy I was to the burning intellectual passions of the man I was becoming.

Of all my father's children, I turned out to be the one who would follow directly in his footsteps. The trajectory of my life and career has, in many ways, been identical to his. Like him, I was chosen quite by chance to embark on a unique educational opportunity. Upon my father's graduation, he became a teacher and invested himself in the task of uplifting the people of his community. Upon my graduation, I taught history to O- and A-level students.

Not unlike my father, I was led by a seemingly random series of events into a life of public service. A career in politics was not something I'd ever planned for myself, just as it was never something my father had planned for himself. It came as even more of a surprise for me to find myself in the political arena because of my experience during that first coup d'etat and my father's resulting detention.

My social activism began while I was interacting with my students, realising how little they understood of their own history, our shared history. Through the years, my activism continued and it became a non-negotiable part of my life, a political endeavour, when I realised that we are each given a voice with which to speak and that my silence and inaction would serve no one, least of all myself and the people I claimed to care about.

After I ran to become a member of Parliament and won, my father gave me all of his books and papers. He would often talk to me, long into the night, about his experiences in politics, sharing the lessons he'd learned and cautioning me about the pitfalls and impediments I might encounter. Sometimes, in the midst of those talks, I would sit next to him, tapping my toes on the floor as I listened, and I would be reminded of that day in the headmistress's office.

"This your little boy Dramani," she'd said. "I think he has the potential to make you really proud."

I would be reminded, too, of the drive from Bole to Accra with my mother, of how scared I truly was to be taken to live with my father, though at the time I refused to show it or even acknowledge it. Whatever was I afraid of? Throughout my life, my father was my best friend, my mentor, coach, and confidant. He was my everything.

Even though my father is long gone, there are times when I am with my own sons, or going about my official duties, or simply sitting at my desk writing, and I can almost feel the light touch of his palm against my back, just below my neck, as though he were standing beside me, saying, "Well done. Well done." And I know that the headmistress's prediction has come true.

OF SILENCE AND SOLIDARITY

IT WAS WITH much consternation that we came to realise that the brand-new member of our class 3 group was a bona fide bully. It took a while, at least the first few weeks of the term, for that truth to come to light because initially he tried to blend in. I think it was his way of studying us, taking note of our individual constitution and our collective consciousness, so that when he was ready, he would know how far he could go—because people will push you only as far and as hard as you allow them to. Feigning kindness and friendship was his due diligence.

The boy's name was Ezra, and despite his best efforts to fit in, it was apparent from the start that it would be a most difficult task. There were ten of us in our dormitory, and Ezra was the tallest. He was a couple of years older than us, and even though I'm sure the other kids were curious as to why he was even in our class, nobody asked. It would be impolite and in poor taste. And it would make no difference. After all, whatever the reasons, Ezra was in our class, wasn't he?

Something else that made Ezra stand out was that he was

very muscular, which was quite strange for a child. His phy-
sique resembled those of the men we sometimes saw on the
campus grounds clearing the underbrush with long, slightly
curved cutlasses. Their skin, which was blacker even than a
starless sky at midnight, would be glistening with sweat.

The rest of us were of average size. We weren't weaklings,
nor did we look as though we had *kwashiorkor*, though standing next to Ezra, you might be inclined to wonder. I wasn't at
all surprised to learn that his father was a farmer, though I
would have guessed that it was an animal farm and not a cocoa
farm, because Ezra looked as though he had been born, raised,
and fed in much the same way as livestock.

His father, though uneducated, had made a lot of money for
himself. He wanted his son to attend Achimota, the school
where the doctors, lawyers, politicians, and other members of
the upper echelon sent their kids. With good reason: Ezra
was a bush boy; he was tactless and uncouth. Little by little
as the days and weeks wore on, he revealed more of his true
nature.

I believe that little children view difference as a motivation
to be more inclusive, though as we grow older and become
adults we begin to see it as the opposite, a reason to exclude.
Since most of us in our group had been boarding together
since we were six, we all got along wonderfully. We wanted
Ezra to fit in and not feel like the odd one out.

We went out of our way to be nice to him. We would invite him to play with us. We would let him stand at the front
of the queue in the dining hall. We did all of this to welcome
him into our circle. It was a show of our hospitality. Ezra saw

it as a deficiency, his invitation to crown himself king of us all.

ACHIMOTA'S SCHOOL MOTTO IS *Ut Omnes Unum Sint,* "That All May Be One." It fell in line with the statement of unity that the founders were trying to make. They wanted Achimota to be a leader in the practice of breaking down the walls that divided by gender, by race, by ethnic group, by religion, by political persuasion. By the mid-1920s, women in the United States had only just won their battle for suffrage. And women all across the world, from China to Guatemala to Great Britain, were waging their own battles for equality in matters of suffrage, ownership of property, and education. The idea of a school like Achimota, one that embraced and even advocated gender equality, was extremely revolutionary—especially in West Africa. The student population at Achimota seemed to be evenly divided between girls and boys, though some years there might be a few more of one than the other. Our dormitories were segregated by gender, but other than that, the boys and girls attended classes and did most everything else together.

THE SCHOOL CREST IS A black-and-white drawing of piano keys. It was in keeping with the motto and founding principles. One of Achimota's founders, Dr. James Kwegyir Aggrey, is famously quoted as saying, "You can play a tune of sorts on the black keys only; and you can play a tune of sorts on the white keys only; but for perfect harmony, you must use both the black and the white keys."

It somehow seems just, given the history of the land on which it was erected, that Achimota should have made a name for itself as a safe haven, a beacon of promise and hope for future generations of Africans. The school was built in the middle of the Achimota Forest. The forest, which at one time spanned thousands and thousands of acres, was notoriously dense, the sort of place in which a person could get lost forever. It was officially set aside as a reserve in 1930.

The area that became the Gold Coast colony and is now called Ghana was a key location in the transatlantic slave trade. Ghana contains more slave castles and forts than anywhere else. These buildings have been preserved as historical landmarks or turned into museums. They tell the story of domination and enslavement.

But there are lesser-known landmarks, ones that tell another sort of tale, a tale of defiance and resistance. One such landmark is the forest in which Achimota School is now situated. It was where the captured who'd managed to escape would run to seek shelter and protection from those who wished to enslave them.

Even the name that was ultimately given to the forest is a testament to the fear its trees have witnessed and the secrets their canopies have kept. Achimota, in the language Ga, means "speak no name." That forest was a place of silences, but it was also a place of salvation.

This history is all the more reason I find our experience

with Ezra so significant that even to this day it stands out in my mind.

IT STARTED OUT WITH SMALL errands, little things he wanted us to do for him. Initially, they seemed as though they might be favours he was asking. For instance, if he forgot his toothpaste in the bathroom, he would tell you to go and bring it to him. We'd been excusing his lack of manners and home training for some time, so this rough way of asking seemed to fit the pattern.

The first time may have raised an eyebrow, but it was not a problem. The second and third times were annoying. After the fourth, fifth, and sixth times we were told, "Come here," or, "Bring this," we figured out what Ezra had always known. He wasn't asking us for favours. He was ordering us around, and his voice was becoming more authoritative with each command. Ezra had taken us as his servants.

"Dramani," he would bark like a military captain, "I am going for my bath now. Bring my sponge and soap and towel." I would dutifully collect the items he listed and I would walk, my head hung low with shame. He always followed, a few short paces behind, until we reached the bathroom. The other students would watch me as I passed by. They would never say anything, but they'd show solidarity with their eyes, which seemed to be saying, *I'm with you.* I would offer them the same supportive look when it was their time to fetch some items for Ezra.

Why did we do it? We were frightened of him. Had he

arrived at school and tried that nonsense the first day or two, we would not have had any time for it at all. "What do you mean?" we would have asked indignantly. "Who born you by mistake?" And we would have reported him to the auntie of our dormitory at once.

But Ezra had skilfully indoctrinated us. We had shown him our hearts, taken him into our trust, and this had somehow broken down our defences. We had made ourselves too vulnerable. We had taken him at face value, especially given his name. As irony would have it, in its original Hebrew the name Ezra means "helper." Far from being any kind of helper, Ezra had become our personal bully, and now we were stuck with him. He became so powerful that he was second only to the dorm auntie. Whatever he said was law.

One day Ezra issued an edict. He called us all together and announced that, effective immediately, when we went for our afternoon snacks we were to bring them directly to him and he would decide what should be done with them. We were gobsmacked. Ordering us about was one thing, but now Ezra wanted us to give him our snacks! What next? How far would this situation go?

"Understood?" Ezra asked after he'd finished giving us our orders. We all nodded.

The school provided us with three sit-down meals—breakfast, lunch, and supper—and two snacks. Our morning snack was offered to us during a brief break from class. We'd have about fifteen minutes to get our snack, eat it, and play before returning to our studies.

It was our afternoon snacks that Ezra was interested in pilfering. After we had finished with our classes, we would return to the dormitory for a siesta to replenish our energy for our sports practices later on. Between siesta and sports, we were given a snack. Usually it was something like sweet plantain chips, little cakes, rock buns, or groundnuts.

The day after the edict was issued, we all queued at the dining hall for our afternoon snacks. We looked at each other knowingly as we took our portion of fried plantain. My stomach growled in anger. I was unable to bring myself to look at the snack for fear that I would eat it and then have to face the wrath of Ezra. All nine of us marched with our snacks to the dormitory, where Ezra was sitting in state. One of the students had been ordered to collect Ezra's snack for him so he wouldn't even have to leave the dormitory.

He sprang up as we entered, craning his neck to see what the day's delight was. Once he saw that it was plantain, he smiled. Ezra loved plantain. One by one we walked up and stood before him, as though he were a priest offering a communion wafer—except we were the ones giving the offering. He took each of our snacks and divided them imperfectly in half. He kept the bigger "half" for himself and left us with the other "half" to eat.

That's how it was from then on. We would bring him our snacks and he would take what he pleased, then send us away. He would eat some of the snacks he'd taken from us right away; the rest, he would wrap and keep under his bed. He would enjoy his loot before siesta or in the night while the rest of us were readying ourselves to go to sleep. It frustrated and angered us, but still we told no one of Ezra's bullying. We quietly let him have his way.

My two very close friends, David and Agyeman, and I began

to conspire on the playground. We would huddle in a corner and list all the reasons why it was unfair for us to give Ezra our afternoon snack. This was oppression, plain and simple. We would wonder aloud how it was that we'd found ourselves in such a situation. "Why should he be the boss of us?" we would emphatically ask each other. Those sessions seemed to steel us for the inevitable. We would have to confront Ezra.

The three of us would meet, and we would complain and brainstorm and plan. We devised a Plan A and a Plan B; we even had a Plan C and a Plan D. We predicted every possible reaction that Ezra might have to our actions. This was serious business, and we treated it as such. We had to rid our lives of him, the ruthless dictator in our dormitory.

WHAT WAS HAPPENING TO MY group of friends and me in Achimota, around 1967 and 1968, was truly a microcosm of what was happening all throughout Africa. Dictators were sprouting up one after another, bushmen with bad manners and violent tendencies. They held their communities in fear and felt entitled to what did not belong to them. They betrayed the vision of unity and progress that Africa had established for its future during the struggles for liberation from colonial rule.

We were merely three boys on a playground. What kind of revolution could we begin? We did not know that it was within our power to stop it, to effect change in our lives and in the lives of others. But out in the larger world beyond our campus, from the cities of Accra and Addis Ababa to the apartheid-burdened South Africa, there were men who did. Those men gathered in threes and fours to complain and plan and prepare for the moment when they would take a stand, damn the consequences.

We would hear the news reports on the radio and read about them in the papers. In 1967, the African National Congress and the Zimbabwe African People's Union joined forces for armed battle against the Rhodesian army; that same year in Bolivia, a friend of African independence, Ernesto "Che" Guevara, was executed.

In 1968, Equatorial Guinea, Mauritius, and Swaziland all gained their independence; several African countries joined forces with the Soviet Union and various Islamic and Caribbean nations to threaten a boycott against the Summer Olympic Games in Mexico City if South Africa were allowed to participate; the Association of Senegalese Students and the Dakar Association of Students staged a strike and boycott of examinations that resulted in on-campus riots and nearly a thousand arrests. That same year in the United States of America, another friend of African independence, Dr. Martin Luther King Jr., was assassinated.

So much was happening so quickly. Africa felt like too big a subject, too expansive a continent, for us to ever fully know or understand. It seemed like a world far beyond our reach. Perhaps our season of Ezra was our initiation rite into this new Africa, one that was changing so rapidly and radically from the Africa for which our fathers fought and the Africa of which our grandfathers dreamed.

David, Agyeman, and I set a date for our protest. On that

day, we would enter the dining hall and collect our snack as we normally did. However, instead of taking the snack to Ezra, we would eat it right then and there. We'd even prepared and recited a statement that we would make when he confronted us.

The three of us talked about this day and we looked forward to its arrival, but when it finally came, David and Agyeman grew nervous about the consequences we might face.

"Maybe we should wait a little longer," David suggested. He remains, to this day, the most pragmatic person I've ever met, analyzing and overanalyzing everything before taking a decision or an action.

"Wait until when?" I wanted to know. He shrugged, letting the bones protruding through his skin at his shoulders rise as high as his earlobes.

That day all three of us were understandably anxious. We could barely concentrate on our classwork. After siesta we rushed to the dining hall to queue. We stood together, one in front of the other, but I was the first in that chain. I took my snack, a small cake, and in obedience to the pact we'd made, I bit into it. I turned, rather satisfied with my accomplishment, and looked at the others. David and Agyeman were still holding their cakes, looking cautiously at them, then at me, then at each other.

"You won't eat your snack?" I asked while we were leaving the dining hall. As we walked to the dormitory, David explained that they felt it would be best to delay the protest by a day, just one day. Tomorrow, they promised, they would be ready. Their voices were trembling nearly as badly as their hands.

"What about me?" I asked, blocking their path to the entrance of the dormitory. I'd eaten half of my snack already. "What am I supposed to do?" David and Agyeman said they would provide some explanation to Ezra on my behalf, but I suspected that it would not be a wise plan of action. Taking half a snack would be worse than taking no snack at all. Ezra wasn't interested in compromise; what he wanted was full compliance. I turned and walked through the door of the dormitory. The other kids in our class 3 group were behind us, rushing to get to Ezra with their snacks before the time cutoff. As soon as David, Agyeman, and I entered the dormitory, I shoved the remainder of my cake into my mouth.

"Dramani," gasped Agyeman. He slapped a hand over his open mouth. I looked at his long fingers. He dropped his hand and asked, "Why did you do that?"

"Oh boy . . . ," sighed David, shaking his head. They were afraid for me, but it didn't matter anymore. Whatever my fate, it had now been sealed. I couldn't undo what had already been done.

Once we were all in the room, Ezra called each boy up and went through the ritual of division.

"Dramani," he barked when my turn came. I hated hearing my name spoken in that tone of voice. Even at his angriest, my father never called my name with such ferocity. I stepped forward, empty-handed. "Where is your snack?"

"I ate it," I said in a matter-of-fact, what-else-was-I-supposed-to-do-with-it way.

"You ate it? Why?" Before the rage set in, quickening his breath and shifting his already dark shade to an ashen charcoal, a flicker of surprise illuminated his face. I saw then that Ezra had never prepared himself to be challenged. He'd correctly assumed that he wouldn't have to exert much effort to subjugate us. This new realisation made me more determined to not back down. I launched into the speech that my suddenly spineless friends and I had crafted.

"Our fathers pay our school fees," I huffed. "The school fees pay for the snacks, so these snacks are being paid for by my father. He is buying them for me, and not for you."

The other students who were listening seemed impressed by my argument. I saw the solidarity in their eyes. They believed in every word I had spoken; they supported my cause wholeheartedly. I knew all this, but I also knew right then that saying, "I'm with you," silently was not enough. I needed somebody to stand with me. That would have made all the difference in the world.

Ezra unleashed his punishment in one fell swoop. I barely felt the blow, but it landed me on the floor. He kneed me; he gave me knocks on my head. He really maltreated me, but I did not die. I did not die.

I went to bed that evening prepared to face Ezra the next day with David and Agyeman at my side. Would he really beat all three of us—bam, bam, bam? Well, with Ezra, it was a possibility. Even so, what would he do the following day after we had convinced one or two others to join in? And then the following day with more people? Our numbers would keep increasing until our entire group was standing up to Ezra. And then what? He couldn't beat the whole of our class 3 group day after day until it was time for us to leave for our long vacation.

Why hadn't I seen before that our strength, our key to victory, was in our numbers, our unity? I slept well that night; I felt as though I had stumbled upon something significant, a vital piece of knowledge.

David and Agyeman didn't see things the same way. Even though they had promised to delay their involvement by only a day, the beating Ezra gave me unnerved them. It served as a deterrent.

"No, Dramani, no," they pleaded as I opened my mouth to take a bite of my afternoon snack. I didn't mind them. I bit into a long, thin, sweet plantain chip and started chewing. After what had happened the day before, if I delivered my snack to Ezra, I would end up being his biggest servant. He beat me again that day, though not as severely. I didn't care; and again, I didn't die.

On the third day I ate my afternoon snack and, once more, prepared myself for the beating that I knew was going to come, but it did not. When everyone had assembled in the room to deliver their snack, Ezra made an announcement. "Dramani has been exempted," he said, trying to sound as official as possible. "But the rest of you have not. You must still come with your snack as before." I suppose Ezra had decided to cut his losses. Perhaps he had seen the same potential for strength and for unity that I had seen, and he didn't want to chance having me spark a chain reaction of defiance. Smart, very smart.

I left the room as the others were being called to present their snacks. When I passed David and Agyeman, I looked them straight in the eyes with an expression that said, *My brothers, you're on your own.*

WILD LIONS AND LITTLE BOYS
WITH CATAPULTS

O H , H O W I wanted to become a game warden. It seemed like such an enviable career. We would see them sometimes, my brother Alfred and I, in Damongo town after they had closed from work, looking rather smart in their green khaki uniforms with their high-laced boots that were always shiny even during the dustiest days of the harmattan. Game wardens always seemed to travel in pairs, and they carried big rifles that were powerful enough to bring even an elephant to its knees. I'd always admired game wardens, but it was at the start of the long vacation in Damongo with the wild lion and the territorial snake that I actually set my sights on becoming one.

After the marriage between my mother and father broke down, my mother returned from my father's house in Bole to her hometown, Damongo. At first, when she'd been living in Bole, he made the twelve-hour journey between Bole and Accra, where he was based for his work, fairly regularly. Before long, the visits became less frequent, slowly decreasing in number until there was an unspoken acceptance of the fact that he would no longer be coming.

Alfred lived with Dad, who upon his release from detention had moved from Accra to Tamale, which was in the northern region of the country, much closer to Damongo. In Tamale,
Dad set up a rice farming and processing business. I still lived
at boarding school and spent most of my vacations in Tamale,
where my brothers and I would often help Dad out on his rice
farm. But Dad made certain that Alfred and I spent at least one
vacation every year with our mum. Mallam, our dad's driver,
was also from Damongo, so the task of escorting us there and
back naturally fell to him.

Mallam was somehow related to Mum, though nobody
ever really took the time to explain to us how and when it was
that his blood joined ours. But everyone in that town seemed
to be related in one way or another. After Mallam had dropped
us off at Mum's house and paid his respects to her and all his
other relations, he would leave so that he could return to
Tamale before nightfall.

"Come," Mum would say to Alfred and me just as we were
about to get comfortable. "Let's go." I'd twist my mouth into
a frown and let out a short exhale through the sliver of space
between my lips. That was the closest I could come to defiance. Mum would make us quickly go and take a bath to clean
the day's dust off us. We would then put on a fresh shirt and
pair of pants and report back to her for inspection. After she felt
we were clean and presentable, Mum would make us slip on
our sandals so she could take us through the town to greet our
relatives, which essentially meant greeting the entire town.

It was torturous. We would be paraded from house to house,
where we would politely offer the same plastic smiles and answer the same boring questions. We would walk and walk and

walk until our legs were pulsating with pain. What made them seem to hurt even more was the knowledge that we would have to repeat the whole ritual once more the day of our departure; such was the custom.

Damongo was a sizable though hardly bustling town. It was, in fact, a district capital from as far back as the colonial times. One of the main roads in the area, the only road that connected Tamale, which was the capital of the northern region, to Wa, another major city in the north, cut straight through Damongo. The town was the halfway point between the two cities. It was where vehicles would stop and people would get down and stretch their legs or buy something to eat, like groundnuts or *kose*, a type of fried bean cake.

Typically, only a few vehicles passed per day. The hawkers would line up by the roadside, talking and singing and organising their wares, waiting for their opportunity to make a sale. The road was laterite gravel, as brown as the mud houses in which nearly everyone lived. When a car was approaching, the air would fill with billows and billows of dust.

Despite that dust, Damongo was a wondrous place, drenched in the most vibrant array of colours. The sunsets went from orange to violet; the sky was a pristine blue, save whatever feathery white clouds were floating through. Between earth and sky were as many shades of green as imaginable, trees and bushes and shrubs and more trees, more bushes, more shrubs.

Damongo is situated right next to Mole, which is the largest game reserve in the country. It occupies more than 4,800 square kilometres and nurtures hundreds of species of animals, from elephants to gazelle to butterflies, offering the sort of atmosphere that encourages a relationship with nature and reminds you that you are part of a larger cycle of creatures and events.

The absence of certain recent conveniences such as electricity and ready-made products also encouraged creativity. The games we played were the ones we invented; the toys we played with were the ones we constructed. The village kids, the majority of whom were of some distant relation to Alfred and me, were the most clever and original people I'd ever met. When we were with our dad, if either Alfred or I wanted a toy car, all we had to do was ask and he would buy one from the store. If the boys in Damongo wanted a toy car, they'd make one themselves out of empty milk tins and old rubber slippers.

When we were there, Alfred and I spent nearly all of our time with them, letting the rigidity and sophistication of the city fade away. After we had eaten breakfast and bathed, the boys, barefoot and scrappy, would come and take us out to do all the things that little children in a village should do. We climbed trees and picked fruit, our hands and feet searching the knobby, fragile limbs for safe resting places. We ran to the riverside and swam, watching as the fish altered their routes so they would not collide with us.

There were usually always at least ten of us together at any given time. Our large numbers made us feel more secure, especially when we were hunting. One of the village boys, Kipo, a short and soft-spoken little fellow, taught us how to make catapults. That's what we would use as our weapon of choice to hunt squirrels, grasscutters, and other small animals. After we'd killed the animals, we'd make a fire out in the bush and roast the meat. It used to be that you could go onto any farm and as long as you were not picking crops to sell, you could take whatever you wanted and nobody would accuse you of stealing.

Between the few cobs of corn we'd taken from a nearby farm, our roasted animals, and the mangoes, pawpaws, or *gaya* we'd picked, we would have a feast. We would sit, nibbling and laughing, well into the evening.

Idyllic as it may all sound, Damongo was not without its dangers. On one particular vacation, when I was ten and Alfred was twelve, word spread through the town that there was a wild lion on the loose. It seemed to be only a rumour that first day. There was an air of ease to the villagers' discussions that suggested a level of disbelief or dismissal; most of the statements that I overheard the adults making began with, "I learned they say a lion . . ."

Nobody had any real proof of this lion's presence amongst us. Then one night a man was killed, viciously mauled until his body was nothing more than a bloody pile of bones, cartilage, and shredded flesh. This was all the proof that was needed. Panic spread as quickly as the bushfires that charred the dense forest every year during the dry season.

The chief immediately sent a report to the Game and Wildlife Department, and they dispatched several game wardens to Damongo to capture the lion. Never had I seen a game warden in town on official duty. They were ordinarily stationed inside the game reserve, making certain the visitors did not disturb the animals and the animals also did not disturb the visitors. It was an agreement of peace between hunter and prey. The problem is that when such an agreement is broken, as it inevitably is, it is often difficult to determine which will be the hunter and which will be the prey. For this reason, the game wardens were also vested with the duty of protecting the animals in the game reserve from poachers.

Because of their extensive training and knowledge of whichever reserve they serviced, game wardens were often called to assist in the prosecution of poachers. They knew how to track an animal's footprints to ascertain its pattern of movement. They could easily tell from trails that had been left whether an animal was injured, whether it had been in flight, or whether it had been dragged.

Poaching is a serious problem in Africa, one that will find many currently unprotected animals endangered and many already endangered ones extinct. Whereas once there were dozens of species of rhinoceroses on the continent, now only five documented species remain. In the 1930s, there were five to ten million African elephants in existence; by 1989, when they were placed on the endangered species list, there were a little over half a million of them left. African lions are especially vulnerable because the poaching of one lion ultimately leads to the deaths of as many as six to ten others. When the dominant male of a pride is killed, the male who then takes over as the dominant one will kill all of his predecessor's cubs. Currently there are only about ten thousand to fifteen thousand free-roaming lions in Africa; a decade ago, that number was as high as fifty thousand. Deforestation is also a huge problem that is affecting the ability of animals to survive in their natural habitat. Only 30 percent of Ghana remains forested, and that figure is decreasing steadily at a rate of nearly 1.5 percent every year.

In the days of my youth, there was only a laterite gravel road separating Damongo from the Mole Game Reserve. There were no fences or gates or other contraptions to keep the animals in and the poachers out, but somehow the understanding of boundaries was fairly clear. When the animals violated the sanctity of that boundary, which was not very often, the consequence was death; when the poachers violated it, the consequence was imprisonment. It was even written into law. Animals found on the right side of the road were fair game, as it were, to be captured or killed by anyone who chose to do so. The instant a human crossed the road to the left side to do the killing, he officially became a poacher; and all poachers were arrested and put on trial.

IT IS TEMPTING FOR US as humans to believe that we are superior to all other creatures and, as such, have the right to dominate them if and when we so choose. Even as small boys we believed this. We felt powerful, as though we were a force to be reckoned with, walking around with our little homemade catapults. We felt entitled to do as we wished in the narrow stretch of the village that we considered our kingdom. Then one day during that same vacation, as we were hunting in our pack, the tables turned on us and we became the hunted.

Just about a kilometre from the town is Damongo Scarp Forest Reserve, which is home to over a hundred different species of birds. The scarp itself is a perpendicular rock face that rises up about eighty metres into a swooping plateau with a magically wavy outline upon which there is lush vegetation. We must have trudged through the forest and climbed the scarp a dozen times already during that vacation alone to go hunting in the shrubs and tussock grasses that covered the plateau. This time felt no different from the others.

"Snaaaaaakkkke!" Awudu screamed. The thing I remember most about Awudu is that he had a massive nose. We used to teasingly call him "Oxygen Catcher." As he screamed, I imagined his top lip rising sharply and then disappearing completely under the wide umbrella of his nose. We'd encountered snakes before during our expeditions. Mostly they minded their own business, slithering quickly away from the thunder caused by our collective march. To them, our footsteps must have sounded like an approaching herd of elephants. But there was an urgency and fear in Awudu's voice. I looked up just in time to see a massive reptile about two metres long, with its scaly coal-black body coiled beneath it, lift its head high and then flatten its neck as though it were preparing to strike.

"Aaaaaaaayyyyyyyyyyyyyyyyy!" we screamed in unison. Some of us even dropped our catapults. The snake was no more than ten metres away from us. We turned around in perfect formation, as though we were one single body instead of ten, but then after that, when we started sprinting away, it was every boy for himself—and the snake for us all.

I have never run that fast, before or since, in my life. It was a primal flight, as though my body were hurtling forward on its own volition. I could feel my heart pounding in my mouth as if it were literally going to burst. The fear was palpable, like a living, breathing thing, encasing my body tighter and tighter as I progressed. As I ran through the shrubs and tussock grasses, each time my leg grazed a blade or branch or leaf, it would make a rustling sound that I imagined to be the snake gaining ground, coming closer to its victory.

It was when we arrived home, Alfred and I, still running and gasping and sneaking glances behind us to see if the snake was there, that our mother told us about the man who had been mauled the night before. She ordered us not to venture too far or, better yet, just to stay within the town at least until the lion had been captured. After the harrowing experience we'd just had with the snake, we were extremely happy to oblige.

DURING THE WEEK THAT FOLLOWED, the lion made its way into town every night, leaving some gruesome evidence of its visit. Chickens and goats went missing; feathers and unrecognisable pieces of animal body parts were discovered here and there in the town. Everybody was afraid.

It used to be, before the lion started coming into the town, that after the sun had set, people would sometimes stand outside their houses for a bit to socialise and enjoy the night air, their faces lit by the glow of their paraffin lamps. Not anymore. Now, even before the last few rays of the sun had been stained into darkness, the villagers would have locked their animal pens, completed all of their outdoor chores, and barricaded themselves safely in their houses. Nobody went out at night except the game wardens, walking around stealthily with their rifles at the ready.

We could see them when we looked out of the window in our mum's bedroom, where Alfred and I slept with her in a bed that was so enormous, it took up nearly all of the space in the room. It was comforting to know that the game wardens were out there searching for the lion. Whenever I saw them I would choose one, usually the most muscular and courageous looking, and envision my own adult face on his body. Yes, I thought, that would be me in a dozen or so years. I too would be entrusted with the well-being of an entire village. With that, I'd drift into slumber all too satisfied with the decision I'd made for my life.

It was only in the light of day that doubt crept in. Alfred and I still played with the village boys. We didn't wander as far, and we avoided the forest reserve altogether. We carried on as though nothing had changed, but it was apparent that something had. We now walked with a slight trace of apprehension, were startled by the mere snap of a twig underfoot and the sharp flap of a wing overhead. Our confidence had left us.

Whenever I so much as flinched, I would ask myself, Is this what a future game warden should do? I tried to carry myself in the appropriate manner of my chosen profession, but the pressure soon became too much. It dawned on me, with much sadness, that those shiny high-laced boots I desperately wanted to one day be issued were too big for me to fill. Especially right then, even in my wildest fantasies. I was, after all, only a small boy. A small boy who was ready to return to the city, where it was so cluttered with people and machines that wild animals dared not enter.

ONE MORNING IT WAS ANNOUNCED by one of the chief's circle of elders, through the traditional beating of the *gongong*, that the lion had been killed. The news of its death had actually started circulating the night before, but nobody trusted the information as fact. They erred on the side of caution and stayed indoors.

When he spoke, the elder said that the entire village was to congregate at the chief's palace so that they could see the slain lion with their own eyes. It was the only way to assure people that they could finally return to their normal routine. It was now safe.

Overjoyed, everybody started rushing to the chief's palace. We children, stirred by the excitement of all the commotion, joined the crowd. We craftily wove ourselves around the adults and took whatever shortcuts we could concoct so that once we arrived at the palace we would be at the very front of the audience that was being formed.

As promised, there it was right in front of us, the dead lion. I was speechless, and a bit nervous about standing so close. Its eyes were squinted shut as though it were having a siesta; the tip of its nose looked as if it would be wet and cold to the touch; the straw-coloured mane that encircled its face was long and shaggy. The game wardens stood beside the dead lion, looking very cool and proud of their achievement. The women started ululating and praising them for their bravery, while the men stood around remarking on the size of the lion and telling "once upon a time" tales of their own encounters with wild animals.

When the game wardens addressed the assembled group, they explained why it was the lion had started coming into the town. Lions don't usually attack human beings, not when they are strong and active. Apparently, this lion that had terrorised us all for over one good week was old. Its best hunting days were behind it. Hunger and the inability to run fast enough to chase its food were what had driven it to come into the town, where food, in the form of humans and chickens and goats, was plentiful and simple enough to catch.

After I had been studying the lion's face for some time, I noticed the wound from where it had been shot. It was small and round, about the size of a fingerprint. I looked at the game wardens' rifles and tried to picture a bullet flying out of one of them, the hot metal cutting a straight line through the air and entering the lion's skull in one smouldering second. The thought of it made me feel weak and nauseous. I knew then that, no, I could never be a game warden. I could never come face-to-face with an animal, during a situation of one-must-die, take aim, and shoot, not without dropping dead from sheer fright.

At the end of that vacation, Alfred and I painstakingly made our rounds through the village to say good-bye to all our various relatives. When Mallam arrived to collect Alfred and me, the village boys gathered around the car and watched as our mum saw us off. Our departure was always bittersweet, filled paradoxically with both the longing to leave and the desire to stay. With each visit to Damongo came a lesson, an education that could be gained only in a place where nature's welcomes and warnings are almost indistinguishable and you can tell the difference only by allowing the sounds of your breath and the beats of your heart to align themselves with the innate rhythms of the world around you.

FULL MOON DANCE

THE YEAR OUR driver, Mallam, went mad is the same year I saw ice blocks falling from the sky and discovered that the recipe for love is a full moon and a good *conductay*. It was the long vacation before my twelfth birthday. By the time my boarding school had closed for the break, Mallam had already completed his descent. Madness had fully taken hold of him. My father had to send a new driver, Abudu, to collect me from the airport and bring me home.

I was nervous about seeing Mallam again. I had never known a madman before, not personally, but I'd seen plenty of them. They would walk aimlessly around the city, fully engaged in loud and animated conversations with people only they could see and hear. Sometimes they would even be naked, bathing by the roadside. I was afraid of them, not because they seemed dangerous, but because they behaved in ways that I'd been taught were not correct.

"Don't be afraid," said my father as Alfred and I were leaving his house to spend part of the long vacation with our mother. "He's still Mallam, just different from the way you knew him before. He is very ill." Not knowing what else to do or say by way of response, I nodded. What my father said gave me much to consider. I had never thought of madness as an illness before, like tuberculosis or polio or yellow fever, something that was possible to contract. Maybe the rumours about how Mallam had become mad weren't true after all. Maybe he'd simply fallen ill one day, had gone to sleep with a high fever and woken up a lunatic. If that was the case, then his madness wasn't his fault after all.

The drive from Tamale to Damongo just wasn't the same without Mallam. I missed him very much. He had been Dad's driver for as long as I could remember. He had accompanied me to nearly all of my significant life events, sitting behind the wheel of my dad's Mercedes, making eye contact with me through the rearview mirror during our conversations.

I could draw the back of Mallam's head from memory because I had been staring at it for so long. He had a big head, but it was perfectly oval. It complemented the trendy Tokyo Joe haircut he liked to sport, which was low in the back and rose into a small, sharply pointed, almost arrow-shaped mound in the front. "Topio Joe" is what we kids called it. I wouldn't have minded sporting one myself, but it was not allowed. We younger boys all wore the same hairstyle, short with a part on one side that was not shaved in but rather made with a comb.

Abudu was not at all like Mallam. He remained silent the entire ride, while Alfred and I talked and shared stories. After we had exhausted our trove of anecdotes and jokes, we fell silent and just stared out the window at the clusters of trees we passed every few kilometres, the blackfruit, the baobab, the acacia, ebony, neem, and shea nut trees.

There are two seasons in the northern region of Ghana: rainy and dry. The rainy season there is one continuous period of precipitation from May to October. The dry season begins in November and stretches through April, with the temperatures climbing higher and higher as it progresses. The dry season includes harmattan, which is when the hot winds blow down from the Sahara.

During the dry season, all the leaves would fall off the trees and it would be brown everywhere, not a drop of moisture in the atmosphere. It was as if God had decided to take the air, wring it like a cloth, and pin it up in direct sunlight to bake dry. Your skin would be completely ashen; your lips would get so dry, no amount of saliva could soften them, and if you didn't rub shea butter on your feet, the skin of your heels would crack.

As with anywhere else in the world, the seasons in Damongo were not entirely predictable. They came with their own blessings and refusals. Some rainy seasons were torrential, stopping short of the need for an ark; others offered barely enough water to fill a well or make a river rise.

When we'd left Tamale that day, the rain was merely a fine mist, not even so heavy as to be considered a drizzle; but before we were even halfway to Damongo, it had started coming down in sheets. By the time we arrived at our mother's house, the downpour had cleansed me of all my anxiety. Because it was raining torrentially, I knew that I would not be seeing Mallam that night. I knew, too, that Alfred and I would not be walking through the town to greet our relatives. "Tomorrow," Mum said to us as Abudu was pulling our belongings from the boot of the car.

When I was not away at boarding school, I went back and forth between my two homes, and each one felt as though it contained its own life, the only life that belonged to me. Stepping into my mother's house was like stepping into the skin of a new Dramani.

It was a beautiful house, one of the nicest in the village. My father built it for her back when he was living in Damongo and working as a clerk to the traditional council. As with all the other houses there, ours was made of earth. Only a few houses in town, the houses of affluent people, were roofed with corrugated aluminium sheets. Ours was one of them.

In the north, compound houses are the most common sorts of residential structures. The "house" was actually a series of structures organised in a rectangular shape with an open courtyard in the middle. That was where all the cooking and washing was done. Facing the courtyard, along the sides of the structures, were eaves created by the overhang of the aluminium roofing sheets. It was almost like a little veranda.

If you were a kid in the village, you were everybody's child. You were welcomed inside anybody's house, and the grownups fed, spoiled, and disciplined you as though you were one of their own. Whenever Alfred and I were in Damongo, the local boys liked to spend most of their time with us and at our house.

When we weren't on one of our adventures, we would stay in the courtyard and play games or talk as my mum and aunties went about their routines. It wasn't unusual for us to find ourselves in the courtyard playing when suddenly the sky would break open and release a million raindrops, then close up just

as suddenly and allow the sun to return. Whenever this happened, we would dash under the eaves, every so often sticking
out our heads, with our tongues hanging out, or our hands,
with the palms flattened and facing upward, to catch a few of
those drops.

One day at the onset of a shower like that, we kids started
running, as usual, straight for the eaves. There was something
different about these drops. They stung when they hit my flesh,
as though my legs and arms and face had been caught in an
attack of stone pellets.

"Eeiish," remarked Awudu as he was taking his final few
steps to make it under the eaves. We were all stunned by the
violence of the rain. That's when we heard the sound the rain
was making as it hit the aluminium roofing sheets and the
concrete in the courtyard. It was not the splatter of liquid
meeting a hard surface. This was the smack of one solid object
colliding with another. We all leaned forward small to see what
these things falling from the heavens really were. They looked
like little lumps of rock or stone. Awudu ran out from under
the eaves and picked up a few of them.

"Ice blocks," he exclaimed as his eyes widened with wonder. Awudu's eyes were now almost as large as his legendary
nose. The rest of us were dumbstruck. *Ice blocks? Falling from
the sky? In Ghana?* Then, as if a pistol had sounded to indicate
the start of a race, we all made haste into the courtyard to
join Awudu. Certainly none of us had ever heard of hail before or had any idea what it was. Even as it was happening, it
seemed surreal. Alfred and I looked at each other, wondering
if our brothers back in Tamale would believe us when we told

them that ice blocks had fallen from the sky in Damongo. No, they probably would not, but I was there. I saw it myself. I touched those cold, gritty pebbles with my own hands. I spent hours playing with my brother and friends in the freezing hailstorm, dressed, as children in tropical climates dress, only in shorts.

After we'd finished playing, my mother gave us a very hot bath and sent us off to bed. By sunrise, I was ill. Within two days, I'd been admitted to Damongo Hospital, where they diagnosed me as having pneumonia.

The hospital was run by the Catholic Church, which took great pride in its charity and missionary work in Ghana. It was neat and spotless with modern beds, clean sheets, and kind-hearted nurses.

I'd never been that ill before. It frightened me, but not because I thought I was going to die. At eleven years old, I was not so profoundly aware of, or concerned about, my own mortality. What I feared was madness. I feared getting lost in the euphoria of the illogical, fever-induced dreams I was having. They were, in the way of dreams, dramatic scenes in which the most unlikely people, headmistresses or barbers, would appear in the oddest places, like the forest in Damongo or the airport in Tamale. They would speak in non sequiturs that somehow made perfect sense to me.

Every morning I would wake up confused and frightened, unsure if I was still in the dreamworld or if I had been returned to reality. Then I would have a few normal conversations with the nurses or one of my visitors, like my mother or Alfred, and I'd know that I still had my wits about me. Within a week I felt better, the fever went away, and the dreams stopped. I was given a clean bill of health and sent home to enjoy what was left of my long vacation.

WE WERE AT AN AGE of change. Since my last visit to Damongo, several of the boys I knew in the village had hung up their catapults in favour of musical instruments. Instead of killing animals, they were now interested in admiring girls. Only admiring; they hadn't reached the point of flirting. I was one of the younger members of our little group, and I was not yet convinced that girls were anything special. It was difficult for me to empathise with the urgency of the other boys' desire to be near them or their need to be chosen by the *conductay*—a word that was an obvious bastardisation of *conductor*—to play in the band during Simpa, the local full moon dance.

The first time during the long vacation that I saw Mallam, I had just parted company with a few of my friends. They had cut short my visit with them so they could rehearse their instruments. The full moon was less than a fortnight away, and the *conductay* would soon make his selections. They wanted to be ready.

As I was sulking back home, I saw Mallam. He looked like all the other madmen I'd ever seen. His hair was no longer in a Tokyo Joe style. It had grown out and was matted and dirty. His clothes were torn and dirty. He was barefoot and his heels were caked with mud. Everything about him was dirty. Could madness really change someone that dramatically? The Mallam I knew was a handsome and stylish young man whom you would care to notice. This man in front of me made me want to look away.

When I first came upon him he was talking aloud, either to himself or to an invisible companion, but he recognised me immediately.

"Dramani," he called out in a voice so clear and familiar, it forced me to blink. I wanted to make sure my eyes weren't playing tricks on me. I smiled and approached him.

"So how is Daddy?" he asked. Nothing about the conversation I had with Mallam would have convinced me that he was anything other than a sane young man in need of a bath, a shave, and a clean pair of trousers. His English was as impeccable as ever. He was remarkably lucid, to the extent of being intuitive. I believe he could tell that I was having trouble reconciling the image before me with the voice that was speaking.

"I know I am sick," he confessed. "Soon your father will come for me and take me to the hospital and I will get well."

I didn't doubt what Mallam was saying. My father had always had a soft spot for him. They met while my father was living and working in Damongo. Mallam was completing middle school. What my father saw was a bright and promising boy. When he was elected as a member of Parliament and had to move to Accra, my father took Mallam and several other young boys, who he felt were full of potential, with him. He knew how limited their possibilities were in the village.

In Accra, they worked for him in various capacities, and he saw to it that they finished their schooling. Some were able to take the opportunity as far as it led, completing university and then travelling abroad for advanced degrees in subjects like engineering and medicine. Mallam worked as my father's driver.

He was a good employee, a reliable and honest young man, but he was too enticed by city life and eventually lost himself, or at least the person he'd once been, a village boy who wanted to excel and become as successful as life would allow.

With the exception of the hours he spent working for my father, Mallam's life in Accra was one of flash and debauchery: women, drink, discos, expensive clothing, jewellery, and, soon enough, marijuana, or *wee*, as everyone referred to it. Word got out quickly that Mallam had started smoking *wee* regularly. People kept saying that if Mallam continued to smoke *wee*, he would go mad, because that's what it did: it drove its users mad. Of course, as a child I didn't know what *wee* was or what its effects were. What I did know was that my brothers and I would often see Mallam smoking behind the house, by the hedge. We assumed it was cigarettes, but once Mallam did indeed go mad, we realised that what the other drivers and houseboys had been saying was really true. Mallam had been smoking *wee*. Why, I wondered, would he do that to himself? Why would he do that to us?

When I was three years old, my mother took me to go live with my father and brothers in Accra. Mum and I sat quietly in the backseat for most of the long journey as Mallam drove. At one point, as we were driving through the mountains, I noticed Mallam nodding off, his head tilting suddenly to one side as though it were no longer being supported by his neck. It remained there for a moment, and then Mallam suddenly jerked it back to a stiff, upright position.

A few minutes passed; then his head fell forward toward the steering wheel in that same limp way. This time it remained where it was for a while before he once again jerked it back up.

I looked over at Mum to see if she had also noticed Mallam's odd head movements, but she was staring out the window dreamily. She'd been doing that for most of the drive.

"Mummy," I whispered, tugging at the arm that she'd wrapped around my body, "I think Mallam is sleeping."

"Oh, Dramani, you too," she said dismissively. "What do you know about driving? Have you driven before? Let the man do his job."

Mum leaned forward until her face was almost touching the back of the driver's-seat headrest and asked, "Mallam, are you okay? Is everything all right?"

"Yes, sir, madam," he replied with a voice that was rough and hoarse from having not been used for hours. I saw him glance at us through the rearview mirror. His eyes were a pinkish red, as if he'd been crying, but his face was dry. When our eyes met, he smiled and I smiled back. I snuggled my head back into the curve of my mother's arm, in the pit just beneath where shoulder and collarbone meet, and drifted off.

As I slept, I had the sensation of tumbling, of rolling over and over, my body being tossed about as though it were weightless. It wasn't a pleasant sensation, not like the one I'd felt during the dreams I'd had before about flying, soaring high above everything until I'd vanished into a cloud. This feeling was frightening. I kept willing myself to wake up, and in the distance, through the haze of the dream, I could hear my mother doing the same.

"Dramani, Dramani," she kept saying. "Dramani, wake up. Open your eyes."

When I was finally able to lift my eyelids, I discovered that what I'd felt hadn't been a dream at all. As we were coming down the Aburi mountain, approaching Accra, Mallam had drifted off to sleep and driven right off the edge of the precipice. The car had somersaulted and somersaulted until, thankfully, a tree had broken its fall.

The villagers in the area had formed a makeshift rescue team. They'd walked down to where we'd landed to find out the extent of the damage that had been done to us and to the car. As soon as they discovered that we were all a little banged up and bruised but essentially all right, they helped us to get out of the smashed vehicle and climb up to the roadside. Mum gave one of the villagers my father's information, and that person contacted another person who knew another person who owned a motorbike. He agreed to drive to my father's home in Accra to send word that we'd been in a near-fatal accident.

My father immediately got one of his other drivers to take him to Aburi to collect us. The following day, he made arrangements for the car that Mallam had been driving to be towed away from the scene of the accident.

When I first found out that Mallam had gone mad from smoking *wee*, I remembered that accident. I wondered whether he had been smoking *wee* that day. Was it exhaustion that made him too drowsy to concentrate on the road, or was it the *wee*? I firmly held my suspicion, but I did not dare ask, not that first day when I spoke with him in Damongo or any of the several other days when I saw him and exchanged pleasantries. I only wished that whatever the cause of his insanity, he would find some way to someday return to the Mallam I once knew.

THE EVENT CALLED SIMPA USED to take place in some villages in the northern region each month during the full moon. It was a tradition used for the informal initiation of courtship. Every village in Ghana has an open space or central square where events are held and social activities take place. Starting at twilight, all the young people in Damongo would gather in that space. They would bring benches and stools, but there wouldn't be that many seats, so the majority of the people would stand. On a regular day, the young ladies would go about village life in their wrappers, but on this occasion they would dress up and adorn themselves with beads. The young men would also tend properly to their appearance to make themselves worthy of being chosen. By the time the moon was huge, round, and electric white against the black sky, Simpa would begin.

All the young people would sing, and the ladies would dance seductively. The singing and dancing were always accompanied by live music. A full brass band would play in one corner of the open space. The *conductay*, who directed the band's performance, wielded a lot of power. He decided who could join the band, which songs the band would play, and how they would be performed. This made him a highly respected person in the village. He would stand directly in front of the band dressed in a white short-sleeved shirt, white khaki-style shorts, and tight white socks that covered his muscular calves and stopped just below his knees, but no shoes. The *conductay* never wore shoes.

At all times during Simpa, the *conductay* carried a stick. It was what he used to direct the band's tempo and volume, to alert them to his desired starts and stops. He used it just like a more formal conductor's baton, but it was not manufactured.

It was a stick from a tree: straight, peeled of its leaves, painted white, and polished. To watch the *conductay* wave his stick was really something; it was as though life on earth, as we knew it, depended on the precision of his movements. And perhaps for the young people of the village, it did.

Even though the dancing began with the young ladies, who literally took centre stage, before long everybody was dancing whether they had a partner or not. But the people with partners were the envy of the crowd. There was a kind of poetry to the flirtation. It was full of nuance and innuendo. The beauty of the art belied its complexity. As the evening went on under the light of that moon, people would find partners not only for dancing but also for life.

Simpa took place the entire time the moon was full and visible, which meant it was sometimes held for as many as three consecutive nights. Once the moon started to wane, it ended. It was the only entertainment people looked forward to from month to month. But it has pretty much died out now. It went out of fashion once electricity became widespread in the villages. Now people sit in front of their televisions and watch the flirtations of foreigners on the telenovelas and soap operas that are imported.

When I was younger, what I liked best about Simpa was the music. In addition to popular highlife songs, the band would play hits from other countries. James Brown was an all-time favourite. Everybody knew James Brown's songs, from the very first note; we knew the melodies, the breaks, and the various instrumental solos. What most of the villagers, including the *conductay*, did not know were the words. They'd make them up as they went along, either by using elementary sounds—*dit, dat, boom, bah, la-la-la-la, oooh-oooh*—or by substituting words in Gonja, Dagbani, or pidgin. If James Brown sang, "Looka here!" the *conductay* would sing, *"Gbubiya!"*

Gbubiya is a word in the Dagbani language that means "hold it" or "grab it." The band members heard it not only as a lyric, but as a direction, and they would hold their notes, intently watching the *conductay* and his white stick to find out what to do next.

I also used to like watching the people who were dancing. We all did; we treated Simpa as though it were a spectator sport. Alfred and I would hide ourselves in some corner with our group of friends and giggle at the emotional and physical negotiations of love we witnessed: an arm slung around a woman's shoulder in such a way that the man's hand could graze her nipple; a not-so-secret bottom slap; a spirited shove of feigned rejection. We mimicked the contorted faces of the men who sang along to the music while pressing their partners so close, it seemed impossible for them to breathe. It used to seem all so silly to us.

I could tell during that long vacation that it was no longer silly to the other boys. Even Alfred had fallen under the influence of the full moon and its magic. He had started crossing the threshold into manhood, leaving me behind in my boyhood. His dark, lanky body now towered over my much shorter and scrawnier one. He and the other boys would stare longingly at the young ladies, and when the ones they fancied found partners, I sensed that it wounded Alfred and the others in a way and in a place they could not yet name.

Mallam showed up at Simpa. I saw him briefly but then lost him in the crowd. I thought about all the girlfriends he used to have when he lived in Accra, and I wondered how it must feel for him to not be desirable anymore. I guessed that, being mad and all, he probably didn't care; love was probably the last thing on his mind. I discovered the following week when I saw him in town how very wrong I was. Love always matters.

There were three mad people in Damongo. There was Mallam, there was another young man who was about the same age as Mallam, and there was a woman who was a few years younger than the two men. As Mallam and I were talking that day when I saw him, the two other mad people passed by. It was clear that they were both at the centre of a universe of their own creation; but it was also clear, in a more subtle way, that they were both also inhabiting another universe, a third space of consciousness, together. They were a couple, if a word like that could be used to describe a pair like that.

"He is a disgrace to mad people everywhere," Mallam said, sneering at the man. Mallam told me that in the night the madman would go and find the madwoman and sleep with her. I wasn't sure if what I heard in Mallam's voice was enmity or envy, but in his eyes was the same wounded look I'd seen on my friends' faces during Simpa. Maybe when I'd seen Mallam at Simpa, he'd been there hoping that he might find a woman who'd been touched by the full moon, if only momentarily. It was the beginning of my understanding of love and the particular brand of insanity it roused in everyone, even people who were already mad.

The week before Alfred and I were scheduled to leave Damongo, Abudu came for Mallam. Our father was sending him to the mental asylum for treatment. I'd believed it when Mallam told me he knew Dad would help him get well; there had been a sanity to Mallam even in the midst of his lunacy. There were two Mallams; of that I became certain. There was the one that was well and the one that was ill. What I was not as certain of was whether one had only recently surfaced or whether the two had always existed simultaneously and we had just become aware of the other's presence.

If madness was truly an illness and if it felt anything like the illness I'd experienced during my week at Damongo Hospital, then it must have presented numerous opportunities for the doubt and disbelief of what Mallam perceived as his reality. But, I grew to learn, the same could be said of what we like to believe is sanity. It sometimes forces us to question the miraculous moments, the metamorphoses, and the lost ceremonies of our lives: like ice falling from the sky in West Africa, the new and inexplicable yearnings of boys turning into young men, and how a tradition that had been handed down through the generations could die with just the flick of one switch.

HOW I GOT MY CHRISTIAN NAME

MY STEPMOTHER, GRACE, WAS a practising Catholic. This meant that on Sundays she would gather up the whole lot of us, dress us in our finest Western wear, and march us off to mass. Because I attended boarding school at Achimota, I didn't go every week like my brothers and sisters, but I attended often enough to view it as an indelible part of my life's routine.

At first the youngest of my siblings, myself included, would attend the children's section of the church, where we would sing songs and play games. Eventually, as we got older and our attention spans lengthened, we graduated to the regular church, where we had to sit, like everyone else, through the whole service. Our family was big enough to occupy an entire pew. We would slide in, one after the other, until we were all seated in one long row with Vick, the oldest among us, at one end and my stepmother at the other end.

For my stepmother, her unquestionable faith notwithstanding, church was a type of social event, and with it came limitless opportunities to interact with other members of the community. There were the various women's ministries and the

Christian mothers' clubs. And she also got on well with the priest, who would always greet her after mass. The two of them would stand and speak, surrounded by us, the throng of Mahama children, fidgeting and barely attempting to hide our profound boredom.

For us children, going to mass was like travelling to a foreign country, a place with its own unique customs and clothing and language. We were fascinated by the rituals, the carefully choreographed sequence of kneeling, then sitting, then standing, then singing. There were the Stations of the Cross, from Pontius Pilate's house to the Crucifixion at Calvary. Through the eyes of a child, those pictures were intimidating and they cast a slightly sombre mood over the entire proceedings.

The priests wore long robes; the nuns wore habits. Church was the only place in the whole of Accra where you would see anybody dressed in such a way. The holy communion wine was served in an ornate silver goblet, which just looked peculiar and exotic. And the entire mass, from the first word to the last, was officiated in Latin, a language none of us understood; a language I would later learn nobody spoke, not in Accra or anywhere else in the world, because for centuries it had essentially been dead and relegated chiefly to medical terminology and religious texts.

It was a strange experience, sitting in that pew, staring at images of the long-haired, blue-eyed Jesus Christ with his limbs nailed to a cross and a crown of thorns on his head, while listening to the deep, raspy voice of the priest saying, *"Dominus vobiscum, et cum spiritu tuo."* That phrase remained etched in my memory, even though it would take me forty years before I even ventured to learn its translation: The Lord be with you, and with your spirit.

Our father never came with us to mass. He was not a religious person, not in the churchgoing kind of way. I knew him to be a Presbyterian, and I have two or three childhood memories of attending the Presbyterian church in Tamale with him. As is true of a large number of Ghanaians his age, Dad's religion came by way of his schooling. He had been exposed to Western education, and along with it usually came Christianity; at that time in our nation's development, the two went hand in hand.

Church was a part of life at Achimota School as well. On Sundays we students would be shepherded to the Aggrey Memorial Chapel. Those Sunday services at boarding school were nondenominational and not at all as distinctive as the services in my stepmother's church.

During the years of my youth, Christianity had taken hold mostly in the south of Ghana; it was not that widespread in the north, though a few denominations, like Catholicism, had started to make inroads. You could find a Catholic church in most of the district capitals like Damongo, where there was also a Catholic hospital, the place where I'd spent two blissful and pampered weeks recovering from pneumonia.

There were very few established churches in the villages, but the missionaries had started to slowly and surely set up camp in those places as well. For example, you might find a single missionary living in a mud hut who'd perhaps managed to convert eight or ten others to his faith. Those types of groups were an oddity; they stood out and were sometimes even regarded

with suspicion because for the most part in the northern territories Christianity was still fighting a battle against Islam
and animism.

Though there were definitely people who were devout tra-
ditionalists when it came to their faith and their form of wor-
ship, animism was so intricately woven into our culture by way
of our ceremonies, festivals, customs, and rituals that it wasn't
necessarily viewed as a religious doctrine or defining spiritual
belief; it was just who we were as Ghanaians.

ONCE IN A WHILE WHEN Alfred and I went to visit our mother
in Damongo, she would take us to the village of Busunu to
visit her parents. Busunu is just off the main trunk road between Tamale and Damongo, about an hour's drive away from
Damongo. If Damongo could be considered a village, as it was
back then, I'm not exactly sure what to call Busunu. It was
much smaller and much more rural than Damongo.

There was no electricity. Nobody we knew of had a generator. There was also no running water. Plastic was not as
commonplace as it is now, so instead of metal pails or buckets,
which were rather costly, water was collected in a giant calabash. That's how we took our baths.

Alfred and I would stay in our grandmother's hut with our
mum. Often, if we visited during the harmattan season when
the weather is dry and it gets chilly at night, our grandmother
would build a small fire in the hut to warm up the place. I have
fond memories of those instances, but overall, I truly and deeply
disliked going to Busunu. Alfred and I played with the chil-

dren there as well, but we did not share the same easy and fraternal relationship with them as we did with the kids in Damongo.

Whereas in Damongo, Alfred and I felt as though we were on an endless adventure of discovery on which we could claim each new find as our own, in Busunu we often found ourselves bored senseless—especially after night had fallen. There was nothing to do except listen to the sounds of the crickets.

Every house in Busunu had animals. Actually, every house in Damongo had animals as well. In the north, animals were not raised primarily as food. They served as a store of value; they were like a bank. It was not uncommon for food to be cooked and served without meat in a household that, with dozens of goats and chickens and cows on the premises, was virtually a farm. Whenever we saw an animal being slaughtered, it was usually for a festival or a funeral or the arrival of out-of-town visitors.

The animals were also used for barter. Occasionally, for instance, the head of household might take a goat, tie it up, and carry it along with him to the market. There, he would most likely sell the goat and use the money to buy cloth or kerosene or matches or whatever else was needed at home. The balance of the day and the money would be spent drinking *pito* or some other type of alcohol until both funds and man were exhausted. Only then would he return home.

There was a particular festival in Busunu that involved animals, and every year it seemed that our visits would coincide with it. It was this festival that first made me question the relationship between culture and religion, as well as between folklore, superstition, and tradition.

I suppose technically you could say that our relatives in Busunu were animists, but not fundamentally so. It wasn't as if they spent every morning making sacrifices or pouring libations, but they did take part in the local festivals and celebrations, including doing whatever they were supposed to do to pacify the gods.

Just as a priest or rabbi helps to facilitate people's understanding of their faith, the local chiefs and their circle of elders served as something of a gateway to the gods. They were the ones who set the dates for the various festivals honouring the gods; they were the ones who knew what pleased the gods and what made them cross.

My maternal grandfather was an elder and a very close aide to the chief of the village. Whenever we went to Busunu, I was always amazed at the number of amulets and talismans displayed on the walls and tables in his room. He even had smocks that were adorned with all kinds of fetishes.

The belief among the villagers was that every year, on one particular night, the gods came down from the sky or the heavens or wherever it was they resided to visit Busunu. The chief and the elders in the village, such as my grandfather, were the ones who communicated to the villagers which night that visit would take place. When that night arrived, all the villagers were supposed to remain indoors. The gods were not to be seen by mortals; it was forbidden. And these gods were reputed to be rather aggressive, so much so that they were armed with whips, and they would mercilessly cane anybody who was caught outside.

It took several days to prepare for the gods' visit. One of the first things people did was corral their animals. Any goats, cows, and chickens that were left wandering about would be taken by the chief and elders on the day of the gods' visit and slaughtered in the village square as a sacrifice. This seemed like an especially harsh punishment seeing as how every household in the village was already slaughtering at least one of their animals as a sacrifice to the gods.

It was customary for people to kill their best goat or fowl and then use it to make a lavish meal. The people in the household were allowed to eat some of the food they'd pre-pared, but they had to leave a healthy portion of it, the one with the juiciest and most desirable parts of the animal, for the gods. What I recall most vividly is how those offerings were left outside of each compound, bowls and plates of food—*fufu* with groundnut soup, *tuo zaafi* with guinea fowl. Mum, Al-fred, and I would see the dishes as we rushed home to my grandmother's hut.

Being the curious and inquisitive child that I was, I enjoyed walking in front of each hut to see what had been left. One year, my mum, Alfred, and I found ourselves outside as the sun was setting. Most of the villagers were already inside their homes, and the three of us were rushing to do the same before it got dark and the gods descended. I was drawn in by each of the dishes on the doorsteps we passed by. My mother and Al-fred were far ahead of me before they realised that I was still standing in front of someone's home, staring longingly at a heaping plate of food.

"Dramani," they both yelled, "hurry!" And I rushed to catch up with them. Like everyone else, we were frightened of what would happen if we were still outside when the gods descended and we were unlucky enough to come face-to-face with them.

MY FAMILY, LIKE ALL THE other families in Busunu, Damongo, and Bole, are Gonjas. The Gonja people have a fascinating history. The Gonja state was founded in the late 1500s by Askia Dawud, an emperor of the ancient Songhai Empire. The Songhai Empire occupied the area at the bend of the river Niger where it meets the Sahara desert. As the empire grew, it covered a wide stretch of land, reaching into the territories of what are now modern-day Mali, Niger, Senegal, Guinea, The Gambia, and Burkina Faso. At the empire's height, it even reached as far as Benin and parts of Nigeria. The Songhai Empire was known, among other things, for the transformation of the city of Timbuktu into the largest outpost for the trans-Saharan trade of gold, salt, cloth, and slaves. Timbuktu was also the nucleus of intellectual and scholarly activity. It contained one of the largest libraries in the world, boasting a collection of at least five hundred thousand books, and a university with a student population of twenty-five thousand.

The Mandé, a tribe to which Dawud belonged, were also the founders of the ancient Ghana and Mali Empires. Their leaders were given the title Jakpa. In the 1700s, Sumaila Ndewura Jakpa extended the Gonja territory and is widely hailed as the leader of the modern Gonja state. The Mandé people were closely associated with the Muslim tradition, and legend has it that Sumaila Ndewura Jakpa's chief spiritualist was a Muslim man by the name of Fatimoripe, whose followers accompanied the Gonjas into battle, offering prayers and performing rituals for their victory. It is said that the Muslim followers could predict whether a battle would go well or whether it would go badly, whether people would perish or whether they would prevail. These Muslims were called the Sakpari, and they were the ones who prayed for the salvation of the souls of the Gonja people. By this arrangement, the Gonjas were able, then, to go into battle and lead their secular lives, with the assurance that their souls were being safeguarded, that the Sakpari were interceding with Allah for their victory, safety, and salvation. It was, in fact, Fatimoripe who baptised Ndewura Jakpa and gave him the name Sumaila.

This history is important because it illustrates both a spiritual respect and a spiritual independence in Ghanaian culture dating back to the origins of the tribes that currently exist in the country. Ghana has always been, and still is, a secular state, yet at the heart of its culture it has maintained a deep respect for spiritual faith and practise. It is a magnificent tightrope that not many other African countries have managed to walk. We have successfully and peacefully incorporated myriad spiritual beliefs into one unified nation.

You can wake up at dawn in certain sections of Kumasi or Accra or the various areas of the north and hear the muezzin, facing in the direction of Ka'ba, calling *azan* through the minaret: *"Allahu Akbar. Allahu Akbar. Allahu Akbar. Allahu Akbar."*

Then, too, there is Ghana's large population of Christians. Before the numerous orthodox denominations took hold, there was the movement of syncretism. There were a number of apostolic churches in the north, one of the most prominent of which was Cherubim and Seraphim. What made the Cherubim and Seraphim church stand out was that the women had to cover their hair, the men wore long white robes, and the congregation really belted out the music. There was body shaking and prophecies and speaking in tongues. Unlike the more Western-influenced orthodox churches, which had not yet gained full ground, these churches were unapologetic in their African orientation. They allowed African musical instruments in their services like drums; the *balafon*, a type of African xylophone that is traditional to the Mandé people; and the *shekere*, a West African form of maraca. These types of churches were referred to in the vernacular as *Nyame pe agro*, which, loosely translated, means "God loves entertainment."

We had a distant relation, a carpenter, who belonged to a Cherubim and Seraphim church. He had a little shed out of which he used to work. It was called Young Ambition, and it was the most popular carpentry shop in the north. It's where everybody would go if they wanted well-made furniture. Alfred and I would go there to watch him work. We were captivated by the way he used his planer to shave the surface of the wood. There was a distinctive smell to his shop that I found oddly pleasant. Each type of wood had a different odour. There was the sweetness of *wawa*, which was supple and easy to finish and mould. Then there was *odum*, which seemed sturdier and released a more pungent scent as it was being shaved.

Our relative, whose real name I have forgotten because we merely called him "Uncle," would finish his day's work, then would rush over to the church. Sometimes Alfred and I would stray in that direction and peer through the windows to see all of the people inside in their robes and head scarves. The men would be chanting, almost as if they were in a trance, and the women would be going into paroxysms. People would faint, having apparently been possessed by the spirit. They also performed healings.

The service reached its climax when the priest entered and started dancing. The women would gather around him, singing and hailing him and fanning him with their cloths. It was a wonder to behold. Alfred and I would stand with our faces pressed against the windowpane and our hands cupped just above our cheeks, at our eyes, as though we were holding binoculars. We wanted to take in everything.

SOMETHING HAPPENED THAT NIGHT WHEN my mother, Alfred, and I were in Busunu, rushing to get home before it got dark. We arrived at my grandparents' hut safely, carefully stepping over the plate of food that had been left at the doorstep as a sacrifice for the gods.

Alfred and I were in our beds when the gods descended and began walking through the streets of Busunu. We could hear them singing their usual song:

> *Wofa tim-bri-basanyo*
> *Wofa tim-bri-basasa*
> *Wofa tim-bri-basana*
> *Fular fenkor*

They were singing, "The spirit has whipped two people; the spirit has whipped three people; the spirit has whipped four people. If you come out, we will whip you until you shit."

When they passed by our window, we could hear their voices, deep and gruff and full of force, with an echo that thundered through the air behind them. They waved their whips through the air as they walked. I learned much later that those whips were made of bamboo, which had been sliced again and again in such a way that it became limp enough to swirl. Each time the whip went up and the wind entered those grooves, it made a chilling, unnatural sound. Alfred and I lay shivering with fear under our covers, but as their voices grew more distant, Alfred suddenly got up and crawled to the window.

"What are you doing?" I whispered, frightened that my big brother would end up being caned. He held a finger up to his mouth, signalling me to shut up. I did as he ordered. I was scared, but as usual, curiosity got the better of me. I refused to be left out of whatever it was Alfred was up to. I crawled over to the window and joined him. Alfred stood on his knees and peeked outside. I struggled to squeeze my body into the corner between him and the bed so that I could also have a look. I too wanted to steal a glance at the gods.

Wofa tim-bri-basanyo
Wofa tim-bri-basasa
Wofa tim-bri-basana
Fular fenkor

Their voices were growing more and more distant. It was difficult to see anything in the darkness. I was shorter than

Alfred, so my line of vision wasn't as clear. In my attempt to make more room for myself to get a better look, I pushed Alfred into the piece of furniture that was on the other side of him, and he knocked over whatever was on it. It wasn't an extremely loud sound. Had the night not been so still, and had the crash not happened right in the middle of a pause between the refrains of the gods' chant, the sound would have probably gone unnoticed.

"Heh? What was that?" one of the gods asked in a regular person's voice. Alfred and I nearly tripped over each other as we scurried back to our bed. We pulled the covers over our heads and squeezed our eyes shut.

"Did you hear that?" another god asked, also in a normal person's voice. They turned around and started moving back in the direction of our window to investigate the source of the mysterious crash.

I noticed that the second god who spoke sounded a lot like one of our uncles. The gods returned to the area just beside our window, and they stayed there, standing silently, for a long time. Or maybe it just felt like a long time because Alfred and I were holding our breath, petrified of making any more sounds. We didn't want to be found out and caned.

"It's nothing," the second god finally said. That time I was all but sure it had to be our uncle. I tapped Alfred on the shoulder to get his attention. He didn't mind me. After a few more moments of silence to confirm what the second god said, that it really was nothing, they started to walk away. Alfred and I listened to the footsteps of the gods until they started singing again, and the tenor of their voices combined with the eerie rattle of their whips possessed the night.

Wofa tim-bri-basanyo
Wofa tim-bri-basasa
Wofa tim-bri-basana
Fular fenkor

Those few seconds were all I needed to refuel my suspicion. Our uncle walked with a slight limp. It wasn't especially noticeable when you watched him, but it made the rhythm of his gait unmistakable. Whenever he came to visit us at our grandmother's, we could usually make him out long before we saw his face, just by the sound of his footsteps. I tapped Alfred on the shoulder again.

"Ah, but do you think . . . ," I started to whisper to him. I wanted to know if he had also realised that our uncle was one of the gods.

"Dramani, shut up," he scolded under his breath; then he turned his back to me and didn't speak again. I wanted to wait until the gods or whoever they were had walked far away from our window before trying to pose the question to Alfred again. I waited and waited until, before I realised it, I had drifted off to sleep, and it was daybreak.

The next morning, Alfred and I lingered at home, not doing much of anything. Neither of us uttered a word about the night before. Around lunchtime, our mother told us to get ready. The three of us went to pay our uncle a visit. When we arrived at his compound we found him and several of the chief's elders sitting around, feasting on bowls of light soup with mounds of meat in them. I recognised some of the plates of food from the doorsteps that we'd hurried past in our attempt to get home before dark the night before.

Alfred turned in my direction and gave me a look that told me he knew. So it wasn't all in my imagination. He knew. That wasn't any god outside of our window; it was our uncle. But how? Why? Had be been walking in the company of gods? Or were those other people with him his fellow elders? Later that day when Alfred and I had a chance to talk, we came to the conclusion that even if those other men were gods, we believed the festival to be a conspiracy, a way for the elders to loot animals and food from the villagers one day every year.

I was starting to get a sense of the power that religion and spirituality had over people and how others could so easily use it to encourage trust and devotion or to control and engender fear.

EVERY ETHNIC GROUP IN GHANA has a ritual or formal ceremony for the naming of a newly born child and a way of choosing the name that is in line with their traditions. Though there are details of these rituals and ceremonies that differ from ethnic group to ethnic group, they are governed by the same basic ideas and principles.

When a child is born, he or she is considered a stranger or a visitor. In the north, among the Dagombas, newly born boys are called Saando, and the girls are called Saanpaga, which, respectively, means "stranger boy" and "stranger girl." The infants are kept indoors for a period of time, usually a week; thus the naming ceremony is informally referred to as an "outdooring." It is during the outdooring, upon being given a name, that the child is officially considered a person, a member of the community.

Outdoorings are usually officiated by family elders or religious and spiritual leaders, and they generally take place at dawn. Various rites are performed to welcome the child to the community and the world at large and to prepare him or her for life.

In the north, the outdooring takes place on the seventh day of a child's life. The family arranges for a *wanzam* to come and perform a few of the rites. *Wanzams* are itinerant barbers. They travel from town to town with their tools of trade, a series of sharp blades. Theirs is a trade that is passed on through the generations, from father to son.

The hair with which a baby is born is considered tainted because it came from "the other side." At the outdooring, the *wanzam* shaves the newborn's head so that all the hair that grows from then on will be of this side of life. If the baby is a boy, the *wanzam* will also circumcise him. In many cases, the *wanzam* will also cut distinguishing marks onto the baby's face or body. This scarification is sometimes referred to as tribal marking because it is a practise performed only by certain tribes, but each mark has a meaning and tells an immediate story about that child's history and lineage.

All of our traditional primary names hold meaning, one that is symbolic or somehow of relevance to the family, village, or larger tribe. Some Ghanaian ethnic groups give their children names that correspond to the day of the week on which they were born. For instance, a Sunday-born Akan boy might be named Kwasi and a girl, Akosua.

There are names within ethnic groups that identify children as twins, even signalling the order in which they arrived.
There are names that reveal if a child is the firstborn girl or
boy in a family or if he or she is a single birth directly following the birth of twins. Some names are telling of circumstances or conditions surrounding the child's birth, like if it
was a sunny day or if it was in the midst of a drought. A name
might indicate that the father died before the baby's birth or
that the mother had suffered the deaths of one or two other
babies before the arrival of the one being named.

Regardless of whether they are Muslims, because of the
Gonja people's link with the Sakpari, many northerners be-
stow Arabic names on their children. Imams, leaders in the
Islamic faith, are occasionally consulted before outdoorings
to assist the family with the selection of an appropriate name.

The usage of paternal surnames is a Western convention
that has only recently made its way into our culture. Previously it was not unusual either for a child to have no surname
or for each child in a family to have a different surname. This
was because in addition to the primary name that is given to
an infant, the family might attach the name of a departed relative or a respected elder. That second name, by Western standards, would serve as the child's surname. You'll even find a
person's hometown or village being used as a second name,
distinguishing them from others with the same primary name,
such as Fatima Navrongo or Seidu Bunsunu.

Within my family, the use of a paternal surname began with
my father. My grandfather, the Gbemfu Wura, was named
Adama. With the exception of his chiefly title, that was his

primary and sole name. My father was named Mahama. When he began attending school, he was required to have a surname, so his father's name was used. Following the standard protocol of academic attendance rosters, the student's surname was placed first, followed by a comma and then his primary name. My father's name was thus written as "Adama, Mahama."

This proved confusing to the teachers, the majority of whom were Western and unfamiliar with Ghanaian names; it was unclear to them which was the primary name and which was the surname. Complicating matters further was the fact that a lot of the students had the same names, except in different combinations. There could easily have been another student with the name "Mahama, Adama." To simplify everything, the teachers just ignored the comma between the two names. This is how my father's primary name evolved into a surname.

Children who were not being educated at a *makaranta*, the Hausa word for school or madrasa, were being educated at Western-style schools and were most likely being taught by missionaries. Those children were required to have Christian names preceding their indigenous names. These days it seems that all Western names are referred to as Christian names, but when my father was in school and while I was growing up, these were proper Christian names, taken right out of the Bible.

At school, my father was given the name Emmanuel. Thus, he became Emmanuel Adama Mahama. In his adulthood, to preserve the name his family had given him, my father used only the initials of the ones that had been imposed on him,

E.A., and allowed Mahama to stand as the only name that was written or spoken in full. By the time my father's children were born, the use of paternal surnames had become common among the educated and elite, so in addition to the primary names we were given, we were given what had now become our father's surname, Mahama.

OUR FATHER NAMED ALL OF his children according to tradition. At the outdoorings, a *wanzam* came and performed his portion of the rites. The name I was given at my ceremony was Dramani. I was named after a relative, one of my paternal grandfather's brothers who had died.

In Ghana, it is not often that you will hear someone use the word *granduncle* or *grandaunt*. It is even more rare to hear *greatgrand* anything. We take all of those relations to be our grandfathers and grandmothers. In our collective society, as an extension of respect, grandparents are called Nana, and it is considered rude to call them by their given names.

Naming me after my grandfather was a way to honour his memory, but it was also a way to anoint me with his qualities or traits that were most loved. It was believed that a part of him lived on in me through his name. As a child, and until this day, many of my aunties and uncles would not call me by my primary name. They called me "Nnana," which means "my grandfather," conferring the reverence due him to me, the holder of his name.

My brother Peter's given name was Issah, Alfred's was Abdulai, and Adam's was Adama, after our paternal grandfather.

My sister's name was Meri, but we called her Mama. Like our father, they were all made to take Christian names as soon as they started school. Dad, who'd recently been made the regional commissioner, decided to enroll the children at a new school in Tamale that was run by a family of British missionaries. I was not yet living with my father.

One day, during their first week at the school, Dad gathered my four siblings into the living room. He produced three sheets of paper that he'd received from the school's headmaster. On each one was written a name, a Christian name. He gave one of the sheets to Mama and told her that the name on the paper would be her Christian name; it was Mary Magdalene. Since Adama had been our grandfather's name, and since that name had inadvertently become our father's as well, Dad decided to Anglicise it to Adam for his son. He also gave Adam the Christian name he'd been given, Emmanuel.

There were two pieces of paper left. Dad asked Issah and Abdulai to each take one of the pieces of paper. Being the oldest, Issah chose first. He took the paper with the name "Peter" on it. Abdulai's paper had the name "Alfred" written on it. Abdulai said his new name out loud a few times: "Alfred. Alfred. Alfred." He liked the sound of it.

Issah did the same and promptly decided that he didn't want the name "Peter." He much rather preferred the sound of "Alfred." The two boys started to quarrel. It struck Issah that they were arguing over names they didn't know anything about. Where did these names come from? Who had settled upon those two? Were there others from which they could choose?

"But Daddy," asked a baffled Issah, "what is the meaning of these names?" Our father told them all about Alfred the Great and Saint Peter the Apostle, who is sometimes referred to as "Peter the Rock." Those were the people whose names they were being given. After hearing about their new namesakes, Issah decided to let the name "Alfred" go. He didn't mind being "Peter" after all.

Not long after that naming incident, Dad brought my newly "christened" siblings to Damongo to visit Mum and me. The instant our father called me Dramani, Peter wanted to know what my name was. Our father, misunderstanding, looked at Peter strangely and said, "He is Dramani, your brother."

"Yes, but what is his other name? His Christian name?" Peter asked. Dad told him I didn't have one. This didn't sit well with Peter. If they'd been made to assume Christian names, then I should be too.

"What about 'John'?" Peter asked. "Like John the Baptist. I think 'John' is a nice name for Dramani."

"Yes," Alfred agreed. "I think 'John' would be a good name for him."

Our father didn't protest or disagree. I think that's because he knew it would merely be delaying the inevitable. I'd have to be given a Christian name when I began attending school, so why not do it now and why not have it be "John"?

After his tenure as regional commissioner, while awaiting the announcement of his next government post, my father moved the family south to the capital, Accra. I joined them there and started attending school. Interestingly, neither of the two schools I attended in Accra required me to have a

Christian name. Everybody continued to call me Dramani. It wasn't until I entered secondary school that the name "John" became an active part of my life.

When my dad's political career came to an end, our family returned north to Tamale. At my new school, my name was written on the enrolment roster as "Mahama, John Dramani." Since my teachers and classmates were not people who had ever known me as Dramani, they latched onto John as my primary name. That is how I became John Mahama. The name "Dramani" effectively got lost until I entered politics and started to use my full name officially.

OUTDOORINGS ARE STILL A FUNDAMENTAL part of Ghanaian culture, though aspects of the ceremonies have changed as a result of advances in our health delivery system. Far more women, in the villages as well as the urban areas, are giving birth in hospitals or clinics and opting to have their infant sons circumcised there under more sterilised conditions rather than calling for a *wanzam*. HIV-AIDS has also had an impact on the usage of *wanzams* for other rites that occur during naming ceremonies, such as the shaving of an infant's head or the cutting of tribal marks.

It is now commonplace for siblings born of the same father, like my siblings and me, to all carry his surname. Parents are also giving their children Christian names at the same time they are being given their traditional names. Even so, the Christian names tend to be reserved for formal use, at school and amidst strangers, people who are outside of a family's immediate circle.

There are no set traditions associated with the giving of Christian names. Some parents choose the names of celebrities, some use books to guide them or stick to biblical names, and others recycle the names that were given to their forebears.

Religion and spirituality continue to play crucial roles in Ghanaian society, informing and shaping our culture, sometimes for the better and sometimes not. When I am on my way to church services with my family, depending on the route we take, we'll pass the Catholic church I used to attend with my siblings and stepmother. Whenever we do, I watch the children filing in, wearing their Sunday suits and dresses, and I remember us, my brothers and sisters and me, squirming in the pew, listening to the priest say, *"Dominus vobiscum, et cum spiritu tuo."* I remember, too, the chill of fear that would run down my spine when Alfred and I heard the strange *whoosh* of the gods' whips as they stalked the night, singing:

Wofa tim-bri-basanyo
Wofa tim-bri-basasa
Wofa tim-bri-basana
Fular fenkor

I will lose myself in the labyrinth of those memories with the smells of shaved wood, the sight of steam rising off the plates of food that had been left in front of houses as an offering, the bitter taste of communion wine, and the momentarily blinding flash of a *wanzam*'s blade. Then, finally, we will arrive at our church and my wife, Lordina, will call my name. "John," she will say, "we are here," breaking my reverie and bringing me back to the reality of who I am today.

SANKOFA

W HEN MY FATHER was released from detention, he was like a completely different man. I was away at boarding school, so I didn't see him, but my brother Peter did. He told me that Dad had a full beard, not the kind that people grow on purpose, trimming the edges and the loose, wiry hairs that stand straight instead of curling like the others. Dad's beard was scraggly, unkempt, like that of a castaway. His hair was the same, thick and wild.

"I looked at him," Peter told me, "and I said, 'I think I know this man. I think he is my father.' He was almost unrecognisable."

Dad hadn't shaved or had a proper haircut in more than a year because it wasn't allowed in detention. Naturally, when he got back, that was one of his top priorities. He wanted to see himself, and for others to see him, as the man he'd once been. But it soon became apparent that even clean-shaven and properly coiffed, he was no longer that man. Our father had changed. I noticed it immediately when I came home on a break from school. The change wasn't enormous, in such a way that you could point to a single thing and say, "You see?" It was more a series of minor changes, shifts in his outlook and personality, attitudes and behaviours that had not been present before his detention.

Some days Dad behaved like a man who'd been blind his whole life and had just been given the gift of sight. He took everything in as if for the first time, like the gradually increasing brightness of the sun as it rose in the morning or the particular arrangements of colours in the wing or tail feathers of a bird flying past. When he looked at my siblings and me, he seemed to be studying our faces, comparing them perhaps with the faces of the children he'd left behind, taking note of how much we too had changed during his absence.

On other days Dad behaved in the opposite way, as though he had been submerged in darkness and was desperately searching for an opening of light. He would sit quietly, staring off into the distance, not looking at anything. Just staring.

"I will never return to prison," Dad would say, abruptly breaking the silence. "Never again. I will always be a free man."

He said it often enough, with the firmest resolve I'd ever heard him say anything, that it sank into my head and stayed with me. I'd never had reason to consider the concept of freedom. I don't think any of us in my household had. I guess we'd always taken it for granted. Unlike Dad, we'd never been detained. We'd also never lived under colonial rule. Even my older siblings who'd been born before Gold Coast became Ghana were too young to know the freedoms that distinguished a colony from an independent nation.

What I learned in my childhood, though, while watching my father reconstruct his life were the freedoms that distinguished a man before his detention and that same man upon his release.

AFTER THE 1966 COUP D'ETAT, a governing body was organised ad hoc by the military to oversee affairs in the country; it was called the National Liberation Council (NLC). The NLC had set up a formal Commission of Inquiry to investigate officials, like my father, who had served in Dr. Nkrumah's government. This investigation had taken place through a series of interrogations while those officials had been detained. Their release coincided with the presentation of a report by the Commission of Inquiry that outlined certain restrictions and sanctions for each of those former government officials. All of them, for instance, were barred from participating in party politics or holding any public appointments for a period of ten years.

My father's assets and bank accounts were frozen or seized, leaving him financially crippled and effectively turning him into a pauper overnight. The house in Kanda Estates where we'd been living before the coup was an official government residence from which my father had essentially been evicted. He owned another house in the nearby Ringway Estates neighbourhood of Accra. As luck, or fate, would have it, my stepmother had been in possession of that house, so it was not among the assets that were either seized or frozen.

Because the coup had caused our family to be separated, my father gathered his children, one by one, from where we had been taken and moved us into the house at Ringway Estates with him. It would be our new home, where we would live for almost two years while Dad was figuring out a way to move forward. He didn't have employment, nor did he have any viable prospects. He couldn't even return to teaching because Ghana's educational system was public and he had been barred from holding public appointments. He had to feed his family and plan for our future, and every day posed a new challenge.

For us children, it was an easy reconciliation. We quickly regained our closeness and fell back into the same relationships we'd once shared. We were carefree, as kids should be, all but oblivious to the tremendous weight of worry our father was carrying. We roamed the streets of our new neighbourhood, making friends with the other kids who lived there, discovering new ways and means to have fun and make mischief. Those were the challenges that our days posed.

Ringway Estates is directly next to the Osu neighbourhood, where the main strip, a lively collection of shops, restaurants, and boutiques, is now affectionately referred to as "Oxford Street," a not-so-subtle comparison to the well-known thoroughfare in West End, London.

I used to walk there with my brothers and our new friends, to buy ice-cream cones and other treats. On the way back home, right at the place everybody called the "Jehovah Witness Junction," because that's where the church's headquarters were, we would pass a house that had a ferocious dog on the property. Posted on the gate to the house was a sign that warned, "Beware of Dog." We never minded the sign. In fact, we would even make it a point to cross the street just so we could walk by the house. Whenever the dog would hear people passing by, it would run directly to the gate, barking ferociously and hurling the full weight of its body against the metal.

We would taunt the dog by growling back with our hands curled like claws beside our cheeks, our mouths wide open and teeth pronounced as though in midbite. It was a game to us. We'd laugh and laugh at the bulldog, caged and helpless in his rage, until our jaws ached and our ice cream began to melt.

One day we stood in front of the gate and started taunting the dog as usual. He lurched forward and pushed his front paws against the gate. We did the same, which was how we noticed that the gate hadn't been properly secured. Our lurch forward had pushed the gate inward, and now it was partly open. We could see the bulldog eyeing his exit and us, his tormentors, standing right across the threshold.

We bolted out of there and ran for dear life. We'd been running for only a short while, with the dog in hot pursuit, when he stopped suddenly, as though he'd hit some kind of invisible barrier, then turned around and sulked back toward his gate.

"That's because we went past his territory," my brother Alfred explained to us knowingly. "Dogs are territorial. They often fear going beyond the places and things they know." We lapped up our melting ice-cream cones, and this newfound knowledge, as we sauntered back onto our street.

SANKOFA IS AN AKAN WORD that means "go back and get it." It is also two of the symbols of the Adinkra, a traditional cotton cloth attributed to the Ashanti people. The Adinkra symbols, each of which is representative of a proverb or virtue, are either woven into or stamped onto the cloth. One of the Adinkra symbols for *sankofa* is an ornate drawing of a heart. The other symbol is a bird with its head facing backward, using its beak to lift an egg off its back. The egg is meant to suggest the future, that which is unborn.

The proverb that is associated with both *sankofa* symbols is *Se wo were fi na wosankofa a yenkyi.* It translates literally as "If you have forgotten and you go back and get it, it is not a taboo." It is also loosely or figuratively interpreted as "We must look to the past and take the best of what it has offered us in order to successfully move forward." The entire proverb has become encapsulated in the word *sankofa,* which for well over the last half century has been embraced by people of African descent throughout the diaspora as something of a "home call," a reminder that finding the essence of one's self often requires a return to one's roots.

After African countries gained independence, diasporans felt a greater urge to "return" to the continent to claim what had been lost or forgotten in the Middle Passage during the transatlantic slave trade—an identity, a lineage, a nationality, that rightfully belonged to them. The author Alex Haley had his finger directly on the pulse of that urge when, in the 1970s, he published the novel *Roots,* which illustrated to the mainstream of America and in effect the entire world the importance of that journey into one's past.

"In all of us," Alex Haley explained, "there is a hunger, marrow-deep, to know our heritage—to know who we are and where we have come from. Without this enriching knowledge, there is a hollow yearning."

That yearning to go back and reclaim heritage was equally

as present in post-colonial Africa. Just as diasporan Africans were discovering their roots and shedding their English names to embrace traditional African names, newly liberated nations were also shedding their colonial names and adopting more indigenous ones. Gold Coast became Ghana; Basutoland became Lesotho; Nyasaland became Malawi; Bechuanaland became Botswana; French Sudan became Mali. Over the course of the three decades that it took the majority of Africa to become free from colonialism, a number of other countries would do the same. It was as if the ideology of *sankofa* had become the mandate of an entire continent.

In addition, many countries attempted to marginalise their colonial tongue and nationalise an indigenous language. This would prove difficult to a number of new nations, such as Ghana, because of the presence of so many indigenous languages. As a result of the artificial borders that had been constructed in the course of colonisation, dozens of ethnic groups and languages spilled over from one nation into another. The decision of which one should take precedence was all but impossible for leaders to make. The borders these nations inherited divided not only territories but ethnic groups and families; they split allegiances, sometimes forcing people to choose between tribalism and nationalism. It is, unfortunately, a tug-of-war that is still ongoing for many people, many tribes, and many nations.

AT SOME POINT, IT DAWNED on my father that the only way for him to move forward was to go back to his roots. He was a northerner through and through, and the south wasn't being especially welcoming to him in his attempt to start anew. His sole purpose for moving to Accra had been to represent and serve the interests of his people in the north. The coup had brought an end to that, so after trying for almost two years to make some sort of living for himself and his family in Accra, he packed up and returned to the place and the life that was most familiar to him. Since there was no other field of work available to my father, he decided to become a farmer.

Ghana's "land tenure" is a specific administration of land occupation and ownership. To ensure that the lands remain in the hands of the daughters and sons of the soil, there is no such thing as true ownership. From region to region, the rights of the land are ancestral and within the control of the various tribal hierarchies. In much of the northern portion of the country, land is held in trust by the chiefs for the people, so if an individual wants a parcel of land, he or she has to go to the chief to make a request. If the individual is deemed eligible, and after he or she fulfils whatever necessary protocols, the chief will allocate the land.

Through this system, my father was able to build a home right at the edge of Tamale and lease over two thousand acres of land in Yapei, a small village on the outskirts of the city, about twenty-six kilometres away in Gonjaland, where my father was of royal lineage.

The house in Tamale was a big, comfortable three-bedroom bungalow situated on an acre of land. As was typical in Ghana, there was also a boys' quarters, a kind of outhouse where the domestic workers resided. The boys' quarters were also a three-bedroom structure.

The edges of the yard were dotted with mahogany and eucalyptus trees, and there was a straight row of neem trees behind the boys' quarters. We had a small garden in front of the veranda in which my father planted a variety of flowers. The ones I loved the most were the forget-me-nots. I'm not sure what enthralled me more about them, their unusual name or their tiny paper-white bloom with a small yellow eye in the centre. There was also bougainvillea that grew along the hedges in the most vibrant array of pink and white petals.

Because Dad had grown up in a self-sufficient household, and also because he was about to engage in the business of farming, he believed it was necessary to grow one's own food. The rest of the plot surrounding our house was used for growing vegetables. We planted every vegetable imaginable, from onions and carrots and tomatoes to peppers and eggplant. There was rarely a need for us to go to the market. Whatever we desired was right outside, ready to be picked and brought into the kitchen for cooking.

Dad intended to use the farm at Yapei for growing rice. He'd surveyed the possibilities and come to the conclusion that the best agribusiness opportunity for him would be in commercial rice farming. He felt that it could be a sustainable, if not lucrative, endeavour. Rice was something Ghanaians ate in abundance, yet the local production did not meet the demand.

As soon as Dad had organised the house and got the farm up and running, he moved all of us kids from Accra to Tamale to live with him. For Dad, one of the benefits of living in Tamale was that northerners attended school free of charge. Ghana was still making tremendous efforts to provide greater

access to education in the north, so it had put in place a programme called the Northern Scholarship Scheme that enabled
kids from the north to attend school, from primary straight
through to the end of their education, with the government
providing for tuition, room and board, full uniform (including sandals), and books. All of my siblings were transferred to
boarding schools in the north. I remained at Achimota because Dad wanted me to complete primary school there.

The education my brothers received upon their arrival at
Tamale Secondary School was not one simply in academic
studies. It was the first time they'd come in contact with ex-
treme poverty. Some of the students, they told me, would come
to school with nothing except the clothes on their backs. They
brought no provisions, no sponges, soap, toothbrushes, or bags
in which to carry their books. My brothers learned, through
conversations with those children, of the crushing day-to-day
struggles in the villages where they lived.

Even taking advantage of the free education provided by
the Northern Scholarship Scheme proved difficult for many
families who were too poor to pay for the transportation to
get their children back to school. My brothers told me of a fellow student who had to miss a term because his family had to
wait for the yam crop to be harvested and sold before they
would have enough money to send him back.

It was an eye-opening experience for my brothers. They
saw for themselves the opportunities that an education promised those children, the freedom from abject poverty and the
chance to create a better life for themselves and their families.
It gave my brothers, and ultimately me, greater insight into

our father's passions, namely his passion for education and his commitment to helping develop the north. Throughout our lives, our father had been consumed with the self-designated task of expanding the possibilities of the people who lived in the north, people whose conditions mirrored the ones from which he had been spared through his own access to education. And now we understood why.

On breaks and short vacations, I would join my family in Tamale. Although I was not yet attending school in the north like my brothers, just being there also provided me with a vital education. I had moved to Accra when I was still very small, and in the process of growing up there I'd learned Ga, which is a language spoken in Accra, and Twi, which is an Akan language that is also widely spoken in the south. While I was picking up these new languages, I was also slowly losing my ability to speak my native languages, the ones I'd first learned while living with my mother in the north. Living in Tamale forced me to relearn Gonja, Dagbani, and Hausa and, as a matter of course, regain a vital part of my identity as a northerner.

Going home to Tamale was always a special treat for me because I got to fly. When I was younger, I used to have the most awesome dreams of flying, of soaring higher and higher until the city beneath me was out of sight, until I was surrounded by clouds. Now, travelling between Accra and Tamale, I got to live those dreams, except in an airplane.

I would leave Achimota and be taken to Kotoka Airport in Accra, where I would board one of the Douglas DC-3 Dakota airplanes that Ghana Airways operated. The planes sat on the tarmac in such a way that their rears were very low to the ground and their noses were pointed up, as if they were already in the midst of takeoff. They were old airplanes. The height of their use and popularity had been in the mid twentieth century. By the late 1960s and early 1970s, they had been officially retired, all except the ones that had been sold to developing countries in Africa, planes that had been used and overused for decades in countries like England, Canada, India, and the United States.

When my flight arrived in Tamale, Abudu would pick me up from the airport and take me straight home, where my brothers, especially Alfred, Adam, and Peter, would pull me headfirst into whatever latest obsessions they were nurturing or trickery they were planning. We were constantly inventing new ways to amuse ourselves and toe the edge of trouble. It was almost always harmless, but it was also almost always at somebody else's expense.

The appliances that we consider common these days were luxuries back then, especially in the northern regions. Television sets were rare. They tuned in to only one channel, Ghana Broadcasting Corporation, and the pictures were displayed only in black and white. GBC began its programming at five in the evening and ended it at ten. During those hours, my brothers and I were glued to the television set, watching *The Wizard of Oz*, *The High Chaparral*, *Hawaii Five-O*, *The Twilight Zone*, and *Soul Train*.

Refrigerators were also rare, and ours became the centrepiece for many of the tricks we played on people. We used to put water in the fridge and let it get as cold as possible. We would then purposely serve it to those of our dad's visitors who'd come from the villages, knowing full well they'd most likely never had ice-cold water before.

In Ghana, it is customary to immediately offer water to visitors once they enter your home. Since many people travel long distances by foot or public transportation in the scorching heat, this is a particularly hospitable gesture. It is also customary for visitors to accept the water and take at least one sip of it. Our watchman in Tamale, Salifu, once told me traditional legend held that you should beware if a visitor entered your home and refused to drink water because it meant he or she was really an apparition in human form.

When someone came over whom we'd decided we wanted to play this cold water trick on, my brothers and I would rush to the kitchen before the house help had a chance to get there and we would take the water from the fridge and pour a tall glass. We would come back to the living room and serve it to the visitor, then stand off to the side and watch as the visitor took the first large gulp. We'd watch the expression of curiosity on his face when he held the chilled glass. His eyes would grow wide with alarm as the water made its way down his throat. After he'd swallowed, he would usually express some sort of bewilderment, saying something that would make us laugh hysterically, like "Oh, it cool my teeth" or "The water freeze my tongue."

One person we used to play this trick on all the time was a local farmer called Dagbando. The plot of land right next to our house also belonged to Dad. It was vacant, so he allowed Dagbando, who lived in the neighbouring village of Gumbihini, to farm on it. Dagbando and Dad became good friends. He was tall, as black as burnt metal, and brawny. He looked to be in his early forties, and his face beamed with kindness. A lot of the local farms were operated by individuals who used old-fashioned methods. The farmers used to plant the seeds in the ground and hope that everything else would fall in place for their crops to thrive. Since Dad used more modern farming practices and equipment like tractors and combine harvesters, he would often give Dagbando practical advice. Sometimes he would also give him fertilizer or teach him how to spray herbicide. Dagbando in turn as a show of his gratitude would bring us guinea fowls as gifts.

Whenever Dagbando was thirsty or had to use the bathroom, he would come next door to our house instead of walking the almost one kilometre or so back to his home in Gumbihini. This gave us kids the opportunity to serve him water. The first time we did this, he, like all the others, was startled. "Aeeiiiiii, aeeiiiiii," he said, squinting his eyes and shaking his head. The next few times he didn't say anything, but his physical reaction was the same. One day when he came over to ask for water, as my brothers and I were marching off to the kitchen to get the water from the fridge, much to our dismay, Dagbando said, "Please, not the one in the glass that sweats." And that was the end of our fun, at least with him.

MANY OF THE TREES IN Ghana have roots that sprawl; they extend beyond one small area of space. Many of the families here are like that as well, with mine being no exception. In our culture, no matter where you were born, depending on your ethnicity and whether that tribe is matrilineal or patrilineal, you claim the hometown of either your mother or your father. And they in turn claimed the hometown of their mother or father. In this way, the origins that we claim are ancestral, dating back multiple generations. Yet the roots of our family trees are sprawling, covering the ground of everyone to whom we are related. If our roots fix us sturdily in soil, then our heritage places us in something more adaptable, something that allows us to embody the apposite influences of those with whom we have come into contact.

Our family stretches out into Côte d'Ivoire, Nigeria, and a few other countries in the West African subregion. Some of our relatives were born in those countries, and others are transplants. Once, during my teen years, a distant relative of ours who lived in Côte d'Ivoire, Alhaji Daudu, paid us a visit.

Alhaji Daudu and my father were sitting out on the veranda, talking and laughing. I've forgotten what the conversation was about, but what I can recall is my shock at hearing my uncle describe himself as a "Frenchman."

"Oh, you know me," I remember him saying in response to a statement my father had made. "I'm a Frenchman. You know how we are."

My uncle, like every other person from a Francophone African country I've ever met or known, spoke with a distinctive accent, a combination of the guttural West African and the toothy French. When he spoke, he randomly inserted French words that we pretended to understand.

I took great offense at the statement he'd made. I felt that labelling himself that way was a denial of what and who we were. I looked at him, his features. He was a tall man, but his girth dwarfed him. He had a dark, pie-shaped face and a laugh that sounded like a succession of hiccups.

How can you be a Frenchman, I asked Alhaji Daudu in my head, *when you are an African?* The answer to that question is obvious to me now in a way that it could never have been then, in my childhood. My uncle, in some moments and mannerisms and by way of certain behaviour, was indeed a Frenchman in the same way that my father was an Englishman. They were gentlemen of a specific age and era. Both were born and raised during colonial times, when fragments of other cultures were being subsumed by African culture.

My father was a big tea drinker. He woke up every morning at six A.M., and one of the first things he did, even before having his bath, was to drink a cup of tea. Dad drank his tea with sugar and cream, as would be expected of an Englishman. He would have another tea in the afternoon, except this time he would drink two cups. It was a ritual he maintained until the day he died.

All the local banks, and even foreign banks, like Standard Chartered, had started lending heavily to the agricultural sector. Standard Chartered used to have a programme through which every year they'd send the best farmers in Ghana, fully sponsored and fully financed, to the United Kingdom to attend the Royal Agricultural Show, which was organised by the Royal Agricultural Society of England. For several years, Dad had the honour of being chosen as one of the best farmers in the country.

After one of those sponsored trips to England, Dad returned with an automatic tea maker. It was called Teasmade,

SANKOFA 121

and it was outfitted with a clock that had an alarm and a timer so that you could schedule the machine to make your tea for whenever you wanted to drink it. There was also a pot in which you placed the tea, and a kettle into which you poured the water.

My father was extremely proud of his Teasmade machine. In the evenings, before he went to bed, Dad would meticulously pour the right amount of water into the kettle and drop the teabag into the pot. He would set the alarm for six A.M. and set the timer for a few minutes before that so when he woke up all he'd have to do was fill the cup he'd set on his bedside table and start drinking.

Every weekday morning, my father arrived at his office no later than eight. At this point, Dad's agribusiness venture had expanded into a major enterprise. He was running both a rice farm and rice processing mills. He employed dozens of people and had even started exporting rice to neighbouring countries.

After spending a gruelling morning at the office tending to various administrative duties, Dad would knock off at about half-past noon and come home for lunch. After eating, he would have a one-hour siesta, usually between two and three. Before his siesta, Dad would prepare the Teasmade machine. He would set the alarm and timer so that by the time he rose from his siesta, there was a fresh pot of tea awaiting him.

In the afternoons, Dad would take his tea sitting outside by our little garden. Friends and relatives who knew his schedule would stop by and visit with him during his teatime. If their discussions weren't private, he would invite us kids to join them. We didn't particularly fancy tea, but we would drink it anyway because we were thrilled to be included.

Then there were the extra-special times when it was just us
with our father, sitting by the garden. We would listen as Dad
talked and sip ever so slowly, hoping to stretch out our time
with him and make the one hour that he allotted for those two
cups of tea last as long as possible. After that, he would return
to work.

I suppose it's not the first scene that comes to mind when
one thinks of an African family spending time together. And
believe me, there were many other, perhaps more stereotypical
or predictable scenes and memories; but this one was as true
as any of those others to the core of who we were and how we
lived.

As much as I disliked tea in my youth, it is now a part of my
daily routine. When I wake up in the morning one of the first
things I do, even before having my bath, is drink a cup of tea.
It is a part of my past that I have gone back and reclaimed, one
of the many legacies that my father handed down.

TEENAGERS IN TAMALE

I WORE A huge Afro, bell-bottom trousers, and heavy platform shoes. It was the early 1970s, and that was the definition of cool. Black American culture had taken West Africa
by storm. More accurately, there seemed to be a cultural exchange taking place between black America and West Africa,
especially Ghana.

Black Americans had traded in their blue jeans, suits, and
shirtsleeves for batiks, tie-dyes, and dashikis sewn from the
popular Ghanaian cloth called "Angelina." Meanwhile, we in
Ghana had taken to wearing hipsters, miniskirts, and polyester
shirts that were left unbuttoned straight down to the navel.

As funky as the fashion was, it was merely a by-product;
the music was the main event. Jackson 5 mania was spreading
through the continent like an infectious disease. Those brothers
were our idols. We memorised their songs, copied their dance
moves, and tried to dress like them. Everybody I knew wanted
to be like Michael Jackson, and I was no exception.

As luck would have it, I had more in common with Michael Jackson than any of those boys who purposely spoke in
awkwardly high voices or stood in front of the mirror every

morning and diligently picked their Afros. For starters, we were almost the same age. Michael was only three months older than me, to the day. His birth date was August 29, 1958, and mine was November 29, 1958. To children, small coincidences like that hold a great deal of weight and meaning.

Another thing that Michael Jackson and I had in common was the size of our families. His was big, and so was mine. If any group of kids in Tamale could fit the image of the Jackson 5, it was us, my brothers and me. We had enough children in our family to make not one or two but nearly four singing groups just like the Jackson 5, except a couple of them would have to be of mixed gender. Soon enough, a couple of my brothers did end up in a musical group called Oracles 74, but it was nothing at all like the Jackson 5.

My father had nineteen children, the result of four marriages and several relationships. In those days the more children you had, the more respect you were given in the family and in the larger community. Unlike his father, who was a village chief in Bole, my father was not polygamous. Whenever Dad got married, it was to one woman with whom he would live exclusively and permanently until, of course, the union ended.

Between marriages, or sometimes toward the final stages of a marriage that was ending, Dad also had relationships with other women. There were children born of these unions as well. People were not as squeamish back then about those things as they are now. Small, nuclear family units headed by couples in monogamous lifetime relationships are a fairly modern phenomenon in Ghana.

My father raised all of his children under a single roof until we came of age or moved out on our own. Even if we didn't begin our lives under that roof, we all eventually ended up there. It usually, though not always, happened like this:

A child's mother would deliver him or her to Dad's office. More often than not, Dad would have sent for that child, explaining to his or her mother that "it is time." The child would sit, with a small bag of clothing and toiletries on his lap or by her side, in Dad's office and wait for him to finish working.

At the end of the day, Dad's favourite driver—for a long time it was Mallam, and then it became Abudu—would place the bag of belongings in the boot, then open the rear door of the car for the child to get in. Dad would get in on the other side and slide all the way in until he was seated right next to his son or daughter. He would hold the child's hand the entire ride home.

Whenever we heard Salifu, the watchman, opening the gate to let our father's car in, we would all stop whatever we were doing so we could run outside to greet him. Like most of the ministers of state, members of Parliament, and other politicians from Dr. Nkrumah's time, our father drove a Mercedes-Benz 220. They all loved those cars. So many of them owned those Benzes that it was like the unofficial official car. It came with status. Whenever people saw a Benz approaching, they took notice because they knew that whoever was inside the car had to be a "big man," an important somebody.

We knew the sound of the engine well, so we could hear

our father coming from at least five houses away. He so loved our welcoming ritual, especially as the group of children grew larger and larger. He adored his brood and in his own way, from that very first day in the backseat of his Benz, maintained a unique connection with each child.

After he'd gotten out of the car, Dad would walk toward us, his welcoming committee, with a child hesitantly holding on to his hand. When Dad was only a few steps away from us he would let go of the new child's hand, nudge him or her toward us, and say, "This is your brother," or "This is your sister," followed by the child's name. "Take him"—or her—"to your room."

Over the years, more brothers and sisters kept arriving. Our house was virtually a dormitory. There were several bunk beds in every room except our father's. Whenever a new sibling joined us, we would do everything within our power to let him or her feel loved and wanted. Most of us had once been in that position and understood what it was to be the new kid in the Mahama household.

Some of the siblings, like our older sister Rose, who was married and had her own flat, did not live in the house. Even so, our father made certain that we remained in close contact. They would come to visit the house regularly, and Dad would also take us to visit them. He didn't want us to feel any type of distance or sense of separation whatsoever from our siblings. We were one, unified by the same blood, the same name, and the same doting patriarch.

Even though I was one of those who did not live at the house full-time, the bond we Mahama children shared was so strong that whenever I returned home to my family, it was as if I had never left.

AFTER THE COUP D'ETAT BROUGHT Dad's political life to an abrupt halt, he turned to commercial farming. Agribusiness may have been new to my father, but it wasn't new to Ghana or Ghanaians as a whole. More than 80 percent of the population was somehow engaged in the business of agriculture. Northern Ghana's introduction to commercial agriculture began in the late 1960s, and it was passionately embraced. There were large maize farms and large farms of sorghum. Interest in agriculture was so high that even the most unlikely people were involved in it, like judges and top civil servants. In fact, the richest people in the northern part of Ghana were the farmers.

Whereas the northern territories were once the most underdeveloped in the country, all of this agricultural activity and revenue made the area quite bustling for those in the know. There were still some who viewed the northern territories of Ghana as socially and culturally barren. Typically, a civil servant who was posted from Accra or some other southern locale to a northern town would be reluctant to go. He would invariably try to find a way to manipulate the system so he could stay in one of the southern areas. It was usually only upon the threat of being dismissed from the civil service that people would agree to go to the northern territories.

After the agricultural boom, it was remarkable how the attitudes of those formerly reluctant civil servants began to shift.

Once they had settled into their routines in the north, they would befriend the locals, usually other civil servants. They would start to notice that the locals spent weekends at the farm, which was often on the outskirts of whatever town they were living in. Maybe a month or two would pass, and as the friendship among the civil servants developed, the southerner might accompany the local to his farm once or twice or more.

If one of the visits was during harvest time, the southerner would see firsthand the kind of revenue that his colleague was bringing in from the farm. Even in a worst-case scenario, it would be far more than the annual salary of a civil servant. Before long, the civil servants who'd been posted in the northern towns would also begin to farm on a commercial scale. After a few years, when it was time for these civil servants to rotate posts and return to a southern city, they would resign so that they could remain in the north and continue farming. That's how lucrative Ghana's agricultural industry was.

In addition to the farm in Yapei, Dad decided to build a rice milling plant to produce quality polished rice that at the time was in high demand but was only being imported from outside of Africa. It proved to be an extremely visionary decision.

IT WAS A GREAT TIME to be young—not just in Ghana, but the world over—and Tamale was the perfect city for us, the Mahama boys. It had all the conveniences of a big city, but it was not as congested as Accra, so we had room to move about and to feel a little free. We would have parties, and we often invited friends over. As we all grew older and wanted more privacy, Dad dismantled our bunk beds so that there were fewer of us in each room. He also allowed us to take over the rooms in the boys' quarters. At the time, Dad was deeply engrossed in his business, too consumed to quibble over trivial matters. He trained and disciplined us, all right, but not with corporal punishment. He never beat us. A stern word from our father was enough to keep us on the right track.

He liked for us to have all the things that he did not have while he was growing up, because his family either was not aware of them or, despite his father being a chief in the village, could not afford them. He especially indulged us in our love of music, buying us top-of-the-line music systems. We had permission to go to nightclubs and dances. Dad would give us pocket money and stipends so we could afford to buy whatever records we wanted. He even bought us a little convertible MG so that we could zip around town whenever we wanted to. By then, he could afford it. The risk he'd taken was paying off well; his commercial rice farm was wildly successful.

Ghana's leadership had been something of a revolving door of names since that first coup d'etat in 1966. Major General Ankrah was put in place as head of state after the coup but was forced to resign over accusations of bribery. Following Ankrah's departure, Brigadier Afrifa stepped in as head of state but served for only a short while, after which time a presidential commission was formed to transition the country back to constitutional rule. Elections were held in 1969, but the ban on political participation that had been placed on all of the members of Dr. Nkrumah's government had a debilitating effect on what had been the country's most popular political party.

During Dr. Nkrumah's presidency, the organisation of Ghana's government somewhat mirrored the organisation of the U.S. government, with one individual heading the executive branch and serving as commander in chief. Before the 1969 elections, the organisation of Ghana's government was changed and fashioned after the Westminster system, whereby voters elect a political party, not a specific candidate; the head of the political party that is elected assumes the role of head of state. It was in this way that Dr. Kofi Busia, who was the head of the Progress Party, became prime minister of the Second Republic of Ghana.

Dr. Busia served as prime minister for a little more than two years. One of the first pieces of legislation introduced by the Busia administration was the controversial Aliens Compliance Order, which required all illegal aliens residing in Ghana to return to their home country. A large majority of the aliens affected by the order were Nigerians, who were forced to return despite the fact that their country was in the midst of a civil war.

In January 1972, following a coup d'etat by the armed forces, Colonel I. K. Acheampong became the military head of state. Not long after Colonel Acheampong took office, he introduced a programme called Operation Feed Yourself. The mission of this programme was to encourage Ghanaian citizens to grow their own food so that we as a country could sustain ourselves at the most basic level of human necessity. To ensure the success of this programme, the government subsidised fertilizer, improved seeds, and recruited a lot of agricultural extension officers to help farmers employ modern methods of farming. These efforts were fruitful, as evidenced by the huge agricultural boom in the northern regions. Commercial farmers such as my father, who had only recently begun his foray into agri-business, benefitted greatly from this programme.

IF THE 1960S WAS A season of politics, then the 1970s was a season of song. The sounds of Motown and Stax Records filled the airwaves in Ghana with James Brown and the Jackson 5 and Otis Redding. The passion that was once roused by our political leaders was now being channelled into song. The icons of the previous era had all been executed, assassinated, exiled, imprisoned, or otherwise silenced. There was no Patrice Lumumba; there was no Sylvanus Olympio; there was no Kwame Nkrumah; there was no Abubakar Tafawa Balewa; there was no Nelson Mandela; there was no Martin Luther King Jr.; there was no Malcolm X; there was no Amilcar Cabral. There was only us, and there was music.

Fela Anikulapo Kuti was gaining international recognition for his significant contributions to the sound that would forever be known as Afrobeat. There were many other sounds as well. There was Bumbaya, and Hedzole, and the sound of the Uhuru Dance Band. A lot of bands used to tour throughout Ghana, travelling from town to town. Whenever one of the bands, like Geraldo Pino & the Heartbeats, was coming, the whole town would be agog.

In 1971, there was the concert of all concerts, the Soul to Soul Music Festival, which was staged on March 6 as a celebration of Ghana's fourteenth anniversary of independence. It was held in Accra, at Black Star Square, which is now called

Independence Square, and it was fourteen hours long, ending at dawn. A number of Americans came to perform, like Wilson Pickett, Ike and Tina Turner, the Staple Singers, Santana, and Roberta Flack. For months before and for months afterward, Soul to Soul was the talk of the nation. Every town attempted their own mini replica, inviting multiple bands, trying to pack the venues and keep the show going until the crowd was knackered.

All the bands that came to Tamale usually performed at a place called the Legion Village. Not many kids our age could afford the gate fee, but Dad would always give us money if we needed it, enough for us to be able to get in and buy drinks. My older brothers drank beer, but Adam and I stuck to water and minerals, or soft drinks, as they are commonly referred to elsewhere.

The kids in Tamale flocked to our house; because there were so many of us, it was like a ready-made community. Also, they knew that we would always end up taking our closest friends along with us to whatever performance or event we were attending, even if it meant having to pay for them as well. This alone guaranteed that half of the town's kids were always hanging around at our house, hoping to be chosen.

Discos were also sprouting up all over the place. When there weren't any bands coming to town, on Fridays and Saturdays my brothers and I would go to a disco. The most popular one in Tamale was the Right Spot. The music would be so loud that you could feel the vibration of the beats in your chest cavity. Alfred, Adam, Peter, and I would dance, lifting and kicking those clunky platform shoes to perform all kinds of moves that we had seen on *Soul Train*. We enjoyed showing off to one another, being silly, and just generally having a good time.

My interest in the opposite sex was developing, so one of the highlights of going out to these performances and discos was the prospect of seeing a pretty girl. I had not graduated to the level of meeting them or even having a conversation with them, unlike Peter. I admired his confidence and the sure stride that he would use to walk up to a girl he liked and wanted to start a conversation with. He had this way of standing and looking at a girl with a slight grin and his eyes, like flags, lowered to half-mast. When Peter did that, any girl he was talking to would immediately melt. She would giggle foolishly and look away, pretending to be shy but all the while making cat-and-mouse small talk with him. I was at the stage in my development where I could only stop and look. That's all I was physically capable of. If a girl I thought was pretty came to talk to me, I would find myself unable to speak. Or the words that would manage to come out of my mouth would sound silly and juvenile and I would immediately regret having said them.

OUR FATHER TRIED TO DRILL in our minds an understanding of the inevitability of change. "You should always be prepared," he would tell us. "Life is like a cycle, everything goes around and comes around again. One day you're up, but the next day you might be down." He liked to remind us of that because he didn't want us to take for granted the privileges we had or to become so comfortable with a lifestyle of luxury that we did not know how to work hard and earn an honest day's wage.

Alfred and I often divided our long vacations between our mother's home in Damongo and our father's home in Tamale. When we were in Tamale during the long vacation, we would work at Dad's rice mill. Dad would pile us into his car, drive us to Yapei, and hand us over to the factory manager, Mr. Yahaya Crusoe. What I remember most about Mr. Crusoe was that he was no respecter of persons; he didn't care if you were a day labourer or the owner's son, there was work to be done.

The rice mill had various sections, and Mr. Crusoe made certain that we were deployed to each section for at least a week. He would always make me start at the station where the paddy rice was fed into the intake pan. It was the station I hated most because it was extremely dusty and the work was gruelling. I would have to drag sacks of rice to the intake hole. There was one worker at the intake hole with a knife whose sole job was to slice open those bags. After the bags had been opened, I would then have to push over the bags, one by one, so that the paddy rice would pour into the intake hole. It would take every ounce of strength I had in my skinny body to do that. It felt like rolling a boulder up the side of a steep mountain.

The paddy rice would travel by conveyor belt to a section where a machine called a stoner would remove all the little stones and pieces of gravel. From there, the husk would be taken off of each grain; then the rice would go through something called a polisher, which would convert it from its original brown colouring to a stainless white. Polishing was what made the rice nice, shiny, and bright, the way people liked to see and enjoy their rice when it was served at a meal.

After that, the grains would go into a grader, which would separate the different types of rice. There were four grades, some of which were for either semibroken rice or completely broken rice. The completely broken rice, which was good for making rice water or *omo tuo*, which are rice balls, would be separated from the grade 2 rice, which was only semibroken. The grade 2 rice would be separated from the long grain, wholly unbroken rice, which the grader would take to one side; and so on and so forth. Each type of rice had its own price and its own specific market.

After the husk is removed from a rice grain, there is another layer that is also brown in colour; this layer was removed during the polishing process. It's called rice bran, and it went to a whole different section, where it was bagged for the poultry industry. I hated working in that section, too, because the bran was powdery. At the end of my shift, I'd be covered from head to toe in a fine film of rice bran; I'd look as though I'd been trawling headfirst through a pile of fine sawdust.

My favourite station at the plant was the bagging section. After the rice had gone through the processing, it would be put into bags and the bags were then sewn shut. I got quite adept at operating the machine. I could have stayed at that station for the entire long vacation and never grown tired of doing that job. But like all the other stations, it was only temporary. Mr. Crusoe would insist that I move on to the next station.

After the rice was bagged it was placed, according to grade, on loaders. Grade 1, for instance, was loaded on pallets; the next batch of pallets would be for grade 2 rice; and on and on until all the pallets were full. Only a certain number of bags could be loaded onto each pallet. That was because it had to be within the load limit of the factory's forklift that would take the pallets and place them onto one of the articulated trucks that would come from the southern part of the country to collect the rice.

Trade in rice, at that time, was mainly a women's business undertaking. Men were rarely involved. It was the women, mostly the market women from Accra, who would hire the articulated trucks, bring them to the factory, load the bags of rice, and then take them down to the south for sale.

That's how it was in my mother's hometown, Damongo, as well. It was one of the major maize-growing areas in Ghana. It was the women who would bring the trucks, buy the maize, load the trucks, and take them down to the markets in the south. Rice was also processed in Damongo, but it was no-where near as elaborate a production as in my father's mill. The rice in Damongo was processed by pounding. The women would boil the rice and then they would spread the grains out in the sun to dry. Once it was dry, they would put the rice in a large mortar and use a rounded pestle and just pound gently. This was how they would remove the husks. After they had been pounding for some time, they would pour the rice from the mortar into a bowl. As the rice was falling from mortar to bowl, the wind would blow away the loosened husks.

That was the entirety of the processing that took place in Damongo. Their rice, however, was not being produced to feed urban tastes, which were rapidly becoming Westernised.

It was local rice, brown rice, natural rice; it was what my mother and aunties used to make *jollof*; it was the kind of rice that accompanied the various stews they cooked; it was the rice that I, and most of my Ghanaian contemporaries, grew up eating.

IN THE MID-1970S, THE cedi still held strong value against the dollar. It had started to lose some value, but those numbers were relatively inconsequential when compared with the dramatic drops we would see during the 1980s, 1990s, and early part of the 2000s. After a month of work at my father's rice mill, my brothers and I could earn as much as 11 cedis, which was a humongous amount of money for a young boy. If I stayed in Tamale, which I sometimes did, and worked the entire three months of the vacation, I would return to school with 33 cedis. That amount of money could buy all of my provisions for school, and during the time that I was at Achimota, it could also buy me a very good time with my friends in Accra for the better part of the school year.

In 1975, when the head of state, who had now become "General" Acheampong, visited the north on an official working tour, he saw how productive our agribusiness was. In addition to visiting smaller farms that produced crops primarily for feeding local families and not large-scale sales, General Acheampong visited the commercial farms—the vegetable oil mills, the rice mills, and the factories that produced *pito*, which is a type of alcohol made of fermented millet or sorghum. He toured other types of food factories as well, such as tomato and meat factories. General Acheampong was so impressed that he labelled the north the "granary of Ghana."

Around this same time, because Ghana had attained self-sufficiency in rice production, my father applied for permission to export rice. General Acheampong's government gave him the permit. Working through the Bank of Ghana, my father's company started to export rice to Burkina Faso and Mali. It made him an enormously wealthy man.

Following his own advice, my father was ever prepared for any shift or tremor that might suddenly place him on the downward curve of life's cycle. Be that as it may, I don't think he was prepared for the suddenness of the descent on which we would find ourselves in the not-too-distant future. I believe he thought, what with that first coup and his detention, that he had seen and survived the worst. So there he was, raising his children and reinventing himself as a businessman in agriculture; and there we were, working at the plant and thinking about music: the next band we would hear, the next disco we would go to, watching girls swoon to their favourite songs. We were just being teenagers in Tamale, spending the cedis we'd earned and having what we thought was the time of our lives. Little did any of us know that the worst was yet to come.

FROZEN FIRE

OUR WATCHMAN, SALIFU, was a former serviceman with the British Brigade. During World War II, he had served in the Second West African Infantry Brigade as a member of one of the three battalions of the Gold Coast Regiment. He'd been stationed in Burma during his tour of duty, and he loved to tell us stories about fighting in the war. Salifu was a thin, wiry man with a gentle soul and an impish streak that endeared him to my brothers and me.

He was an excellent storyteller, and his tales of war kept us staring at his long, angular face and hanging on his every word. They were filled with quick action, courage, and beautiful, tawny-skinned women with inky hair. We realised that most of Salifu's stories of heroism leaned more toward fiction, like the ones in which he was shot multiple times by the enemy but the bullets ricocheted off his chest like rubber pellets. Even so, most afternoons would find us glued to our seats on the veranda, listening to him tell those stories.

When Salifu spoke of his service during the war, he always began with great enthusiasm and pride. Yet all of his stories ended with complaints and unmasked bitterness about how

poorly he and the other African servicemen who'd fought in
the war had been treated by the British. They'd just used the
Africans and then cast them aside, Salifu would tell us, without proper compensation or recognition.

"But everything that goes around comes around. One day
those British will get theirs," he'd say. "They will find themselves trapped between the devil and the deep blue sea."

Salifu was fond of proverbs and aphorisms. When we spoke
to him, he would always respond with pithy statements. He
would tell us folktales that we knew were supposed to teach us
valuable truths about life, though sometimes those lessons were
lost on us. He once told us a folktale that held me captivated.
It echoed a lesson I'd learned years earlier while being bullied
at school, about how people are always more successful in their
goals when they work together instead of apart.

It was the story of three songbirds, Taka, Tika, and Gangale, who were friends. Their names were reflective of the musical notes that each of them sang. The combination of their
names, especially when intoned repeatedly, had a fetching
rhythm to it. They turned it into a song and began this ritual
of flying to the village square every day at sunrise after the
market women had set up their displays of vegetables, fruit,
grain, and sundries.

By the time the customers had arrived and started thump-
ing on the watermelons and squeezing the oranges to see if
they were ripe, the birds would already be circling the air, in-
fusing it with their harmonious music. "Ta-ka-ti-ka-gan-ga-le,
ta-ka-ti-ka-gan-ga-le, ta-ka-ti-ka-gan-ga-le," they would
chirp. They would change the tempo and add breaks, really
turning it into a full-scale performance.

The villagers looked forward to hearing those three birds sing. They'd ply them with gifts, pieces of bread or grain, coins or paper money that they'd hold in their hands while raising their arms high in the air so the birds could swoop down and collect it. The partnership the three friends had was a prosperous one. The entertainment they provided became the main feature at the market.

Then success started to swell their heads with greed. Each one secretly imagined being able to keep all of the gifts. Each started wondering why he needed the other two birds at all. For a while, they kept these thoughts to themselves. One day their trip to the market reaped a particularly huge reward of goods. At Taka's invitation, they'd flown to his nest to feast. After the meal, when everyone was full and satisfied, Taka told the others that he wanted to talk to them. He'd come up with a theory.

"I'm the leader of this whole thing," he said. "It's my name, Taka, that makes us so popular. It's the power of that first note they hear which brings us the presents and food we get." The other two immediately saw where Taka was going with this.

"Of course that's not true," Tika was quick to rebut. "It's my name, Tika, which makes people give us things. It's an unusual coupling of notes, one is high and the other is low. That makes it the most melodic of them all."

"Hey, hey, hey," Gangale interrupted. "What you two are saying can't be. You both only sing two notes. Me, I sing three notes, and they sound like percussion. That's what the people like. It's my name and my contribution they enjoy most."

The argument escalated as each bird started feeling the need to proclaim his talent and protect his interest in the villagers' gifts. The three friends who had been working so well together got angry and decided to be done with their partnership as well as their friendship. Each agreed to go his separate way.

The next morning, Taka arrived at the village first. He flew high with confidence while waiting for the merchants to place the crumpled sheets of newspaper at the bottoms of their produce baskets, then pile the fruits and vegetables inside, tilting those baskets slightly to promote the illusion of abundance. Once the customers had started filtering in, Taka made his debut.

"Ta-ka-ta-ka-ta-ka," he sang forcefully, "ta-ka-ta-ka-ta-ka." It was a monotonous, pecking sound that the villagers found irritating.

"What is that noise?" they asked one another. Once they saw it was the bird flying from stall to stall making the ruckus, they gathered stones and started to toss them to shoo him away. Frightened, Taka flapped his wings as fast as he could and returned to his nest. The next morning when he went to the market to try his luck again, the same thing happened. For several days he remained in his nest, despondent and hungry. He'd grown accustomed to the tasty selection of food that the villagers had been giving him and the other two birds, and now he was left to forage for his meals.

Tika's attempt at a solo career was greeted with the same disdain. He arrived shortly after Taka had left, unaware of the fate that had met his former friend. Tika found a spot atop one of the market women's stalls. It was a central location, a place where everyone would be able to see and hear him. From there, he started to wail, "Ti-ka-ti-ka-ti-ka, ti-ka-ti-ka-ti-ka."

His was an even more annoying sound. The unusually high note that he had to hit when singing his name sounded to the villagers like a screech. A few of them, unable to concentrate on the bargaining and bartering that was taking place between them and the merchants, abandoned their shopping and left.

"Ah, this bird will lose me customers," one of the market women exclaimed. She picked up the largest stone she could find and threw it right at Tika, barely missing him. Shocked, he flew away and didn't return. Like Taka, after a few days alone in his nest, he started to yearn for those happier times, when they had been well loved and well fed.

Gangale waited a few days before going to the market. He'd been rehearsing his song, flying from treetop to treetop in a forest just outside the village, singing out his name, trying to find the right pitch and rhythm. When he felt he was ready, he went to the village square. It was bustling with activity. The shoppers had already arrived and were milling about. He cleared his throat and began.

"Gan-ga-le, gan-ga-le, gan-ga-le," he sang. Then he paused for a beat and continued again. "Gan-ga-le, gan-ga-le, gan-ga-le." Some of the villagers appeared to be enjoying his song. They shuffled their feet and nodded their heads to the rhythm. Gangale continued. "Gan-ga-le, gan-ga-le, gan-ga-le." After a few rounds of this, he heard one of the villagers asking, "But is that all this bird can sing? What nonsense."

"Mmm, maybe there's a worm stuck in his throat." This made them laugh.

"Go away," they insisted. "Come back when you can add

more to your song to make it sweet." Saddened and ashamed, Gangale decided to leave.

"Oh, what has happened to our birds who used to come?" he heard one of the market women ask as he was flying away. Instead of returning straight to his nest, Gangale went to visit Tika. He wanted to find out how the villagers had received his old friend. When he arrived at Tika's nest, Gangale could see that the bird was forlorn. Tika, having known Gangale for years, could also tell right away that he was unhappy. They knew what they had to do. The two of them made their way to Taka's nest.

Taka was a vain bird and refused to let the others know how miserably he'd failed, but they could see past his pretence.

"I think we've all been foolish," Gangale told them.

"Yes," Tika added. "None of us was the leader or had the most to contribute."

"What they loved," Gangale continued, "was the music we made together."

"You are right," Taka had to confess. "Without each other, what we have is not a song."

They agreed to renew their friendship and to return to their partnership. The following morning, they arrived at the market square bright and early as they always did when they sang together. When they started chirping, "Ta-ka-ti-ka-gan-ga-le, ta-ka-ti-ka-gan-ga-le, ta-ka-ti-ka-gan-ga-le," it was to a welcoming and spirited audience.

"Heeeeyyyyyy, our songbirds are back," everyone cheered. The villagers gave the birds more food and money than they'd ever received in a single day. They returned to Gangale's nest

to eat the bread, fruit, and grain and to count and equally split
the money. After each bird had received his fair share and was
content, Taka, Tika, and Gangale vowed to never again allow
their pride to stand in the way of their progress.

WHEN MY FAMILY MOVED BACK to Tamale, my brothers started
attending Tamale Secondary School, which everyone called
Tamasco. It was located within the city limits, but it was a
boarding school. There was a common entrance exam that
students were required to take in their final year of primary
school. At this time, the students were asked to list their first,
second, and third choice of secondary school to which they
wished to be granted admission. There was also a fourth choice,
but it was for a region, not a school. The schools admitted
students based on their academic performance on the common entrance exam.

If, based on a student's scores, he or she couldn't be granted
admission into their first, second, or third choice of school, then
any school for which he or she qualified in the region that
had been listed could write the student a letter of acceptance.
This system produced a diverse student body, because the pool
of applicants from which a school had to choose was com-
posed of different ethnic groups, faiths, and regions within the
country.

As with anywhere else in the world, there were schools that
were considered prestigious and difficult to get into. Tamasco,
one of the oldest schools in the north, was among those in
that top-tier category. There were also second- and third-rank

schools. In addition, there were other new schools, ones that had not yet gained a reputation or formed a pedigree.

After Ghana became independent and Dr. Nkrumah took over from the colonial government, education became one of his main areas of priority. He wanted to expand access to secondary and tertiary education, which had previously been limited to a few, the elite and the fortunate. Dr. Nkrumah built the University of Cape Coast in the Central Region; he also built the University of Science and Technology, which now bears his name, in the Ashanti Region. At the secondary level, Dr. Nkrumah built a number of new facilities across the country that became known as the Ghana Education Trust Schools.

What I most anticipated after completing my final year of primary education at Achimota was attending school with my brothers. We'd always gone to different schools. They had attended day schools, and from the age of six, I had attended a boarding school. The only time I'd been able to see them and spend time with them had been during my short breaks and the long vacation between academic years. Now we'd be living at home and we'd be boarding at the same school, and I just couldn't wait.

My father had other ideas about my schooling. From the very beginning, he'd made sure I'd been on a different educational track from that of my brothers, and that wasn't about to change for secondary school. I'd done quite well on my common entrance exam, and Tamasco had been my first choice. They'd offered me admission, but so had some other schools in the region of my choice, Northern. My father enrolled me in one of those other schools. It was called the Ghana Secondary School, Ghanasco for short, and it was fairly new, one of the Ghana Education Trust facilities. When I found out, I was crushed. I would have spent the entire long vacation pouting and feeling sorry for myself had it not been for Salifu's stories and the new group of friends my brothers had made at Tamasco.

They were a motley crew, my brothers and their new friends, but they were great fun. The one to whom I gravitated right away was a boy by the name of Sumaila al-Hassan. Though he was friends with Peter and Alfred, he was my age, so we got on well. He was a mild-mannered boy who'd been raised in a conservative Muslim household in the Sabonjida quarter of Tamale. Sumaila was committed to his faith, but he was also a teenager whose interests and curiosities were extending him beyond his insulated childhood. He loved the city life and took every opportunity to hang out with us when we were going to the discos and shows. Sumaila spent a lot of time at our house, so he got to know Salifu and was often with us out on the veranda, listening to folktales and war stories.

Some nights when Salifu had finished telling us his stories, he'd pick up his guitar and play. He'd strum for a while and then he'd start singing. He was so skinny that the veins in his hand protruded, and they became more pronounced when he plucked the strings. His voice expressed emotions the same way whether he was speaking or singing. Every word was suffused with passion, hope, disappointment, or joy. It was as if he'd stepped into the story or song and was living the lines right there in front of us. I felt compelled to listen to the words of songs in a way I never had before.

My brothers and I had been obsessed with music for some

time, carefully placing 45s on the little record player our father had bought Peter, going to discos to dance and shake and jump until we were soaked with perspiration. Those songs had words as well, and we would sing them aloud to one another as we danced, sometimes holding a tightened fist up to our mouths and pretending it was a microphone.

Those songs, with their heavy bass lines and loud choruses, seemed geared toward moving the body. The ones that Salifu sang seemed geared toward moving the heart. They were songs that made you feel deeply and think hard. They were songs about the world, about how we should bring together what was falling apart. They were songs like "Imagine" and "What's Going On?"

"*Yesterday I got a letter,*" Salifu would sing, swaying his head.

From my friend
Fighting in Vietnam
And this is what he had to say:
"Tell all my friends
That I'll be coming home soon."

Nearly all of the songs that Salifu sang were about a world in crisis. At first I thought it was because of his experience as a serviceman in the war. I thought that somehow Salifu had gotten stuck in the events of those times, like how the needle on Peter's record player would get stuck in one place and keep repeating the same word until we made it stop. Eventually I realised that wasn't the case.

In the evenings when GBC, our only TV channel, began

its four-hour broadcast, Peter, Alfred, Sumaila, and I would huddle in front of the television. The first show that aired was the news. Even though it was boring, we suffered through it while waiting for our favourite shows to come on. Listening to the news made me understand that Salifu was not stuck in the past. The songs he sang to us were about the present. Over a period of time, I noticed that there was trouble brewing on every continent. Our world *was* in crisis.

There were numerous wars: a war in Vietnam; a war between Pakistan and India that led to the secession of East Pakistan, which took its independence and called itself Bangladesh. There was the Yom Kippur/Ramadan War. There was also an escalating Cold War, though no matter how often Salifu tried to explain to me how a war could be cold, it didn't add up.

Every night there were reports of violence and brutality. Eleven Israeli athletes were massacred at the Olympics in Munich. The British police shot into a group of unarmed protesters in Northern Ireland and fourteen of them died. Every other week somebody in Argentina was being kidnapped or assassinated, and every other month an airplane was being hijacked.

One by one, governments were being toppled. Richard Nixon resigned as president of the United States after the Watergate scandal was exposed. Sri Lanka was under emergency rule because of a major rebellion against the government. There'd been a coup in Chile, a coup in Uganda, a coup in Ethiopia; Libya had only recently had a coup, and there had even been another coup in Ghana. It felt as though everything was coming undone, descending into chaos.

"That's because the lunatics are running the asylum," Salifu would tell us whenever we'd report the news we had heard back to him. "Don't worry, it's only a matter of time."

"Only a matter of time for what?" we'd eagerly want to know, but Salifu never said. If we pushed for an answer, he'd pretend he hadn't heard. He'd pick up his guitar and start strumming. "It's only a matter of time," he would repeat, as though it were the first line of a song, then he'd strum some more and start singing one of his standards.

Ooh-oo child, things are gonna get easier,
Ooh-oo child, things'll get brighter . . .
Someday, yeah,
We'll walk in the rays of a beautiful sun.
Someday
When the world is much brighter.

We talked Salifu into giving us lessons on how to play the guitar. He would grab a stool and sit, facing us. That way we could see his hands. He showed us how to hold the guitar, and he taught us a few basic chords. All of us learned to strum a few songs, however awkwardly. Except Sumaila, who struggled with the strings and sang so off-key that it was comical.

The instrument felt big in my hands and it was a little difficult to manage, but I made out okay. My singing was passable, though probably not good enough to stand on a stage by myself without being booed or having stones tossed in my direction. I didn't care. I liked the sense of release that came with singing and playing the guitar. It was liberating.

Whenever Alfred took his turn with the guitar, he left us speechless. It wasn't that he was great with the guitar. He played about as well as I did. It was his voice that made us all sit up. Alfred sang wonderfully. His voice was smooth, laden with emotion. He was truly gifted. It got to the point where Alfred would set aside the guitar and sing a cappella, amazed at his ability to make music with nothing else but what came from inside of him.

Peter's voice was not as remarkable. His magic was with the strings. Any time Peter held the guitar and started playing, it was wondrous. We were in awe of his dexterity. His fingers were agile and certain. They made it look as if playing the guitar was the most natural and effortless thing in the world.

When it came to making music, Peter and Alfred were two halves of a whole. Sumaila and I would readily serve as their audience, and we'd often join in on a chorus or two under our breaths. Salifu transitioned from teacher to fan. Instead of giving Peter and Alfred directions, he now gave them compliments, smiling approvingly when their playing moved him. When the long vacation was over and it was time for Peter and Alfred to return to Tamasco, Salifu let them take his guitar with them.

At school, Peter and Alfred continued to rehearse. They would go into the assembly hall and bang away. There was another boy at Tamasco who had a guitar, and from time to time, he would join them. One day while they were playing, a teacher heard the music as he was passing by. He stopped and stood at the door and listened until they'd finished. He felt the boys had talent and they should be encouraged. And surely they couldn't be the only ones in the school population gifted with that type of musical ability. He contacted the music master and the headmaster to make an appeal for the establishment of a school band. They reluctantly agreed, and Tamasco purchased everything that was needed for the boys to get started. Soon they were equipped with various guitars, drums, electric amplifiers, and a microphone and stand.

A few other students joined Peter and Alfred to form a band, and they called themselves Oracles 74. The members of Oracles 74 were deeply engrossed in their music. They rehearsed as though their lives depended on it, forgoing all other extracurricular activities to practise. They got their first big break when the police band was invited to play at the school. Oracles 74 was to open for them. They were to play a few songs to get the students warmed up and ready for the main event.

Oracles 74 tried out several of the songs they'd been rehearsing. The students were wild for them, cheering them on to play another one and another one. They played a few more songs. They were onstage for about an hour. When it looked as though the members of the police band were becoming agitated, Oracles 74 played their final number and turned the stage over.

The songs that Oracles 74 had been rehearsing were the songs of the moment, the ones you would hear on the radio stations geared toward younger listeners. The songs the police band played were from a previous generation. The students, who were now completely warmed up and ready to make the most of their Saturday night, were not impressed. They didn't hesitate to express their displeasure, calling out repeatedly for Oracles 74. The police band was forced off the stage. To the students' delight, Oracles 74 returned and continued their performance.

Overnight, the boys in the band became the most popular kids at Tamasco. Other boys wanted to be their best friends, girls flirted with them, and teachers granted them special privileges. Word of their celebrity even spread as far as my school, Ghanasco.

When you're a teenager, music is like a previously undiscovered aperture, shining light on your interior world. It permits you to explore the cavernous spaces of that world in which you'd never before dared to venture. Music speaks both to you and for you. It's a means of engagement and a form of rebellion. It teaches you how to hope.

When they performed, the members of Oracles 74 expressed themselves in ways that went beyond the music. They wore purple raincoats with iron-gray helmets, tight blue shorts with rainbow stockings, a long green dress with huge underwater-style goggles, six-inch-high brown platform shoes, and a white pirate-style shirt. One band member was perpetually decked out in a newsboy cap. We called it a Cooley High, which was the name of an American film that had been shown at most of the cinemas. All the characters in the film wore caps like that. Our stepmother then, Joyce Tamakloe, owned a boutique in Tamale where the band used to shop for a lot of their outlandish clothing.

In addition to their eclectic outfits, the band members adopted stage names. There was "Chikinchi" on guitar, "Tony Marvis" on drums, "Bob Miracles" on congas, and on lead vocals was my brother Alfred, "Frisky Papa."

Oracles 74 may have been unique, especially in Tamale

where there was no other school band, but teenagers all
throughout Ghana were becoming obsessed with music. There
were so many school bands sprouting up that a competition
was put in place called Pop Chain. The event was held in Accra at the Arts Centre every long vacation. There would be at
least twenty-two bands participating. They had such fascinating names, like Corpus Christi, the Slim Jims, the Horns, and
Matthew Chapter 5. Students would travel long distances to
go and support their school band. If their school didn't have
one, they'd still show up to listen to the talent that was being
showcased. When a band gave a particularly good performance,
the entire place would erupt in applause and cheers and shouts.

The competing bands were required to play a traditional
Ghanaian tune, a foreign tune, and an original composition.
The bands were usually superb with the Ghanaian tunes. With
the foreign tunes, it was hit or miss. They would play one of the
popular American songs or one of Fela Kuti's Afrobeat songs.
Their original compositions could be surprisingly good. You'd
hear tunes that could easily find their way onto the radio, but it
was more likely you'd hear arrangements that were awful.

Oracles 74 was the only school band in the north. Even
well-known schools in the Brong-Ahafo and Ashanti Regions
didn't have bands. This made Oracles 74 all the more determined to win the Pop Chain competition. I would accompany my brothers when they went to Accra for Pop Chain. I
was so proud of Peter and Alfred that I could hardly contain
myself. When they stepped on the stage, that pride would
turn to nervousness. As I listened to them play, I would be
praying they didn't make any mistakes, that their voices would

remain in the right key. I would be praying for them to win. They never did, though one year they gave their best performance and came in fourth place. I only wished Salifu could have been there to see them, but he was back home in Tamale.

Sumaila desperately wanted to be a member of the band. He tried his hand at every instrument—drums, bass, keyboards—only to discover, as he had when we were learning how to play the guitar, that he lacked either talent or coordination or both. Singing was out of the question. It was a hopeless pursuit, but for some reason Sumaila never gave up. He never let himself feel defeated. He held fast to his dream. If one instrument didn't work out for him, he moved on to the next and stayed with it until there was no denying that he couldn't cut it with that one either.

If being in the band wasn't going to be a possibility for Sumaila, then he at least wanted to be around the band. There were a couple of other boys who felt the same way. They volunteered to be the band's helpers. They would attend every rehearsal and performance. If a band member needed a glass of water or a towel to wipe the sweat off his brow, one of the helpers would get it. They were the ones in charge of setting up and packing up the band's equipment.

Sometimes when the show was over, the stage lights had been turned off, and the band members were out in the crowd receiving adulation, Sumaila and the other boys would stand on the stage and hold the instruments. They wouldn't play them, they'd only stand there and hold them for a few minutes while staring into the empty chairs in the audience. They'd let the energy of their dreams seep through their hands and into the instrument, as if it were a Bible or the Koran. Maybe one day, they prayed, their dream would come true. Eventually, the other boys grew weary of being so close to something they wanted but knew they couldn't have. They stopped coming to rehearsals and shows. But Sumaila didn't. He continued to dream and believe.

The band members were still the most popular kids at Tamasco, but once their novelty had worn off, people started questioning their choice of names. *What kind of name was that? Were they trying to imply that they themselves were oracles? Could it be that they were involved in the occult? Was that why they dressed the way they did?*

The band members didn't like the things they were hearing. They held a meeting and decided it was time for a change. Some of them, like Peter, would soon be graduating. They would have to recruit new members during the long vacation, before returning to Tamasco. That would be a perfect time to choose a new name to debut when they got back to school.

The name they settled on was Frozen Fire. It was odd but catchy, a paradox.

"How can fire be frozen?" I asked Alfred when he told me what the band would now be called. He shrugged.

"Ah, Dramani," said Salifu, shaking his head. "You have to learn to think past the literal. Fire gets frozen all the time, in people and in places. Ask anybody who is married. Or even just look around. We are living in a frozen fire. Ghana is a frozen fire. Africa is a frozen fire. Hmm. . . ."

Salifu shook his head again, then picked up his guitar, which Peter and Alfred had returned to him after Tamasco had bought the band their own instruments. Salifu started strumming.

"It's only a matter of time," he said while strumming. "Only a matter of time." Then he started to sing, "Every day things are getting worse."

It would take the vantage point of adulthood for me to see, through hindsight, that Salifu was right. During the 1970s, we in Ghana were living in a fire that had been frozen. Most of Africa was. The entire continent had been caught in a state of suspended animation. The flame that had been sparked by Ghana's independence and subsequently blazed a trail of freedom throughout the continent had indeed been frozen. We weren't making any progress whatsoever. The sole reason the fire hadn't yet been extinguished was the presence of hope. That was the only thing keeping it alive, the only thing keeping us alive, the hope that things would get better. It was hope that burned inside us, inside the songs we sang.

SUMAILA'S PERSEVERANCE PAID OFF. One of the members of the band played the *shekere*, which is a West African maraca. Unlike maracas from other parts of the world, these do not contain beads or seeds inside the instrument. These maracas are made with a woven net of beads wrapped loosely around the outside of a calabash.

Though the band considered it a vital part of their ensemble, in terms of crowd popularity the maracas were a low-key instrument. The maraca player didn't have the same name or face recognition as the other members of the band. When they performed and the girls called out the names of the band members they favoured, his was not among them.

He slowly started to lose interest in the band. He would sometimes miss rehearsals, and even when he did show up it was evident that his heart was no longer in it. There were other activities he wanted to try and other interests he found more gratifying.

One day when Frozen Fire was scheduled to perform, the maraca player didn't show up. They waited and waited, but he never came. They didn't know what to do. There was no backup because nobody was really interested in playing the maracas. They didn't consider it an instrument with star power.

When the band was about to take the stage, they asked Sumaila if he would sit in for the maraca player. They worried about putting Sumaila onstage. It was common knowledge that music was not the boy's calling, but they had no other choice. Sumaila had been with them since the beginning. He knew their entire repertoire, every note of every song. They only needed to get through that show and then they'd find themselves a new maraca player, one they could rely on.

What the band members didn't know was that Sumaila had seen this opening coming, and he was more than prepared to step through it. When he'd noticed the maraca player's growing dissatisfaction with his role, Sumaila had taken the cue and started teaching himself how to play.

Frozen Fire always began their first song by introducing the instruments one at a time. The first player would play solo for a while, and then the lead singer would raise his right hand in the air, snap his fingers, and call for another instrument to join in. They would jam together for a while, and then the lead singer would call for the next instrument to join in.

The lead singer made eye contact with Sumaila to let him know his turn was approaching, then he raised his arm, snapped his fingers, and said, "Marac." Sumaila started playing, and everybody was astounded. Not only was he performing in perfect rhythm with the band, he had crafted his own style to go along with his playing. He could toss the maraca from one hand to the other, throw it up in the air, and clap his hands to the beat before catching it and playing again. The crowd broke into thunderous applause.

After the show, while the new crop of helpers was packing up the instruments, the band members asked Sumaila to officially join Frozen Fire. Of course he accepted. Sumaila was elated that everyone was finally able to acknowledge and experience what he'd known all along; there was talent inside of him, there was music inside of him. It was just a matter of finding the right way to let it out. That's exactly what he'd done, and now Sumaila's dream was becoming a reality. They gave him a stage name, Joe Mara, which is what everybody called him from that day on. The previous maraca player may have faded into the background, but Joe Mara blended in seamlessly. He remained a member of Frozen Fire until he graduated from Tamasco.

During breaks from school, Joe Mara would still come over to our house. If Peter was around, he, Alfred, and Joe would perform. Salifu and I would sit and watch them, taking much joy in the private concert.

"Who do they remind you of?" Salifu once asked as the

boys were playing. I'm sure he was thinking of a musical group, maybe one he'd told us about or whose songs he'd played for us on his guitar. As I looked at those three friends who'd been virtually inseparable since they'd met perform so beautifully together, only one thing came to mind, so that's the answer I gave.

"Taka, Tika, and Gangale."

PRAISE FOR THE POWERFUL

YENTUA! IT'S AN Akan word that means "We won't pay." When Colonel Ignatius Kutu Acheampong came into power through a coup d'etat in 1972, this was his answer to the question of what to do about the outstanding national and international debt assumed by previous administrations.

Colonel I. K. Acheampong, as he was generally known, was Ghana's fifth head of state and its third military ruler. When he became head of state, Acheampong set up a governing body called the National Redemption Council, of which he was the leader. The constitution was suspended, all political activity was banned, and those whom Acheampong felt were a threat to the state were placed in detention.

Ghana found itself back where it had been so many years before, with the military cutting short the tenure of an elected leader instead of allowing democracy to take its course. Acheampong considered himself a nationalist, something of a cultural revolutionary. His goal was to redeem the country, to see it gain self-sufficiency and achieve national unity. He started putting programmes in place to meet that goal. One of the first was Operation Feed Yourself, which had had such a direct and positive impact on my father when he first entered the business of agriculture.

The political life had been a turbulent one, and now what my father craved was a quiet, uneventful life with his family. The time he'd spent in detention, having to live every hour of every day in a small confined space, gave him greater appreciation for the lush expanse of land he'd grown up with in the north. He wanted space. Space and freedom.

He'd built our home on an entire acre of land, and he'd bought the plot right next to it to ensure that nothing and nobody caged him in. Every day while we were living in Tamale, when Dad stepped outside to go to work he'd take a deep breath. He'd suck in all the air his lungs could contain. When he exhaled it was like a sigh of relief, an expression of gratitude.

With the exception of the younger ones who were not yet ready, all of the kids who lived with Dad attended boarding school. When we were home, we ambled through our days, working at the rice mill, spending time with Salifu, the watchman, listening to music, going out to dance, or playing football with our friends. Our lives were uncomplicated, the best definition of normal that we knew.

The plot on the other side of our house was occupied by the manager of the Ghana Commercial Bank. Public servants in Ghana are provided with accommodation. It only made sense, since they were subject to transfer. Based on our system of rotation, public servants worked a certain number of years in one location and then would be reassigned to another location. Over the course of the time I lived in Tamale, I saw at least three or four Ghana Commercial Bank managers come and go. While their positions were not permanent, they were long-term, lasting for as many as three years, so the managers moved with their families.

The house next door, the one that the Ghana Commercial Bank manager lived in, had a wall around the property. It wasn't very high. We could see over it into their yard, but there was never really any reason to look. The managers were usually middle-aged, potbellied men with their wives. If they had children, they were often in university or grown-up and living on their own.

When I was sixteen and in my third year at Ghanasco, a new family moved in. We assumed they were like all the others, but one day as my brothers and I were playing football with our friends, we looked over the wall and saw a boy who was about our age. He was outside playing in their yard, kicking a football aimlessly. We called him over to join us.

We'd been playing for about an hour or two when his sister came out to call him in. What I remember is that I was fully absorbed in the game, my eyes keenly on the ball. I looked up for an instant, almost instinctively, and I saw this girl. She was beautiful, slender, and dark-skinned. Everything about her glowed, as though she were walking with her own spotlight.

I tried to turn my attention back to the game, but I couldn't. I felt funny, as if I were underwater, moving but without precision. When my brother kicked the ball to me, I rushed to meet it, but I couldn't get there fast enough. I ended up fumbling and falling, giving way to someone on the other team to take possession.

"Ah, but what's your problem?" Alfred asked. "That was a clear pass. It was yours."

"Thomas," said the girl, rescuing me from the wrath of my brother. "Mummy says you have to come home now."

"Hi," I said as she passed by me to get to her brother.

"Oh, hi," she responded, looking back at me. I watched her walk across our yard, which we'd turned into a makeshift field. I felt as though something, some powerful force, had grabbed hold of my body and pulled me even deeper underwater. My heart was beating fast. The other boys ignored her. They treated her like the intrusion she was. Even her brother grumbled at her presence. He said his good-byes to us, kicking the dirt as he walked back to their house.

Thomas and I became friends, partly because we were about the same age and he was good company and partly because being around him gave me the opportunity to see his sister again. Her name was Alice, and I'd never before felt the way I did when I was around her. I'd seen and met lots of pretty girls when my brothers and I went to the disco, but this was different. She was different. We hadn't ever said a word to each other beyond the "hi" and "hello" we exchanged when our paths crossed because of Thomas, but that was enough. It was enough to make me think of her all day and dream of her while I slept at night.

WHEN MY FATHER WAS RELEASED from detention, his assets had been frozen. Although he had been able to purchase the plots he needed to build his house and start his farm due to the land tenure system in the north, which rested in the hands of the chiefs, getting his rice mill business off the ground was another matter altogether. He needed capital, and the only way he could get it was to secure a loan from a bank.

Dad formed a limited liability company. He asked two of his friends to help him out by signing the required forms. They were men who had their own lives and occupations. They had no interest at all in Dad's business. Dad provided all the collateral and everything else that was needed for the loan to be approved and the business to take off. He would take care of the day-to-day management and whatever else was needed for the business to run. His friends, the two other shareholders, were, for all intents and purposes, ghosts, names on a sheet of paper.

During one of his visits to the north, Acheampong imposed a ban on the importation of rice in order to give the local farmers a chance. He asked the Bank of Ghana to give direct commodity loans to the rice mills so that they would be able to purchase rice from the local farmers. Since my father was a rice farmer and he also owned a rice mill, the ban and the Operation Feed Yourself programme were especially beneficial. With the state essentially funding the purchase of raw materials, Ghana's rice industry was thoroughly revitalised.

Acheampong's vision was becoming a reality. Insofar as food was concerned, within a short period of time, Ghana had become self-sufficient and was now even entering the export market to sell its surplus to other African nations.

Whenever Colonel Acheampong travelled to the north, he would stop by the house to personally greet my father. The two were not close friends, but they had a cordial relationship, one based on respect and necessity. Because of Operation Feed Yourself, my father's rice mill was of strategic interest to the state.

My father, much to his own surprise, liked Acheampong. The colonel was a military man, a coup maker, and that alone could have easily kept him out of my father's good graces. But Dad believed that Colonel Acheampong, despite the way he came into office, had Ghana's best interests at heart. He was making improvements, effecting change.

Acheampong had switched Ghana's system of measurement from the imperial to the metric. In 1974, through another of his programmes, Operation Keep Right, Ghana switched from driving on the left side of the road to driving on the right. It was perhaps one of the most successful radio and television ad campaigns in the history of the nation. A taxi driver would blow his horn four times at another taxi driver—*beep-beep, beep, beep*. Then the first driver would lean out of his window and say the slogan: *"Nifa, nifa, naa nyin."* This, in Akan, means "Right, right, and that is it."

Ghana's stadia were all reconstructed to meet international standards, so the country could now host sporting events with foreign teams. There was the launch of a National Reconstruction programme aimed at employment promotion and the teaching of practical work skills. Streetlights in the major urban areas were repaired, and low-cost housing was built in every region of the country.

My father used to tell us of Acheampong's accomplishments. He was impressed, there was no denying it. One day he decided to sit down and write to Acheampong, who had recently promoted himself from colonel to general. Dad believed in commending people for a job well done. It was a habit he'd formed while still a young man working as a teacher. It was a habit that we, his children, benefitted from. E. A. Mahama was never one to withhold praise. He gave it freely when he felt it was due.

Though he was writing this letter to General Acheampong as a private citizen, he decided to offer him a bit of the insight he'd gleaned from his years as a politician. In the letter he wrote, Dad told General Acheampong that he had done an admirable job thus far as head of state and had proven himself to be an asset to the country. He reminded General Acheampong that in politics, there often comes a time when the pendulum starts to swing the other way. It might be prudent, my father advised, given his popularity and the success of his various programmes, if the head of state started to give some thought to when he would lift the ban on party politics and transition the country back to constitutional rule. If he properly planned and timed his departure from politics, my father continued, General Acheampong would surely be remembered as one of Ghana's most effective leaders.

"Remember to leave," Dad wrote, "when the applause is loudest."

WHILE DAD WAS WRITING HIS letter to General Acheampong, I was writing my own letter. It was to Alice, the girl who lived next door. After several weeks of playing football together nearly every afternoon, Thomas and I had eased into a friendship. I was older than him by a year or two, so he looked up to me and was always happy to be in my company. Peter, Alfred, and our friend Joe Mara would join us for football, but outside of the pitch they ignored Thomas. After our matches, they would go off and do their own thing, and we'd go off and do ours.

One afternoon while we were sitting and talking on the veranda, I confessed to Thomas that I thought his sister was the most beautiful girl I'd ever seen. He looked at me strangely, as though I'd suddenly started talking in a language he couldn't understand. He must have found me silly. This was, after all, his big sister. It had probably never crossed his mind that anybody could think of her in that way. If one of my friends had told me that he thought one of my sisters was beautiful, I'd have had to stop and reconsider his sanity.

But Alice mesmerised me. Every time I saw her, my mind would take leave of my body. I'd trip over my own feet or walk into the hedges. All I wanted to do was stare at her. Her skin was smooth; her cheeks were high and pronounced, especially when she smiled. I would invent reasons to go and see Thomas, just so I could place myself in Alice's path. Telling Thomas how I felt about her was a huge relief.

With the exception of that "you can't be serious" look he gave me, Thomas didn't respond to what I'd confessed. A few days later, from out of nowhere, he said, "You should tell Alice."

My reaction was visceral. My heart pounded one time, really hard, and then it jumped into my throat. I shook my head so violently, it's a wonder it didn't fall off. Me? Stand in front of Alice and actually say something? And not just something, but that I think she is beautiful?

"No," I gasped. "No."

"Then I'll do it for you," Thomas responded. When he said that, I thought I would drop dead right then and there. What was this boy trying to do to me? I didn't even want to consider how Alice might respond. A girl that beautiful had to already have a boyfriend. It reminded me of when Alfred and I used to go to Simpa, the full moon dance, at Damongo, and Alfred and the village boys his age had started liking girls. When the dance started, each of them would choose a girl he thought was the prettiest and become fixated on her.

They'd stare and swoon and then inevitably the girl would choose a partner for the evening, and it wouldn't be one of them. The rejection would hurt the boys so deeply that they'd wear the pain of it on their faces, not really understanding why they should be feeling the way they were. I didn't want to know that kind of rejection, and I definitely didn't want to walk around with that look of pain plastered on my face.

"No," I said again to Thomas. "No. No. No."

I was thinking how much I regretted ever telling him when he said, "I think she likes you, too."

"Ehhnn? She does?" You'd think this news would have made me ecstatic, but it rather frightened me. No girl had ever liked me—not that I knew of, anyway. What was supposed to happen next? When it came to meeting girls, my brother Peter was the pro. I wondered if I should ask him for advice.

"Write her a letter," Thomas said. At first I refused, but the more I thought about it as the day wore on, the more I decided that maybe it wasn't such a bad idea after all. Writing a letter wasn't like talking to someone face-to-face. When it came to talking to girls, Peter had no fears. I wasn't like that.

In letters, you could tell people what you wanted to say and they could interpret it in their own time and in their own way. I decided to do it, to write Alice a letter.

WE WERE AT HOME, SITTING in the living room watching television, when the military men came for our father. They'd been instructed to deliver him to Kamina Barracks for interrogation, the purpose of which was to determine if he should be classified as a threat to the state. Apparently, parts of his letter of praise to General Acheampong had raised some concerns.

Dad went with the military men to Kamina Barracks, where he was questioned for hours. The men combed through the letter Dad had written word by word, sentence by sentence. Dad was asked to provide an explanation for every single statement he'd made. He answered the questions truthfully, never wavering from the compliments that he'd heaped onto General Acheampong or modifying the suggestion he'd made that the head of state should "leave when the applause is loudest."

"It was advice," Dad assured them, "not a threat." He reminded them that he was no longer involved in politics. He was a businessman, doing quite well as a direct result of General Acheampong's policies and programmes. Why would he want to do something that would hamper his own good fortune?

The military men questioning him were able to follow his logic and it made sense to them, but the decision of whether or not to release my father from custody was not theirs to make. They had received their orders from the Castle, the official seat of government. A report would have to be written and sent to Accra. It would be presented to General Acheampong, who would then decide what should be done with my father, whether he should be released or detained.

Our father was kept at Kamina Barracks for several days while waiting to discover his fate, which was in the hands of a man Dad now saw was not any different from every other coup maker.

Dear Alice,
How are you?
I think you are very beautiful and I like you 99.9%.
Take good care.
—John

It was more a note than a letter. Thomas and I snuck into my stepmother Joyce's room, where she kept her clothing, jewellery, and perfume. We sprayed and sniffed the scents from each bottle until we found one we thought Alice would like. It smelled like lemon, overripe mango, and honey. We doused the paper with the perfume, waving it in the air after each spray so the ink on the words wouldn't bleed or smudge. When it was dry, we folded the paper over once, twice, and a third time, then slid it into an envelope. We sprayed some of the perfume on the envelope, too.

Thomas hand-carried the letter to Alice. That whole night my stomach was like a soup, stirring with anxiety and hope and prayer and fear and desire. The next day, neither Thomas nor

Alice emerged from their house. I was disheartened. I took it personally. She hated the letter; I knew it. She probably hated me, too, and Thomas was too ashamed to come and tell me. I decided I wouldn't show my face outside again for the remainder of the long vacation. I didn't want to chance seeing either of them.

The next day, Thomas came over with apologies. They'd left very early in the morning with their parents to attend a funeral in Kumasi and hadn't returned until late in the night. He handed me an envelope that looked similar to the one I'd given him to deliver to Alice. I took it, thinking she was returning my letter unopened and unread. Then I saw my name written on the envelope in a handwriting I did not recognise. I could also now smell the perfume that had been sprayed onto the envelope. It wasn't the same kind Thomas and I had used. This scent was sweet, like toffee, vanilla, and caramel. I ripped open the envelope, removed the paper, and started to read.

Dear John,
I am fine. How are you too?
I think you are cute and I like you too.
99.9%.
—Alice

I was elated. She really did like me. Thomas hadn't just said that to make me feel good or to tease me because she was his sister. After Thomas left, I sprawled on my bed and read the letter over and over. I laid it over my face and inhaled. I looked at Alice's handwriting, which was neat and feminine, filled with lots of loops and squiggly lines. I looked at the creases in the letter, where she'd folded the paper. I imagined her gently gliding her thumbs along the folds to secure them so the paper would lie flat.

The following day, I wore clothes that were neat, with no holes or grass stains. Before leaving the house, I stood in front of the mirror and checked my face to make sure there was no sleep crust stuck in the corners of my eyes, nothing in my nose, and no food stuck between my teeth. I walked next door to Thomas and Alice's house. When Thomas answered, I greeted him first before asking to see Alice. He was visibly disappointed that the visit had not been for him, but he went and called her to come. As Alice approached the threshold, my heart started beating wildly again.

"Hello," I greeted her. She returned the same greeting. Neither one of us had anything more to say. We stood there in silence, smiling at each other. Eventually she asked if I could come back later.

"We can sit in the garden and talk," Alice said. I agreed.

It was evening when I returned. The garden in Alice and Thomas's backyard contained many of the same flowers as ours, including my favourite, white forget-me-nots with the yellow eyes at the centre.

Alice and I sat, mostly in silence, staring at the moon. We weren't sitting close. There were probably ten inches between us, and each one felt as long as a kilometre. Being so close to her thrilled me. My hands grew moist, and a sensation of heat travelled behind my ears down to the nape of my neck.

Alice asked me to tell her about my housemaster. It was typical for boarding students to talk about their housemasters.

They were the ones who enforced discipline in schools. The most entertaining and humorous stories that a person could tell about life in boarding school usually involved the house-master.

There were a number of stories to choose from. My friends and I at Ghanasco were always getting into situations that caught the watchful eye of the housemaster. I chose the tamest of these stories to share with Alice. I didn't want her to think I was unruly, some kind of troublemaker. She laughed politely at my stories, holding her hand over her mouth.

When it started getting late, I walked her the twenty steps to her back door.

"Will you come again tomorrow?" she asked before going inside.

"Yes," I said, "I will."

The next evening we sat together again, under the moon-light. This time it was Alice who told the stories about her housemistress. Alice attended a boarding school in the south. Because her family moved so often, her parents hadn't both-ered to make the kids change schools.

I'm sure she also chose only the tamest stories to share with me, the ones that still cast her in a ladylike, respectful light. I laughed at her stories, as she had done at mine, often and po-litely, even when they weren't too funny. I didn't care what we talked about. Being with her was what I wanted. It made no difference to me what we did when we were together, whether we spoke or remained silent.

Our evening rendezvous continued throughout the rest of the long vacation. By the time we were preparing to return to school, Alice and I had closed that gap of ten inches between us and were sitting side by side, with our elbows or shoulders touching. We'd hold hands and sit for hours, having become relaxed now in our feelings for each other.

Thomas and I continued to play football in the afternoons. I'm not sure how he felt about my relationship with his sister. He never mentioned her name when we were together, and he stayed indoors whenever Alice and I were outside in their garden. I guess he must have felt as though he'd done his part in bringing us together and now he didn't want any more to do with us as a couple.

We all vowed to keep in touch while we were away at school. Both Thomas and Alice said they'd write to me. I promised to write back. I even stole my stepmother's perfume so I could spray the letters I'd send to Alice.

During the school year, I never heard from Thomas. He was probably too busy with his other friends at school, and it wasn't common for boys to write letters to other boys unless they were brothers. Alice did write me several letters. They didn't come with any predictable regularity, but I treated each of them as I did the first. I would sprawl on my bed and read it from start to finish. I would then lay it on my face and take in the scent. I would then study her handwriting. Sometimes I'd even trace the curves of the letters with my finger. I would imagine her as she was writing, sitting at her desk thinking of things to put down on the paper, thinking of me.

IT IS NOT UNREASONABLE FOR someone to believe that he could lead his country better than the individual in power who, more often than not, is an elected official. That is the purpose of the electoral process, the reason why there is an opportunity at the end of every official's term for him or her to be challenged. That is why there is a platform for candidates to campaign, to share their strengths and leadership ability, as well as their vision for the future, with voters.

It takes a certain type of personality, however, to believe that he can do better and then to circumvent the electoral process through a forceful acquisition of power, denying the people their right to choose their leader. This sort of self-aggrandisement becomes more and more apparent as the coup makers, having already taken political power, attempt to elevate themselves even further.

Several years after his 1965 coup in the Democratic Republic of Congo, Joseph-Désiré Mobutu, a military man in his youth, changed his name to Mobutu Sese Seko Nkuku Ngbendu wa Za Banga, which translates to "the all-powerful warrior who, because of his endurance and inflexible will to win, will go from conquest to conquest leaving fire in his wake." Mobutu also affixed his image on the country's postage stamps and currency.

In 1969, after the coup in Libya, Colonel Muammar al-Gaddafi declared that he was "the leader of the Arab leaders, the king of kings of Africa, and the imam of the Muslims." He rejected the titles of head of state or president and instead adopted the official title "Brother Leader, Guide of the First of September Great Revolution of the Socialist People's Libyan Arab Jamahiriya Muammar al-Gaddafi."

In 1971, after the coup in Uganda, then major general Idi Amin Dada promoted himself to field marshal. He then as-

sumed the title "His Excellency, President for Life, Field Marshal Al Hadji Doctor Idi Amin Dada." Uganda's military leader
then started bestowing numerous unearned titles and decora-
tions upon himself, such as CBE (Conqueror of the British
Empire), VC (Victoria Cross), DSO (Distinguished Service
Order), and MC (Military Cross). By the end of his tenure, his
complete self-given title had become "His Excellency, President for Life, Field Marshal Al Hadji Doctor Idi Amin Dada,
VC, DSO, MC, Lord of All the Beasts of the Earth and Fishes
of the Seas and Conqueror of the British Empire in Africa in
General and Uganda in Particular."

In many ways, it felt as though Acheampong was going in
that same direction, his self-promotion from colonel to general being but one example.

The problem with coming into power by force is that it
breeds a distinct type of paranoia. Military rulers and dictators
find it difficult to trust anyone; they fear for their safety, believing, perhaps rightly so, that just as they forcibly removed others
from power, there are people who would like to see them forcibly removed.

Midway through his time as Ghana's military ruler, General
Acheampong dissolved the governing body that he had set up,
the National Redemption Council, and replaced it with the
Supreme Military Council, which was made up solely of a few
military members in whom he had confidence. Citizens viewed
these changes as sly manoeuvring for Acheampong to tighten
his control of the country and make himself president for life.
Our father, whom Acheampong had decided to release from
Kamina Barracks, was also of that opinion.

The loan that General Acheampong had authorised the

Bank of Ghana to give to the rice mills brought a large flow of cash into Dad's company. Money is known to be a destroyer of relationships. My father's friends, the formerly uninvolved and uninterested shareholders, were suddenly interested and eager to get involved. In order to gain greater control of the company and its assets, they took my father to court.

My father called on General Acheampong for assistance. Though Acheampong had chosen not to detain my father, he no longer viewed Dad as an ally. My father's calls went unanswered. Ultimately, the company that my father had built was wrested from his control.

BY THE TIME THE SCHOOL YEAR had come to a close, I'd grown accustomed to being in love and having a girlfriend. Alice and I had been exchanging letters. On breaks, we'd sit in the garden at the back of her house, but we'd also take long walks, sharing ideas and thoughts. That surge of adrenaline I used to get when I first met her never went away. My heart would still beat an accelerated rhythm of bliss. I never tired of looking at her or listening to her talk. I was planning to spend my entire long vacation with her. I'd made a list of the places I wanted to take her, places I'd seen while riding my bicycle as far as Savelugu, nearly eighteen kilometres outside of Tamale.

When I returned home, I discovered that Alice, Thomas, and their parents were moving. The Ghana Commercial Bank had transferred their father to the Volta Region. Another bank manager would assume the post in Tamale and, as part of the package, move into the house next to ours. I was distraught.

We barely had time to say good-bye. When we did talk, the two of us rationalised that it would really be no different from being away at school. We would continue to write, and once in a while we could find a way to see each other. It sounded like a reasonable plan, and it kept me stoic enough to offer whatever assistance I could to help Alice prepare for their departure.

After they left, I told myself that the plan would never work. Maybe for a while she would write to me. In time the letters would become fewer, and then they would stop. Maybe we would even find a way to see each other once or twice, but it wouldn't be the same. We wouldn't be neighbours. We wouldn't have the bench in her garden or the moonlight. We'd be strangers all over again.

For weeks, misery enshrouded me like a second skin. I didn't have much of an appetite. I would take to my bed and surround myself with Alice's letters. I couldn't bring myself to read them.

"It will get better, Romeo," Peter would say whenever he and Alfred came into the room and caught me thumbing through the envelopes or holding one to my nose to smell the perfume. "You'll fall in love again."

"And again, and again," Alfred would add.

They were right. I met other girls, not that long vacation, but over the years. But even as I was falling in love with a new girl who had stolen my heart and inspired me to start writing love letters again, whenever I sat on the veranda and saw those pure white petals on our forget-me-nots with their bright yellow eyes, I would think of Alice. I would always think of her.

UNION GOVERNMENT

MY FORMER LITERATURE professor at Ghanasco was a committed socialist. His name was Mr. Wentum, and he was one of the most affable, down-to-earth teachers in the school. All the kids loved him. He was a soft-spoken man, tall and gangly, with slightly bushy hair that was the colour of tea. He was the kind of person who would not stand out in a crowd. He dressed simply, in trousers and shirts that were almost never tucked in. He also favoured *batakaris*, a woven heavy-cotton smock worn by men in the north.

As a teacher, Mr. Wentum was professional and by-the-book. He stuck strictly to the curriculum. We read works by authors like Chinua Achebe, William Shakespeare, Leo Tolstoy, and D. H. Lawrence. He taught me in O levels, and I was taken by his brilliance. We all were. He was a true intellectual, a lover of words and critical thought.

Outside of the classroom, Mr. Wentum was a friend. He didn't draw that strict line of separation between student and teacher that is common in our culture, especially back in 1977. He considered us his younger friends, and he treated us that way. We affectionately called him Brother Wentum. He would walk with us, come to our dormitories; he'd chat with us about anything and everything, including his beliefs. Most of these discussions took place in Mr. Wentum's flat. He allowed us, his group of young friends, free access to his flat. We could go there and laze about when we were done with our classes. It became our spot.

On-campus accommodation for faculty was limited, so the school had rented Mr. Wentum a flat in town, about a kilometre away. My best friend, Sulley, and I used to walk over there several times a week and linger for hours. Sulley had just started attending Ghanasco. He lived in Wa. He was born in Ghana, but his parents were originally from Nigeria. They'd immigrated to Ghana while it was still the Gold Coast colony.

Sulley was one of the most talented and versatile kids I'd ever met. He had a sharp mind and was witty. He knew how to sew, a skill he'd learned from his father, who was a tailor, and he was practical with his hands in ways that I, and his other bookish friends, envied.

The building Mr. Wentum lived in was fittingly unremarkable. The flat itself was also rather ordinary. It was sparsely furnished, with a couch, a few chairs, and two or three small stools. There were no nice decorative objects, no paintings on the wall, no carvings. The only thing in the whole place that hinted at Mr. Wentum's history or personality were his books. He owned dozens and dozens of books, which he allowed me, Sulley, and the other boys to borrow or read while we were there.

Mr. Wentum enjoyed sharing his worldview with us. "The history of all human society is the history of the class struggle," he would explain to us while preparing one of his delicious meals. "Human beings exist in social classes, and the classes are in a constant struggle for control of power and resources."

When he'd finished cooking, Mr. Wentum would serve all of us a dish of whatever he had prepared and then continue talking to us about the importance of the working class, who were the real instruments of revolution. As we ate, we listened to him talk about how socialism would triumph until it became the entire world's ideology.

Mr. Wentum told us that soon enough socialism would spread to the far corners of the earth, everywhere from America to Israel to Australia, even to Upper Volta, the country that in 1984 was renamed Burkina Faso.

"Upper Volta?" Sulley asked incredulously. Since attaining its independence, the country had been unable to achieve stability. It had undergone a series of coups and military rulers. In an attempt to transition to civilian rule, a new constitution had just been written and approved, and open elections were scheduled for the coming year.

"Why not?" Mr. Wentum asked back. "They are moving toward democracy, and Karl Marx wrote that 'democracy is the road to socialism.'" He would often quote the works of Karl Marx and Friedrich Engels. He would also urge us to read them ourselves. Whenever I left Mr. Wentum's flat, my head would be filled with words like *proletariat, bourgeois, peasant,* and *oppressor.*

Mr. Wentum's passion for socialism was infectious. After weeks of hearing him talk about equality and classless societies, the creation of a nation in which there was full employment and everybody lived a decent life, I could feel myself slowly being converted, but I was not without my questions and doubts.

My father was a businessman, and by Mr. Wentum's definition, that meant he was also a capitalist, an oppressor. This, for me, created a fair amount of intellectual and emotional dissonance.

Mr. Wentum told us that Engels wrote, "A few days in my old man's factory have sufficed to bring me face to face with this beastliness, which I had rather overlooked." When he said it, I became wracked with guilt. I thought about the times when I'd worked in the factory at my father's rice mill, going from station to station. It was hard work, but I felt I'd been paid a fair wage. I wondered whether the permanent workers there also felt they were being paid a fair wage or whether they felt they were being exploited.

I knew my father to be a man of the people. That's the reason he'd entered politics. It's also the reason he chose to join the Convention People's Party (CPP), which was founded and led by Dr. Nkrumah.

The CPP aligned itself with some socialist philosophies, particularly where education and welfare were concerned. Dr. Nkrumah believed that quality education was a right to which people were entitled and that it was the state's duty to provide them access to it. Likewise, he believed that in order to have a healthy, productive population, citizens should have access to free health care provided by the state.

Mr. Wentum's ideas went far beyond the sort of socialism that had been adopted by the CPP. The end goal for Mr. Wentum was a revolution of the working class, along the same lines as the Great October Revolution, and the creation of a Communist state like the Soviet Union, which he regarded as a utopia.

My response to politics had always been personal because of my dad's involvement. He was my father. What affected him, affected me, so I automatically stood on his side. Though the events of my entire life had, in one way or another, been shaped or influenced by politics, I'd never considered or defined my own political leanings. Now I was beginning to.

GHANAIANS WERE FED UP WITH General Acheampong's leadership. He was facing intense pressure to step down and return the country to a multiparty political system with constitutional rule. After Acheampong dissolved the National Redemption Council and instituted the Supreme Military Council (SMC), the military moved into all facets of Ghanaian life, especially the country's economic life.

Brutality and human rights offences were on the rise as soldiers brought the codes and conduct of the barracks into civil life. Since Ghanaians were not living under constitutional rule, soldiers acted with impunity, even bringing summary discipline to civil life. If somebody ran afoul of the law for something as minor as a traffic infraction, it wouldn't be unusual for a soldier to pull the unfortunate person out of the vehicle and beat him up. There were no laws in place to prevent or punish this type of rogue behaviour.

The military was in control of everything. They were the

managing directors of the State Housing Corporation. They controlled the State Transport Corporation and every other state-owned company, of which there were many. Soldiers were in charge at the ministerial level and also at the local government level, which meant they controlled all the places where the state had strong influence on the country's means of production and distribution of goods.

Ours was a command economy, so that gave the soldiers tremendous power and access. Suddenly the military was engaging in the kind of corruption they'd once accused the previous civilian government of. Soldiers started building posh mansions and buying beautiful expensive cars.

Meanwhile, day-to-day survival was becoming more and more difficult for civilians. Imports were restricted unless the individual or business had an import license, and those were all but impossible for the average person to obtain. As a result, there were shortages of everything. We operated under a chit system. In order for civilians to purchase the items that were considered essential commodities, such as soap, tin milk, tin fish, corned beef, and sugar, they needed a chit, an official voucher. They could then take the chit to a state warehouse and collect the items.

Traders would wait at the gates of the state warehouses for people to come with their chits. Often, they would purchase the chit at a black market price, go inside and collect the items, and then sell them to other traders, who would in turn sell them at the market for nearly ten times the price.

These practices introduced shortages, which led to hoarding. When they had the opportunity, people would buy far more of any commodity than they needed and keep the extra for later use or resale on the black market at exorbitant prices. Ghanaians coined a term for this; we called it *kalabule*.

Vendors would hoard merchandise and store it in warehouses. They devised crafty ways of covertly advertising the items they were selling, and the negotiations between vendors and customers took place in code. You might, for instance, find a market woman sitting at a stand with only a few brooms beside her, with the bunch of straws on each broom held together by a strip of cloth. It was not the brooms that were for sale, but the cloth. Cloth, especially imported wax prints, was of tremendous value to Ghanaians; but, like everything else, it was scarce.

Things had run completely amok, a general descent had taken place, and people in civil society started to get angry. They were tired of living in a state of lack and a society of lawlessness. They wanted stability. They wanted accountability.

In response to the public's agitation, General Acheampong and the SMC introduced a concept called Union Government. Democracy, they explained, was a Western creation. This new system of government would be based on an indigenous form of democracy. They argued that in Ghana's traditional system of governance, leaders were not elected but were nevertheless representative of the people. Decisions made by traditional rulers were not at their sole discretion; there was a council of elders with whom the ruler met to discuss issues.

General Acheampong and the SMC maintained that this was truly an all-inclusive form of governance, because according to tradition, every segment of society has a chief who holds a seat in the ruler's court. Those chiefs were essentially the representatives of the society. They advised the ruler, who was then able to make decisions by consensus, decisions that were in the best interests of the whole society.

This summary of Union Government (or UniGov, as most people began to call it) was nebulous. The government went to great lengths to sell this idea to the people. They even printed a book outlining its benefits. What they failed to provide were the specifics of how exactly it would work, how it would be organised, who would be in charge of selecting the representatives, whether they were permanent or subject to replacement, and who would decide if or when the representatives should be replaced.

Book or no book, the concept of Union Government was not well received. People felt it was a ploy for General Acheampong to remain in power because he knew that if there was a full return to a multiparty system, he would have to step down.

The government claimed that it would leave the decision of whether or not to create UniGov in the hands of the people. They scheduled a referendum for March 1978. At this time, citizens were to vote yes if they were in favour of UniGov or no if they were not. The government waged a full-scale campaign to gain a yes vote for UniGov. Numerous ads were aired in the state-owned media to promote UniGov; money and new vehicles were given to opinion leaders so they could try to sway the vote.

Students and professionals were aggressively against the concept of Union Government, and they waged their own full-scale campaign. Massive demonstrations were held on campuses throughout the nation. Police and soldiers would show up and beat the demonstrators. Many universities were forced to close because of the protests and the resulting violence.

When the students went home to await the reopening of their universities, they carried pamphlets written and published by the National Union of Ghana Students detailing the reasons why UniGov should not be approved, the most important of which was the fact that it would ensure that Ghana remained a no-party state in the hands of the same power-hungry ruler. The students would distribute these crudely produced pamphlets to market women, hairdressers, tailors, and other working-class people in the community. They would also distribute them to students at secondary schools.

BETWEEN MR. WENTUM AND BONIFACE, the students at Ghanasco had been fully radicalised. We were firmly against UniGov and were prepared to play our role on the day of the referendum.

Boniface was a university student who had recently attended Ghanasco. He still had friends there, so he would often come to visit. Like Mr. Wentum, who had been a student activist while attending the University of Cape Coast, Boniface was a committed socialist. Unlike the gentle-mannered Mr. Wentum, Boniface was loud and confrontational. During the times when his university was forced to shut down because of the bloody clashes between the demonstrators and soldiers, Boniface would come to Ghanasco to solidify our support.

He was short and slim and looked more like a primary student than a university student. We would see him at Mr.

Wentum's flat, where he'd bring handfuls of "No to UniGov" pamphlets and tell us graphic stories about the events that had been taking place in Accra, where he was attending university.

We cringed when we heard about the excessive force with which the soldiers treated the students. Demonstrators were kicked and slapped, hit with truncheons and clubs; shots were fired into the air and into the crowds. Having seen what he had seen, Boniface was sure that there was no way the military would allow the results of the referendum to reflect the true will of the people.

"If they won't allow us to even demonstrate against it, why would they allow us to vote against it?" he asked.

Ghanasco students could not participate in the referendum because we were not eligible to vote; we were too young. However, Ghanasco was going to be used as a polling centre because the majority of the student population would be on break. We sixth-form students were required to remain on campus to prepare for our university entrance exams. Boniface and Mr. Wentum devised a plan, a way for us to protect the ballot box.

Every night we would meet at Mr. Wentum's flat to go over the fine points of the plan. We would gather in the living room and Boniface would talk to us while Mr. Wentum cooked. He told us about life at university and how different it was from life in secondary school.

"It's the real world," he said. "You can't hide behind childhood anymore." Boniface also answered our questions about socialism.

"Are all capitalists oppressors?" I asked, thinking of my father. Boniface was emphatic in his response.

"Yes. They have to be. That's the nature of the system they're in. When the revolution happens, all of them must go." Go? Go where? I was poised to ask Boniface when he started speaking again.

"Marx said, 'The last capitalist we hang shall be the one who sold us the rope.'" Everyone laughed except me and Sulley, who gave me a comforting look and shook his head slightly as if to say, *Nothing is going to happen to your dad.*

The strategy session would begin after Mr. Wentum had served everyone a steaming plate of food. The plan was that we would stand outside where the ballot boxes were in view and make sure that nobody went inside to stuff them. We were told not to stand in clusters but to disperse and look inconspicuous so we didn't frighten the people who were going in to vote.

In the unlikely event we were confronted by a soldier or policeman, we were to scream for assistance. The others would then come to our aid.

"They wouldn't dare come and harm children," Mr. Wentum assured us.

"Wouldn't they?" Boniface challenged.

We went over the plans at every meeting to make sure each of us knew which ballot box he'd be watching, where he was to stand, how he was to respond if verbally questioned by a soldier, and how he was to escape if he was physically threatened or accosted before help had arrived.

I missed one of the meetings at Mr. Wentum's. There was something or other I had to do in connection with an upcoming exam that prevented me from attending. Sulley and the other boys went without me but promised to fill me in on all the details when they returned to the dormitory.

Boniface's university had reopened and he'd returned to Accra, so he wasn't at the meeting either. Mr. Wentum fed the boys dinner and then began to update everyone on the latest news about recent riots and protests and about demonstrators who had been injured or killed and schools that had shut down. The referendum was taking place in a few days, so he wanted to make sure everybody was still committed to the assignment and knew what they were supposed to do.

Sulley decided to quickly refill his glass of water before Mr. Wentum moved into the review of the lists of dos and don'ts of our mission. Sulley got up and walked into the kitchen, which was adjacent to the living room. He opened the refrigerator to get the water.

Mr. Wentum, who was single, cooked his own food. Since he usually ended up feeding us as well, his refrigerator was often well stocked. This time it must have been overfull, because as soon as Sulley opened the door, something fell out and dropped to the floor. It was some food, loosely wrapped. There were similar parcels on the shelf next to where it had been, except they had been placed in more securely. Sulley bent down to pick it up. To his horror, when he touched it, the parcel paper opened slightly to reveal a hand.

"John, it was hairy," Sulley told me later that night. "And it had five fingers. One of them was an opposable thumb! And its palms were very black, with lines in it just like ours." Sulley sounded surprisingly calm as he described this hand. If it had been me, I would have run right out of the kitchen.

"What did you do?" I asked my friend.

"I picked it up," Sulley said, as if it were the only thing he could have done, "but from the bottom where the wrapper was still intact."

Sulley, who at that point had decided he was no longer thirsty, walked back to the living room and stood in front of Mr. Wentum, holding out the hand from the fridge. The other boys gasped, opening their eyes really wide or simply moving away as if the appendage in the open parcel were alive and could attack them.

"What is this?" Sulley asked Mr. Wentum.

"What do you think it is?" Mr. Wentum asked him back.

"A monkey," Sulley answered, sounding disgusted.

"Well," Mr. Wentum said, smiling, "what do you think you have been eating all this time?"

Upon hearing that, a couple of the boys slapped their hands over their mouths and rushed to the bathroom to vomit. One boy continued to chew the meat that was in his mouth, clearly not caring if it was monkey or beef or mutton. Sulley said he'd initially felt like throwing up as well, but he'd reminded himself that the meals had been nice. There was no reason to pretend otherwise now that he knew what it was he'd eaten. What's done was done.

Mr. Wentum took the monkey hand from Sulley and carefully rewrapped the packaging. On his way to the kitchen to return it to the fridge, he told the boys he believed everything God put on this earth was to be eaten. He didn't understand why people had such strange taboos when it came to food.

"If someone can eat fish and someone else can eat rabbit or snail or antelope, then why can't we also eat monkey?"

ON THE DAY OF THE referendum, we took our positions and watched the ballot boxes, as planned. Back then, ballot boxes were made of steel and painted black so nobody could see what was inside. Voters went and registered with the electoral official; then they placed their ballots and left. We stood there the entire morning. Turnout was low.

A few of our teachers, Mr. Wentum and his like-minded colleagues, joined us on our mission, which was turning out to be pleasantly uneventful. Be that as it may, we had no business being there. We were secondary school students, eighteen- and nineteen-year-old boys, not vigilantes. We had been reading books and exchanging ideas and thoughts about class struggle and revolution for so long, we'd started to imagine that Ghana was on the brink of both. Karl Marx wrote, "This revolution is necessary, therefore, not only because the ruling class cannot be overthrown in any other way, but also because the class overthrowing it can only in a revolution succeed in ridding itself of all the muck of ages and become fitted to found society anew." We believed this.

We wanted Ghana to become a new society, one without hunger, rampant unemployment, and wide separation between classes. If that meant watching ballot boxes to safeguard the vote, then so be it. We were willing to sacrifice our study time. It never crossed our minds, even with all we'd heard about the demonstrators and the soldiers, that we might also be sacrificing our lives.

By early afternoon, when we were convinced that the Ghanasco ballot boxes in the referendum would not be subject to any foul play, a suspicious-looking young man arrived. He approached us and told us to go away. We refused and, contrary to the instructions Mr. Wentum had given during the various planning meetings, entered into a verbal altercation with the man.

He threatened to beat us up. We scoffed at his threat. There was no way he could beat up all of the boys in our group. We wouldn't even have to call for help from the others. The man saw that he was outnumbered. He turned around and started to walk away.

"We'll come back," he said, "and you will see." We had no idea who he meant when he said "we," but it didn't matter. We were proud of ourselves. We watched the man walk back to his car, a brand-new Peugeot, the kind that the government was giving away to entice people into becoming mouthpieces for the creation of Union Government. This made us feel even more victorious: our David to their Goliath.

An hour and a half later, a pickup truck pulled up. It had a tent canopy covering the bed area in the back so we couldn't tell what was in it. We assumed it was ballot papers and that the people in the pickup truck had come to stuff the ballot boxes. We watched them, curious to find out what they intended to do. Another pickup truck came, followed by a Peugeot like the one we'd seen earlier.

The vehicles came to a screeching halt, one after the other. Before the drivers could even turn off their engines, people starting jumping out of the vehicles with clubs and cutlasses. There were perhaps twenty of them. They started approaching us. We noticed that one of them was the man we'd had words with, the one who'd promised us he would return. Now we understood why he'd said "we."

"Who are the ones causing the confusion here?" one of the men asked.

"Are you the ones disrupting the elections?" another of the men asked. We almost laughed. Us? Causing confusion? Disrupting elections? We told them no.

"So what are you doing here?" the first man wanted to know. By this time, all the others involved in our mission had rushed over to where we were.

"Stand," said Mr. Wentum. Some of the boys heeded his call. They locked their knees, straightened their spines, and pressed their arms to their sides as though they were imitating a soldier. The men kept walking toward us. The next thing we knew, a club had come down on somebody's head.

Sulley and I looked at each other and then we ran. One of the teachers started running, too. He wasn't as fast as we were. We could hear him huffing and puffing to keep his pace. As we ran, we could hear footsteps going in other directions of the campus. We could hear people screaming as they were being beaten. We kept running until we were in our dormitory, safely hidden in a place where nobody would find us.

The next day, Sulley and I went to Mr. Wentum's flat to check on him. Some of the other boys were there, too. A few of them had lumps on their heads from being clobbered and bruises on their faces from being slapped repeatedly. Mr. Wentum looked as though he'd been badly beaten, but he was

still moving about. He sat and talked with us about the need
to press onward and continue the struggle. I searched his shelves
for books. I pulled down a few about capitalism and revolution that seemed as though they would be informative and
asked Mr. Wentum if I could borrow them.

"Of course," he agreed. He said he was feeling a little hungry
and told us he had made some food earlier. "You're invited," he
said, limping toward the kitchen. Sulley and I immediately
headed for the door, using the excuse of our studying to make
our exit. A few of the other boys were right behind us, on our
heels. Only one boy remained seated, the one who apparently
didn't have any strange taboos when it came to food.

I clutched the books I'd borrowed firmly in my hand as I
walked back to the campus with Sulley and the other boys.
My days of eating at Mr. Wentum's flat may have been over,
but my fascination with socialist ideology had only just begun.

TRUTH STANDS

THE WORLD MAPS of my youth were always flat. They depicted an earth that was stretched and distorted, with no topography, no shaded relief. The only markings were the names of continents and oceans, the names of countries and their capital cities, the names of rivers and mountain ranges.

According to those maps, the places I knew best did not exist. They were swaths of light-coloured space with no definition, nothing to show the vast forests or plains, the huge scarp that my brother Alfred and I used to scale as children so we could hunt. I would look at the other unlabeled areas of the map and wonder what and who existed in that space.

There has always been something about the earth that has beguiled me. I used to study the maps that were posted on the walls of my classrooms and printed in the pages of the atlas my father kept in his study. I could barely start memorising the names and shapes of the countries before the map I was using became obsolete. That's how quickly the world was changing. Borders were being redrawn; countries were being formed and re-formed, and some of them were assuming new names.

What remained the same throughout were the contours of each continent, like the curve of western Africa and the pointed tip of South America. I noticed that the landmasses, though separated by enormous bodies of water, fit perfectly together, as though they could be one, or perhaps had even been. This was before I learned about Pangea, the supercontinent that is believed to have existed before the continental drift that ultimately led to the configuration we currently know.

In sixth form, I chose geography as one of my subjects of study. The information I learned expanded my knowledge of the earth and made me feel a sense of connection to other countries and continents that I hadn't before. I formed a broad feeling of kinship to the other people of the world, people I realised I might never meet or know.

WHEN I ARRIVED AT THE University of Ghana to begin my freshman year, I was steeped in disappointment. I hadn't been granted the courses of study that I'd indicated were my first and second choices. I'd hoped to study business administration; that had been my first choice. I'd chosen it because it was the most popular major at the university, one to which prospective employers were said to respond. Other than that, I knew very little about business administration and had very little interest in it.

My second choice was law. It wasn't something for which I held a burning passion, but it was practical. University was a time for serious study, a time to prepare for life. I had no idea what I wanted to do with my life, but from all that I'd been

told, a degree in law provided a strong platform for nearly
every profession.

History, which was my third choice, the one to which I'd
been assigned, was not discussed with the same gravity. I had
always enjoyed studying history. In primary school I'd been
given an award in history, and along with geography and eco-
nomics, it had been my other course of study in sixth form.
Yet history as a university major was said to limit a graduate's
career options. It was too specific and offered no knowledge
or skills that could be immediately applied outside of the classroom, in the workforce.

I eventually grew to consider my assignment to history as a
blessing in disguise and recognise that the knowledge I would
gain from its study would carry me far beyond the classroom
and workaday existence. However, in those first few weeks of
university, I felt as though I'd been cheated out of the things I
wanted.

My disappointment and that general feeling of having been
cheated also stemmed from the fact that in addition to not being granted my top course choices, I was not granted my top
choices in halls of residence.

At the time, there were five halls of residence at the University of Ghana—Commonwealth Hall, Akuafo Hall, Legon
Hall, Mensah Sarbah Hall, and Volta Hall. Volta was the all-
female hall. Mensah Sarbah was a mixed hall; women occupied
one wing of the building, and the rest was all male.

Legon Hall was my first choice because I was told it was
peaceful and quiet, a hall of gentlemen. My next choice was
Mensah Sarbah, which I'd been told was beautiful. The residents of that hall were called the Vikings and were said to be

extremely good at sports. Third was Akuafo, which was dedicated to the farmers of Ghana. My fourth and final choice was Commonwealth, and that was where I was assigned.

Commonwealth Hall had a controversial reputation. Its residents were called the "VANDALs." The acronym VANDAL stands for "Vivacious, Affable, Neighbourly, Devoted/ Dedicated, Altruistic, and Loyal." The boys at Commonwealth Hall were said to actually be unruly, rowdy, insulting, and provocative. They paraded on campus virtually half-naked, and they kept a shrine in the hall to Bacchus, the Greek god of wine. Suffice it to say, I did not want to live there.

Unbeknownst to me, Commonwealth was historically one of the most radical of all the halls of residence. A lot of the political ferment, activism, and rebellion that took place on campus was usually hatched by the residents of Commonwealth. Because of this, the university officials had devised an unwritten rule to balance out the types of personalities and temperaments of the students in the hall.

Students whose first choice was Commonwealth were assumed to be of the same ilk, so they were automatically assigned to a more subdued hall. Meanwhile, students like me, who were resistant to being in Commonwealth and placed it last in their list of choices, were the ones assigned there.

The University of Ghana was built on a hill. There is a long, rectangular pond at the front of the entrance. Standing there, facing forward, you can see straight to the top of the hill. When you pass through the main gates, there is a wide boulevard that travels up the steep incline. The boulevard ends at the steps of Commonwealth, forking into two roads that wrap around the enormous building and then continue upward toward the administration's offices.

Freshman students arrived a week earlier than the rest of the student population to go through an orientation. A lot of the final-year students were also on campus, working on their dissertations and theses.

On my first day, I stood at the base of the sweeping concrete stairs. There were a number of final-year students hanging around, singing. They were dressed in strange attire. Some of them had leaves around their neck. One person was wearing a bra and panties. A few were wearing their trousers with one leg down and the other rolled up or cut off into shorts. They were there as our freshman welcoming committee, to help us carry our bags up the stairs to the porter's lodge, where we were to sign in.

After we'd climbed the stairs and were standing at the entrance of Commonwealth Hall, I noticed that a coat of arms was affixed to the top of the arched doorway. Embossed on the coat of arms were the words *Truth Stands*, which is the hall's motto.

This was a cardinal moment for me. I stood there, having just arrived at this preeminent Ghanaian university, looking at the coat of arms and the hall's motto, "Truth Stands." I felt humbled; I felt filled with purpose. It occurred to me that the hundreds of people who had walked through the doors of that hall had uncovered the truth of their lives. I was determined to do the same.

I later learned that the Commonwealth Hall motto, "Truth Stands," was taken from the poem "Satire III" by the English

poet John Donne. This, to me, made the motto all the more
profound.

> To stand inquiring right, is not to stray;
> To sleep, or run wrong, is. On a huge hill,
> Cragged and steep, Truth stands, and he that will
> Reach her, about must and about must go,
> And what the hill's suddenness resists, win so.

By the time I entered the University of Ghana, I'd moved
deeper into my exploration of socialist ideology. I was still
deeply invested in its goals of a classless society, one that was
entitled to the most basic necessities and rights, one that upheld
the value of education.

The violence I had witnessed, and narrowly escaped, on the
day of the referendum for Union Government had left me
shaken. It reinforced the viciousness and selfish motivation that
was characteristic of the political landscape in most of Africa.
If our country was going to progress, then change had to come.
We had to break the cycle of coups and military rule and return
to democracy, which would ultimately lead us to socialism.

My former secondary school teacher Mr. Wentum had put
me in touch with professors at the University of Ghana who
ran socialist cells. I joined one. We would meet once a week for
a couple of hours to better familiarise ourselves with the works
of Karl Marx, Friedrich Engels, and Vladimir Lenin. We would
juxtapose the conditions that led to the Great October Revolution with Ghana's current society and position, debate the
direction in which we felt the country needed to go, and figure
out what part we could play to help it get there.

It had been announced that the referendum for Union Government yielded an overwhelming yes vote, but the public could not be fooled. Even the announcement of the results was mired in controversy. There was too much unrest for things to continue as they had been. General Acheampong was forced to resign by his own Supreme Military Council, a military coup of a military coup maker.

In July 1978, Lieutenant General Fred Akuffo, who had been the number two person in the SMC under General Acheampong, took over as head of state. With the exception of the names of the rulers, nothing much had changed. People were still not able to afford essential commodities. The practice of *kalabule* persisted, so the nation was operating on an artificial economy that was driven by a thriving black market.

In 1979, there was another coup, led by a young flight lieutenant named Jerry John Rawlings, who set up an interim government, the Armed Forces Revolutionary Council (AFRC). Flight Lieutenant Rawlings told the people of Ghana that their goal was to conduct a "housecleaning" exercise and then promptly return the country back to civilian rule. Party politics was now allowed.

After the 1966 coup, my father had been banned from participating in politics or holding any political appointment for ten years. That period of time had elapsed, but when my father wrote what was supposed to have been a letter of praise to then head of state General Acheampong and found himself facing the possibility of detention again, it soured him on politics.

But these were new times, with new possibilities. The Convention People's Party had been refashioned into the People's National Party (PNP). My father, as a senior member of the original party, was persuaded to help them select a suitable flag bearer, one who was capable of winning the election. Unable to resist a call for assistance, particularly if it concerned the advancement of the nation, my father reentered political life, but only as a key adviser.

Dr. Hilla Limann, a career civil servant, was chosen to be the party's presidential candidate. Limann was a virtual unknown. So much so that when my father and the other senior members of the group met and his name came up, someone asked, "Li-who?" It was a question that was asked many more times over the course of the brief period between the coup and the election. Nevertheless, Dr. Limann won and became president of the Third Republic of Ghana.

At the same time that my father was reentering politics, I was being initiated into a political life, albeit at the student level. In those days, the student body was one of the most active unofficial political organisations. We were very conscious of what was going on in Ghana and in the rest of the world, and we participated in all kinds of demonstrations.

There were protests against nuclear weapons in Africa; there were pro-Cuba protests and antiapartheid protests. We students in Ghana stood in solidarity with our brothers and sisters in South Korea who had staged an uprising against their dictatorship, as well as our brothers and sisters in Iran who had revolted against the shah. We held placards and raised our voices in support of Palestine. And, of course, we picketed, demonstrated, and did whatever else we could to bring attention to our own causes in Ghana, be it an issue within the university system or our discontent with governmental policy.

Living in Commonwealth, which I came to regard as the

best hall on campus, coaxed the natural activist in me to come out. There was an ivory tower priggishness and orderliness that went along with university life. It perpetuated the status quo. Life inside of Commonwealth was the exact opposite. It encouraged the formation of opinions and the expression of individuality.

Without a doubt, this manifested itself in odd behaviours. People went around at all hours of the day and night singing in hoarse voices and dressed in curious attire. They felt free to let their hair down and just be themselves. When it came time to stand up for their rights or the rights of others, the Commonwealth Hall boys rose to the occasion. They took their motto to heart and stood for whatever they firmly believed was truth. I'd never really been expressive. I had strong opinions, but mostly I kept my inner thoughts to myself. Living in Commonwealth Hall helped me to start speaking out because I felt relaxed enough to be myself.

The socialist ideology I was espousing was already creating a great deal of internal conflict for me because my father had been a successful businessman and my family had lived in relative comfort. I didn't like the view of my father as a capitalist, an oppressor, someone who exploited the labour and human resources of others. Nor did I believe that lines of definition had to be so inflexible and tightly drawn, with no room for exceptions or explanations.

My burgeoning political views and activism at times clashed with my father's views, especially when it came to government affairs. As a senior member of the party, Dad felt that given the mess they'd inherited, the government was heading in the right direction, making solid long-term decisions.

Acheampong's *Yentua!* policy had shattered Ghana's economic standing in the world and its relationships with international aid organisations. Dr. Limann's government was having ongoing conversations with the International Monetary Fund and the World Bank about entering into a programme that would improve the financing of the budget and inject fresh capital into the system to restore the deteriorating infrastructure.

From our student activist purview, change wasn't happening fast enough, so we took the government to task by marching and demonstrating every chance we could. My participation in these activities caused arguments between Dad and me. When I'd return home during a break from university, he'd ask, "What the hell did you kids think you'd accomplish with that protest?" I would launch into an impassioned rant about the wrongs of the government. My father would just shake his head.

"Things don't happen overnight," he would explain. "Some of these policies are already in place, but it might take a while before you can see the results."

"Long-term changes are fine," I would argue, "but we need immediate changes, too. Something that will put money in people's pockets so they can eat and live." We'd argue back and forth, until he grew tired of trying to explain what he realised my youthful fervour and political naïveté prevented me from comprehending. However far apart we grew in our politics and ideologies, my father and I remained close in our relationship. There was nothing I couldn't ask him for, nothing he wouldn't do to help or support me. His love and presence were unshakable.

I'd been in a leadership role before as a prefect, but that was an appointed role, not an elected one. Every hall of residence at the university had a junior common room, a JCR. Every JCR had executives, who served as the leadership for that hall of residence. All the other halls held JCR elections once a year. Commonwealth Hall being Commonwealth Hall, its residents held JCR election three times a year, once during each term. It was their brand of democracy. They believed that to elect an executive who would serve an entire year was oppressive. This way, if an executive wasn't performing well, the hall residents would not have to suffer with the poor leadership for too long.

I decided to run for JCR vice president. I stood against a tough opponent. He was a VANDAL through and through, involved in the choir and just about every other Commonwealth Hall activity one can imagine. People knew him well. They felt he was one of them and could understand their concerns. Though I was a general part of the Commonwealth Hall community, I didn't take part in many of the activities, particularly not the choir, because the members were a bit wild and their repertoire was full of profane songs.

The mode of campaigning was basic grassroots, going from room to room meeting people, telling them who you were and what you intended to do if elected, then asking them to please vote for you. Many people told me flat out that they would not vote for me, and they even explained why—because I was not involved enough in Commonwealth Hall life. I lost the election, but it was a great learning experience. I had been focussed squarely on my own goals and visions as a candidate. After the loss, I came away with an understanding that in these types of contests what is most important is a candidate's knowl-edge of the electorate and its expectations in the selection of a leader. I carried that knowledge with me the next time I decided to run for an office. During my second year at univer-sity, I ran for the office of secretary of the Students Representa-tive Council. And that time, I won.

If my exploits outside the classroom pulled me headlong into what I considered a whole new world, my instruction inside the classroom enlightened me to the fact that it was a world predicated on prior mistakes and achievements. The history I learned filled in the blank spaces of the maps I'd studied in my youth; it gave definition and meaning to the countries that pre-viously were nothing more than geometric shapes with names. It also gave me a context within which to place my own coun-try, a context much larger than I'd ever imagined.

We studied Socrates, Archimedes, and Galileo. We learned about the Nubians, the Moors, the Incas, the Aztecs, the Ma-yans, the Greeks, and the Romans. We learned about the Chi-nese dynasties and Japan during the Jomon period. We learned about Mesopotamia, between the Tigris and the Euphrates, the rise and fall of the Sumerians, Akkadians, Babylonians, Assyrians, and Hittites, builders of chariots.

To know what and where Carthage, Thrace, Constantino-ple, Cuzco, Thebes, and Timbuktu were is to know who and where you are. Without first understanding the empires of Songhai, Mali, Ghana, Kushite, Luba, and Mwene Mutapa or researching the imperialist Scramble for Africa and the divi-siveness and devastation it caused, I would never have been able to arrive at an understanding of Ghana and the struggles

my country was facing. History sparked within me an awareness of the continuum within which we all exist.

The maps of my youth were actually quite symbolic of my
view of the world, which back then was also flat and stretched,
ignorantly distorted and without definition.

I was no longer as concerned about how my time and studies in university would translate into solid employment prospects. I was more excited about the theories I was formulating
and debating with my socialist comrades, the relationships and
leadership abilities I was developing at Commonwealth Hall,
and the truths I was learning in my history courses. And I
knew, without anybody having to tell me, that eventually all
of those things would stand for something worthwhile.

PERILOUS CROSSINGS

W E S E E M E D T O have crossed the line. Ghana had descended to a place from which there appeared to be no return. It was like a game of political musical chairs. Acheampong was gone; Akuffo was gone. During Flight Lieutenant Rawlings and the AFRC's "housecleaning" exercise, the former military heads of state along with five other top military leaders were executed. Other members of the military thought to have been engaged in corruption were placed in detention. Civilians engaged in acts of hoarding were arrested.

Overall, Ghanaians were supportive of the coup and the subsequent actions taken by the AFRC to rid the country of all the corruption and negative practises that had been pulling it down. The feelings of bitterness and rage that the society had been suppressing were let loose, creating an atmosphere of vengeance and feeding the desire for retaliation. The general sentiment was that blood should flow and that people should be made to pay for the suffering Ghanaians had endured. It was a dangerous climate of mean-spiritedness.

When the AFRC handed over power to Dr. Hilla Limann, presidential candidate for the People's National Party, it had been with a caveat, that if his administration did not perform in such a way that would restore stability and promote economic growth, they would return and remove him from office.

Though my father was at first hesitant to reenter politics, as time wore on he engaged wholeheartedly. He felt that Dr. Limann's government was a chance for Ghana to start anew. Not everyone agreed with him. There were mixed feelings about Dr. Limann's leadership, even within the party. Though opinions differed greatly about whether the administration was on the right course to make the sort of rebound the country needed, citizens took comfort in the fact that Ghana was now back under constitutional rule. If it turned out that Dr. Limann and his government did not meet their expectations, there was always the option of voting them out of power.

After a little over two years of watching the government flounder while trying to find its feet, Flight Lieutenant Rawlings staged a coup on December 31, 1981, and seized power from the Limann administration. This time, the public's reaction to the coup was mixed. The revolving door of leadership was making Ghanaians restive, uncertain about their future.

IN LATE 1980, AT THE time of the coup, I was in the midst of my national service duty. Upon graduation from university, as a means of giving back to society, students who had benefitted from the free education provided by the government are obligated to work for a certain period of time as an act of national service. Back then, the requirement was two years. National service personnel could be dispatched to whatever region or industry in which their talents and services were needed. A small stipend was given to cover living expenses; other than that, national service personnel did not receive a salary.

Having graduated from the University of Ghana as a history major, I was sent to teach the subject to A- and O-level students at Ghanasco, the secondary school in Tamale I'd attended. My friend William, whom I'd met in university, was also sent to Ghanasco to fulfil his national service duty. William, who'd majored in political science, had also been a resident of Commonwealth Hall. He was raucous, good-natured, and fun-loving.

William and I were provided with accommodation in one of the masters' bungalows. They were some of the low-cost houses that were built by the Acheampong administration. Ours had three bedrooms, a large living room, and a kitchen. It even had a little porch, where William and I used to sit and watch the sunset while drinking *pito*. The bungalows were located at the edge of the campus, a distance from the dormitories and main lecture halls.

Most of the administrators and teachers with whom I'd been acquainted during my years at Ghanasco, like Mr. Wentum, were no longer there. The revolution that Mr. Wentum had been so anxiously awaiting had come in the form of the 31st December coup. Now he and the other followers of Karl Marx and Friedrich Engels were busy going about the business of figuring out how to form a classless society.

My brother Eben was a fifth-form student at Ghanasco at the time I arrived to begin my national service. Eben, who was part of the younger crop of Mahama children, was jovial and cherubic. Living on the Ghanasco campus together gave Eben and me a chance to interact more and get to know each other better.

William and I made the most of our national service years. We were university graduates, young men without commitments. We had come of age, come into our own, and were testing the limits and privileges of that newfound agency. At the end of each month when we received our stipends, we'd immediately set aside the amount that we had to give the school matron in order to receive meals for the coming month. The rest of the money was ours to spend whichever way we wanted, so of course we spent it aimlessly, having a good time.

Every weekend, William and I would go to a disco. The country had been placed on an eight o'clock curfew, which was being strictly enforced by the military. This meant that discos opened and closed earlier. We'd finish teaching our courses and rush over to one of the discos in town. Most of them opened well before four o'clock. By six o'clock, when people were done with their day's work and ready to relax, the discos would be packed. At half-past seven, everyone would scurry to pay their cheque, collect their belongings, and set off in order to reach their destination before the curfew.

There was a shortage of beer in the country, and discos were the only places where people could be guaranteed an ice-cold glass. The gate fee that patrons paid to enter a disco included the price of one bottle of beer. If you wanted a second bottle, you couldn't simply buy one; you'd have to go outside and pay another gate fee, which would entitle you to another beer.

William and I spent most of our stipends going to discos and restaurants. Rarely were we able to make the money stretch for more than a week or two. The second half of each month usually found us broke, sitting in our bungalow chatting or reading.

IT WOULD BE AN UNDERSTATEMENT to say that people were struggling to make ends meet. The average Ghanaian was fighting just to survive. It was a time of scarcity. There was a shortage of most everything, and it forced people to be inventive, to turn survival into an art.

Food was difficult to come by, particularly in the urban areas where it was not grown. Even if you had money, which a lot of Ghanaians did not, you might not be able to find any food to buy. People rationed their portions, eating only enough to skim the surface of their hunger. Women started improvising, cooking with new leaves that had not been used before. Meat and fish that had previously been undesirable was suddenly in demand because of accessibility. Stockfish, a type of sun-dried fish popularly called *kpanla,* imported mostly from South America and considered a delicacy in Nigeria but not well liked in Ghana, was one of those.

As a result of the famine and the general lack of access to food, a large number of people became so emaciated that their collarbones protruded through their skin. Ghanaians, with their inimitable sense of humour, even through the grimmest of circumstances, began referring to the condition as a "Rawlings chain" or a "Rawlings necklace."

There was a problem with every mode of transportation,

including walking. There were no shoes available on the market, so people were reduced to making them out of used car tyres. Vehicles were also not available on the market, either new or secondhand. If you owned a vehicle and it developed a fault, it would be next to impossible to find the parts for it to be repaired.

Because the government also could not afford to maintain their vehicles, people either walked to work or stood in long queues for hours waiting for the public transport buses, which had often broken down. Roads were not being maintained. They were dusty and riddled with potholes.

International events were also contributing to the severity of Ghana's woes. A major oil crisis had thrown residents of even the most developed nations into a state of panic and spurred hoarding. In America, queues at filling stations stretched for blocks. In Ghana, fuel was rationed. Taxi drivers would coast down hills to conserve whatever little bit they had in their tanks. When their fuel levels were too low to propel the vehicle uphill, they would not hesitate to ask their passengers to get out and push.

Additionally, in protest of the coup in Ghana, the administration of Shehu Shagari in Nigeria had imposed sanctions, one of which was the suspension of crude oil supplies. The effect of the fuel shortages was that it caused a rationing of power as well. There were constant power outages that in turn affected the water supply, because without electricity the pumps did not work. Our taps would flow for a while and then they would stop flowing for a week or two.

Every container that could store water was filled and set aside for the times when the taps were not flowing. Once we'd gone through every drop that was in those containers, we would scrounge for water anywhere we could find it. Sometimes a day or two would go by when we couldn't find any water with which to have our baths or wash our clothes.

My father's house was in an area of Tamale called Agric Ridge, which was in proximity to the water supply company. The taps flowed with more regularity there. At Ghanasco, Dad had allowed me to use one of his cars that was still operational. During the times when water was not flowing on campus and we had run out of what had been stored, if there was fuel in the car, William and I would drive to my father's house to wash our clothes and have baths. We would pile all of our empty containers into the car so that we could refill them at Dad's house. If there wasn't any fuel in the car, we would walk the eight kilometres so we could at least have our baths.

It all seems now like the worst of nightmares, the kind from which you awake all the more appreciative of the safety and comfort of your reality. But that was our reality, and since we had no alternatives we did the only thing we could, we lived it.

THE MILITARY WAS OPERATING IN a state of anarchy, writing its own rules, sometimes at random, and arresting people who broke them. The punishments they meted out to civilians were cruel and at times even deadly. In many ways it was even worse than before, when Acheampong and Akuffo were in power.

Military brutality was perhaps worse in Tamale than anywhere else in the country because of the presence of so many garrisons, especially in relation to the size of the civilian population. We had the Bawah Barracks, where the airborne forces were based; we had the Kamina Barracks, which was the base of the Sixth Battalion of infantry; we had the Kaladan Barracks, which was yet another military installation; and we had the Armed Forces Recruit Training Centre, where newly recruited soldiers were brought for training.

The soldiers in Tamale drove around haughtily in Pinzgauers, intoxicated with the power they had over people. They could stop anyone at any time for any reason. Their actions were guided only by their own discretion. In some, this license triggered their most brutal and inhumane impulses.

There was a group of soldiers that became notorious for their acts of barbarism. They came to be known as the "Seven Gladiators." The very sight of them was enough to make your heart stop. They strapped bandoliers of bullets around their shoulders as if they were guerrillas fighting in jungle warfare. Horror stories about their atrocities circulated through town. There was one particular story that made everyone fear the unmistakable sound of an oncoming Pinzgauer.

Someone had reported a woman to the military. They'd accused her of hoarding cloth. The Seven Gladiators went to the woman's home to arrest her. They searched her house and found some wax-printed cloth. She explained to them that it was not for commercial sale; it was her personal collection.

It is a tradition in many Ghanaian ethnic groups for a dowry to be presented upon marriage. In our culture, more often than not these dowries are gifts given by the groom and his family to the bride and her family. The list of requisite, or recommended, dowry items varies from ethnic group to ethnic group, but the one item that appears on them all is cloth.

Cloth is also often acquired through inheritance, passed down from grandmother to mother to daughter. The woman told the Seven Gladiators that all the cloth she owned was from the combination of pieces presented in her dowry, pieces her mother had passed on to her, and a few pieces she had purchased herself over the years.

The Seven Gladiators did not believe the woman or did not give a damn either way. They arrested the woman and her husband, led them at gunpoint into their Pinzgauer, and drove off, ostensibly to the barracks. Somewhere along the way, they stopped the Pinzgauer. They told the woman they were releasing her and ordered her to disappear.

"Run," one of the Seven Gladiators told her. "Vanish before we change our minds." The woman turned around and started to run back in the direction of her home. The Seven Gladiators watched her for a few minutes. Just as the woman was in fact disappearing into the distance, one of them fired at her. They started to drive away. The woman's husband was traumatised. He started screaming hysterically. Initially the Seven Gladiators ignored him, but when his screaming didn't abate, they decided to deal with him.

"Oh, you want to go and save your wife?" one of the Seven Gladiators taunted. Responding to the cue, the Gladiator who was driving stopped the Pinzgauer.

"Get down," the first Gladiator said to him. "Go save your wife." The man hesitantly got out of the vehicle. Frightened that what had been done to his wife would be done to him, the man walked backward, stumbling.

"What? You won't go?" the Gladiator asked him. Suddenly the man became afraid that they would fire at him if he didn't turn around and run, so he did. He ran and he ran until he heard the gunshot and felt himself falling onto the ground.

Luckily for the man, a passerby who was rushing home to make curfew spotted him lying in a pool of his own blood. The passerby pulled over, picked up the injured man, and put him in his car. Farther down the road they found the woman, also lying in a pool of blood. The passerby stopped and picked her up as well, and he drove the couple to Tamale Hospital. The man lived; his wife did not. By the time they arrived at the hospital, she was dead.

THE STORY ABOUT THE WOMAN accused of hoarding cloth was especially shocking because of the senselessness of her death. Eventually it took the intervention of the chairman of the PNDC to disarm the Seven Gladiators. But unpleasant encounters with members of the military were common and each one had the potential to be fatal. One evening on the Ghanasco campus, my friend William and I, along with a group of students, had our own unpleasant encounter with the military.

The Ministry of Education had asked Ghanasco to organise a symposium in connection with United Nations Day. The school authorities had asked me and the other national service personnel to oversee the event. We'd invited speakers; some of us had even acted as resource persons and talked to the students about the history and role of the United Nations.

The symposium ended shortly after eight, and the students proceeded to return to their dormitories. William and I were walking with several students when we heard the sound of a Pinzgauer and, seconds later, a call for us to stop. We followed the order. Two soldiers got down from the vehicle and approached us. There was a third soldier, but he remained in the vehicle. They wanted to know what we were doing outside past curfew.

William and I cautiously brought up the fact that we were in a protected environment, one in which we were duty-bound to honour the instructions of the school authorities. We told them that we'd been instructed to organise and host a symposium and that the event had only just finished.

"You can see the students walking back to their dormitories," William said.

"And we are supposed to make sure they get there," I added, "before we can then go to our house."

The soldiers refused to understand. They continued to insist that we had broken curfew; they would have to take us back to the military barracks.

That's what happened when you broke curfew: you were taken to the barracks. Once there, you could be beaten and released or you could be detained. We'd heard of people being taken to the armed forces farms and forced to labour. They'd be gone for as long as a week, and their families would have no idea where they were or what had happened to them.

The soldiers told us to sit on the ground. We obeyed. Suddenly the soldier in the car said, "What they're saying sounds reasonable. Let's let them go." He spoke with an authority that suggested he was the other soldiers' superior, a lieutenant.

"All right," one of the soldiers responded.

"But we can't let them go just like that," the other soldier argued. "We have to punish them small." The lieutenant said nothing.

The soldiers' idea of a small punishment was to give everyone a knock on the head with the butt of their guns. They began with one of the students, a young girl. One of the soldiers held his rifle vertically above her head, with the muzzle pointing skyward, and then came down hard. The other soldier stepped forward to take his turn with the next student. Before he could hit the student, William and I started protesting. We couldn't just sit there and silently watch. We had to speak up for our students. We began explaining again about the symposium, reminding them that we were on a school campus. The soldier walked over to me and pointed his rifle at my face.

"Shut up!" he screamed. I was certain he would not hesitate to pull the trigger if challenged or provoked. I stopped talking right away, as did William. My fear turned physical, producing a ghost pain in my right shoulder, where I'd been shot a few years earlier.

After the soldiers had hit each one of us on the head with a rifle, they told us they would count to five and ordered us to vanish before they opened their eyes, or else. We needed no prompting. We all took off. When they opened their eyes, the soldiers must have noticed William and me running in a different direction from that of the students. They called us to come back. We went and reminded them that we were national service personnel; we didn't live in the dormitories. I'm not surprised the soldiers didn't believe us. William and I were young and looked so. We could easily have passed for Ghanasco students.

The soldiers told us to get into the Pinzgauer. They wanted to verify that what we were telling them was true. How they were going to do that, I don't know.

"Let them go," the lieutenant instructed. This time his voice was more forceful. It left no room for argument. We watched as the two soldiers joined the lieutenant in the vehicle, evidently annoyed that their amusement had been cut short. William and I stood in place. We wanted the Pinzgauer to go completely out of view before taking another step. Once we felt sure the soldiers were gone, we started walking back to our bungalow.

We were almost home when William and I saw two lights moving in the distance, probably the glow of paraffin lamps. When the students didn't have power for their evening study sessions, which was fairly often because of the power rationing, they used paraffin lamps.

We watched the lights move deeper into the campus, in the direction of the dormitories. The Pinzgauer approached the two lights. For a few moments the lights remained still, shimmering side by side next to the Pinzgauer. The lamps didn't illuminate the spot well enough for us to actually see the events as they were unfolding. However, when the lights moved into the Pinzgauer and the vehicle began to drive away, it wasn't too difficult to figure out what had happened.

William remarked on how the soldiers had most likely found some unsuspecting students to harass. I offered my take on the matter.

"It looks as though they're being arrested."

"Poor kids." William sighed.

Under any other circumstance, we would have rushed to their aid, but we just stood there watching, silenced by our feelings of helplessness.

The Pinzgauer drove for less than five minutes before coming to a stop. The lights moved out of the vehicle and once again became still. William and I couldn't bring ourselves to go inside the bungalow. We felt we had to witness the outcome of this confrontation. Would the paraffin lamps start moving, heading once again toward the students' dormitory? Or would the soldiers extinguish those lights and detain the individuals holding the lamps?

Unbeknownst to me, one of the unsuspecting students whom the soldiers had stopped was my brother Eben. He and his friend Fatawo had just left our bungalow with their newly refuelled paraffin lamps. Eben would sometimes come by with Fatawo or one of his other friends to wash their clothes, if the taps were flowing, or to hang out and escape campus life for a few hours. He would also help himself to some of the endless supply of kerosene the school gave to the national service personnel. That was one of the perks of having an older brother working and living at the school.

Eben and Fatawo had lost track of time and were rushing back to their dormitory. The soldiers spotted them and made them get into the Pinzgauer. They were going to take the two boys, sixteen-year-olds walking from one end of their boarding school campus to the other, to the military barracks. The lieutenant interceded. He told the soldiers to let the boys go. Eben and Fatawo got down from the vehicle, but they weren't permitted to leave. The two soldiers also got down. They asked the boys to set their lamps on the ground. Eben and Fatawo did it, terrified that the instant they let go of their lamp's handle, they would be shot.

"You," one of the soldiers said, pointing the tip of his rifle at Eben. "Slap him." He then pointed the rifle at Fatawo, the person he'd ordered Eben to slap. Eben didn't move. He was perplexed by the bizarre nature of the request. He should what? Slap his friend?

"Do it!" the soldier screamed. Eben raised his hand and gave Fatawo a quick slap on the cheek. The soldier was not satisfied.

"That was not a slap," he said, laughing. "This is a slap." The soldier hit my brother across the face with such force that Eben nearly fell down.

"Now slap him again," the soldier ordered Eben. "Properly this time." Eben stiffened his palm and fingers. He took a deep breath and then he slapped his best friend with all his might.

The other soldier leaned toward Fatawo and said, "Slap him back." Fatawo didn't want to be shown what a real slap was; he squeezed his eyes shut and used every bit of strength he could muster to slap Eben. The hit was hard and loud. The first soldier requested that Eben slap Fatawo again, harder. He did. Then Fatawo was told to slap Eben. Back and forth, back and forth, the hands and arms flew until the boys had exchanged over a dozen slaps. It was sadistic.

"Enough," the lieutenant finally commanded. "Let them go." The soldiers, who were laughing proudly at the show they'd staged, waved Eben and Fatawo off. The boys picked up their paraffin lamps and ran to their dormitory. The two of them were close friends. They had shared a lot. Now they could add to that list a distinct humiliation; they shared the knowledge of what those soldiers had done to them and what they'd been forced to do to each other.

Once William and I got home, I went straight to bed. The events of that evening had left me exhausted. I curled up on the mattress with my left hand clutching my right shoulder. Not long after, I fell into a dream about the day I got shot.

It was in 1978, the long vacation after I'd finished writing my A-level papers. My father had a love of guns. He was a sharpshooter. He kept all kinds of guns in his cupboard. There were handguns, revolvers, and rifles with single barrels, side-by-side double-barrels, over-and-under double-barrels. You name it, Dad had it.

Often on the farm, Peter, Alfred, and I would take the rifles and shoot wild rabbits and birds, usually partridges and guinea fowls, and carry them home with us to be cooked in a nice meal. When it came to shooting, Peter was better than all of us. That long vacation, Dad and several of our siblings were at the house in Accra, so Peter was looking after the farm in Tamale. When school closed, I stayed in Tamale to wait for my A-level results and to help Peter.

Dad had a rifle that he favoured most when hunting. It was a .22-calibre semiautomatic with a scope and twenty-four-round magazine. Somehow the scope got dropped and the crosshairs broke. Dad ordered a new scope from a company that was located abroad, but he left for Accra before it arrived. Because Peter was running the farm while Dad was gone, that rifle was in his possession. He'd been using it, even without the scope, when he went to the farm to hunt.

The new scope arrived by express parcel service shortly after I had returned home from Ghanasco. Peter wanted to align the new scope to the rifle barrel, and he needed my help. Ordinarily this is something that's done at a shooting range. Since there wasn't one anywhere in the vicinity, we decided to improvise. We got a piece of paper, drew a round target on it with the bull's-eye, and stuck it to a piece of wood, which we placed on a stand. Peter got another stand for the rifle and placed it at a range of about ninety metres from the target. We then began to zero the scope.

The rifle was equipped with elevation and windage knobs to facilitate the process of zeroing and help create a more precise shot. I was responsible for marking the target and reading out the instructions to Peter. I was supposed to stand directly behind the tree, which was directly behind the piece of wood onto which we'd tacked the target. Any time Peter was going to fire a shot, I would go to my assigned post behind the tree.

After Peter had squeezed off his shot, I would signal him to ensure it was safe before dutifully walking to the target to note where the bullet had entered. I would point my finger at the spot. Peter would use the location of my finger and the bull's-eye mark to determine the direction in which he needed to adjust the scope. When he was done, I would use a pen to cross out the bullet hole so that when he fired again I would be able to distinguish the new hole from the old ones. That was my role.

Peter had fired maybe five or six shots already. He was about to fire another. I was walking to my post behind the tree when

I remembered that I hadn't crossed out the last bullet hole. If I didn't cross it out, we wouldn't be able to tell the difference between his last shot and the one he was about to fire. I quickly went back to cross out the hole.

While I was bent over the target, I felt something brush up against my cheek in that small bridge of space between my nose and my eye. I thought it was an insect or a cricket. I instinctively dropped the pen to swat it off. I think that's when the sound of the shot registered in my mind, at the same time I was touching my cheek and realizing that the flesh somehow felt different against my fingertips. It was unusually rough. I pulled my hand away and looked at my fingers, expecting to maybe find an insect. There was nothing.

My skin still felt uncomfortable, so I rubbed my cheek again. This time when I removed my hand, there was blood. It all happened within a matter of seconds. I didn't make the link between the blood on my face and the sound of the shot I'd heard. I just kept rubbing my cheek, and the more I rubbed, the more the blood flowed.

After the gun had gone off and Peter saw me standing there at the target rubbing my face, with blood streaming down my cheek, he screamed and came running to me.

"John, are you hurt?" he asked. "Are you hurt?" It was then that two and two became four and I put it together that I'd been shot.

"I don't know," I replied. At that point in time, everything I'd ever seen get shot, whether on the farm or on television, had died. In my mind I believed that if you got shot, you died. I thought I was in the midst of dying or already dead, but I could hear Peter talking to me. His voice sounded far away, like the final wave of an echo. Nevertheless, I could hear it. Would that be possible if I was dead?

"Let's go, let's go, let's go, let's go," Peter cried while dragging me to the car. When we got in the car, he took off his shirt and gave it to me to stanch the flow of blood. I pressed the shirt to my cheek. I remember pinching myself over and over, trying to figure out if I was alive or dead, because I couldn't reconcile the fact of being shot with the fact of being alive.

Peter, who was panicked, drove like a madman through the streets of Tamale, weaving in and out of traffic. It was the craziest driving I had ever seen in my life. I was afraid we would get into a crash and die. It was that fear that convinced me I had to be alive. If I were already dead, why would I be so afraid of dying?

"Slow down, Peter," I said. "I'm okay. I'll be okay. You just take it easy."

In the consulting room at Tamale Hospital, Peter and I told the doctor what happened. He was someone our family knew rather well, so we considered ourselves fortunate that he'd been on duty when we'd arrived. The doctor disinfected the wound and placed a temporary dressing on it while waiting for the nurses to prepare the operating theatre.

In the theatre, the doctor pulled the lips of the wound together. He snipped off the excess flesh, stitched up the wound, and covered it with a plaster. When he was done and I tried to get off the operating table, my right arm suddenly turned into a ton of lead. I couldn't lift it no matter how hard I tried. I told the doctor. He said he wanted to examine my arm. As he walked toward me, he noticed a hole in the back of my shirt at the shoulder. He came round to look at the front of the shirt and saw there was a hole there, too.

The doctor asked me to remove my shirt. When I did, it confirmed the theory he'd formulated when he saw the holes. The one in the back was an entry wound and the one in front was an exit wound. The bullet had entered my shoulder from the back. It had gone clear through, and because I was bent over, it had grazed my cheek as it was completing its trajectory. The doctor ordered an X-ray of my shoulder.

The bullet hole was visible in the X-ray. The doctor pointed it out to me as he studied the films to determine what kind of damage I'd suffered.

"John Mahama," the doctor said after he'd finished looking at the films, "God was on your side. You are lucky."

The two primary bones in the shoulder are the humerus and the scapula, which is sometimes referred to as the shoulder blade. These two bones are connected by a ball-and-socket joint. They are all, the bones and the joint, surrounded by ligaments, tendons, and muscle.

The bullet that hit me went straight through muscle tissue. Had the bullet hit my scapula, it would probably have been shattered. My humerus would definitely have been fractured. Had the bullet entered my shoulder anywhere other than where it did, it could have passed through my bicep tendon or my rotator cuff, causing permanent damage.

After the wounds healed, I regained full use of my shoulder. I still carry a mark on my face where the hot metal of the bullet made contact with my cheek. People automatically assume it's a birthmark or a tribal mark, so nobody ever asks me about it. I rarely think or talk about that day I was shot, not anymore, but during those years when the military was out of control, I would frequently revisit it. The very idea of being shot again would spark a pain in my shoulder similar to the one I'd felt on the operating table. It would flash me right back to those long, unbearable minutes of dread when I thought I was dying or might already be dead.

AFTER EVERY COUP, PARLIAMENT IS promptly dissolved, the constitution is suspended, and political parties are disbanded. Members of Parliament and ministers of state are asked to report to the nearest police station "for their own safety." That's how it was always phrased: "for their own safety." With the 31st December coup in 1981, as with the June 4 coup in 1979, the different classifications were announced on the radio— MPs, ministers, party officials—and in some cases, people's names were also announced. They were asked to report to Gondar Barracks with immediate effect.

Dad was in Accra at the time of the 1981 coup. Peter, Alfred, and our friend Joe Mara were running a transport business. The three of them had gone to Takoradi to check on some cargo that had been dispatched. When the coup was announced on the radio, they thought of Dad and feared for his safety. In addition to being a senior member of the party that had just been overthrown, he was on the steering committee. Peter, Alfred, and Joe Mara left everything they were doing and drove back to Accra the following morning, January 1, 1982.

When they got to Accra, there was still a lot of firing going on in the city. The situation on the streets was unsettled, but you wouldn't have known it if you had been inside Dad's house. Peter, Alfred, and Joe Mara entered to find him relaxed, reading in his study, looking like a man without a care in the world. They explained to Dad that they didn't feel comfortable with him just sitting there in Accra, especially not the way things were unfolding. Soldiers had apparently already started going to the houses of politicians and arresting them.

"We'll take you to the farm," Peter told Dad.

It was the tail end of the Christmas season. There had been a few parties and gatherings at Dad's house. Our father wasn't a drinker, so he'd taken whatever alcohol had been left over and placed it on a table near the kitchen. Alfred noticed the small collection of partially empty bottles. He went over and grabbed the one with the most alcohol. It was a gallon-size jug of whiskey, more than three-quarters full. When they got into the car, Alfred stuck the bottle on the flat shelflike space in the back, where the speakers were located, between the headrests of the backseats and the rear windscreen.

Almost all of the entry points in Accra have police barriers, even today. There was a barrier at the gates of Achimota on the street that led out of Accra. The military had pitched a tent there. The soldiers were in their helmets and camouflaged gear, holding their weapons, looking very fierce. There was an armoured tank parked by the gates. They were searching every car that was leaving the city. During these sorts of searches, the soldiers would first ask you to open the boot of your car. They would walk around and have a look inside it to see what you were transporting. On their way back to their post, they would peer through each window to see who or what was on board. If everything they'd seen met their approval, they'd wave you on and let you pass through the barrier.

"Eh," one of the soldiers remarked when he walked to the back of the car. "You people have enjoyed Christmas-o." The soldier pointed out the bottle of whiskey, which was visible from the outside of the car, to his comrades.

"Is this what is left?" another soldier asked. "Give it to us."

Alfred, who'd had the presence of mind to hatch a plan to distract and ingratiate the soldiers, smiled and said, "Oh, you can have it." He pulled out the jug of alcohol and handed it to the soldiers through an open window.

"Heeeyyyyyyyyyyy," they all cheered. "Charley, today whiskey come-o." They were too busy jubilating to care about anything else. They waved the car on without taking a careful look at who was in there. Peter, wasting not a second, pressed his foot on the pedal and went through the barrier.

My brothers had called me before they'd left Accra. I'd driven from Tamale to Yapei to meet them all at the farmhouse. While driving through Tamale, I'd observed the heavy military presence and it made me nervous. I wasn't convinced that Yapei was the most ideal place for Dad to stay. When I discussed it with my brothers and Joe Mara, they agreed. There were definitely too many military garrisons too close by. Also, we remembered how spiteful people had turned after previous coups, fabricating information and reporting their neighbours to the authorities. If the military started looking for Dad, it would not be too difficult to find him at the farm in Yapei.

We decided to take him to Bole, his hometown. It was small, and most of the villagers were people Dad could trust. They were loyal. A good number of them were members of his extended family. Bole had a small police station. There weren't more than ten policemen in the whole town, and there were no military garrisons at all. Peter, Alfred, and Joe Mara drove Dad to Bole while I waited at the farmhouse.

It was well into the afternoon by the time my brothers and Joe Mara returned to Yapei. The four of us were about to sit down to a meal when we heard an announcement on the radio calling for all senior members of the PNP to report to Gondar Barracks with immediate effect. It was an announcement we'd all heard before, but this time it was followed by a list of names, one of which was Dad's.

We'd been listening as the announcer called each name but continuing with whatever else we were doing. As soon as he said, "E. A. Mahama," we all stopped what we were doing, turned our heads, and stared at the radio. The sound of his name hung in the air. Peter, Alfred, and I looked at one another. I could tell from the expression on my brothers' faces that we were all thinking the same thing. Dad was not safe anywhere in Ghana.

We could recall the man our father was when he'd been released from detention. He would sit for hours, lost in the thought of whatever horrors or indignities he'd suffered while there.

"I will never return to prison," Dad told us countless times. "Never again. I will always remain a free man." He said that if he ever returned to prison, he would die. The four of us rushed to the car, jumped in, and headed for Bole.

The scene we encountered at the house in Bole was so characteristic of our father, a man whose personality could only be described as magnetic. He was holding court, surrounded by a large group of friends and relatives who'd come to greet him when they'd heard that he was in town. Dad had finished eating his dinner and was now attending to his guests. He was surprised to see us.

"Ah, you're back," he said. "Why?"

"We have to go," Peter said. We didn't need to explain any further. Dad understood what we were saying to him.

"Is that so?" he asked. We told him it was.

"Okay," he agreed, standing up. He went into the bedroom, picked up his bag and his small radio. He came back into the living room and said, "All right, let's go." He didn't move or speak with any discernable fear or sense of urgency. He was collected as he said farewell to the friends and relatives in the house. He simply told them he had to go to Tamale and would be back soon.

We drove from Bole to Sawla, which is an eighteen-kilometre distance. It was where one of our cousins, Al-Hassan, lived. On our way to Bole from Yapei, we'd stopped at Al-Hassan's house to let him know that we were going to pick up Dad and we needed to get him across the border. Al-Hassan said he'd begin the preparations so that by the time we'd returned with Dad everything would be in place.

When we got back to Al-Hassan's, he told us that he'd sent someone on a motorcycle ahead to clear the way for us. Al-Hassan joined us in the car and we drove along the road toward the Côte d'Ivoire border. Night had fallen, and we had to drive without lights a lot of the way to avoid being spotted. A short distance before we reached Kalba, a tiny riparian village on Ghana's border with Côte d'Ivoire, we met up with the emissary that Al-Hassan had sent ahead and got his report. The man informed us that in order to enter Kalba, we'd have to pass through a checkpoint being manned by customs officers.

The borders that were drawn by the former colonials were done without regard to ethnic groups, tribes, indigenous languages, or families. Subsequently, most of the borders divide things that should have been kept whole. We had a relative in Kalba, Bukari. He was a smuggler. In those days, because of the shortages that Ghana faced, smuggling was a lucrative profession. People would go into one of the three Francophone countries that border Ghana to buy soap, canned food, and other necessities. They would bring these goods into Ghana illegally with the intent of reselling them.

For about 250 kilometres, the Black Volta River forms the official border between Ghana and Côte d'Ivoire. Bukari owned a canoe. He used it to make regular trips from Kalba to Côte d'Ivoire and back again. He was familiar with every inch of land and every drop of water between the two places. He had been alerted to our mission. His was the most crucial part. Bukari was to host Dad for the evening and then, at dawn, use his canoe to smuggle him into Côte d'Ivoire.

Our family spilled over into Côte d'Ivoire as well. Our uncle Alhaji Daudu, "the Frenchman," lived there, and the plan was to get Dad over to "the other side," where he would be safe and warmly received by Alhaji Daudu and the rest of our Ivorian family members.

The emissary instructed us to tell the customs officers at the checkpoint that we'd just gotten word of a death in our family on "the other side." We were to explain that we'd come to formally express our condolences and we'd also brought gifts and money for our relatives in Kalba to carry to the funeral on our behalf.

We got to the checkpoint, ready to deliver our sad story, but it was empty. There was no one there. It wasn't even a real checkpoint. It had been hastily constructed, almost like an afterthought: two thick wooden forksticks that you could tell had only recently been pounded into the ground on either side of a narrow dirt road. The wooden bar that was supposed to straddle the forksticks was missing. Had we not been warned of its presence, we wouldn't even have realised it was a checkpoint and would have been caught off guard by the customs officers. As it was, we were prepared, and they were nowhere to be found. Since the checkpoint was wide open, we drove through.

Bukari was waiting for us. We dropped Dad off, said our farewells, and left. We didn't want to linger. It was a small village, and our presence at Bukari's house might have attracted unwanted attention. We drove without saying a word. We knew the gravity of the situation, but I don't think any of us had thought beyond the drop-off point at Kalba. We hadn't considered a future with our father gone, in some other country. Now that Dad's departure was no longer a plan of action but a reality of our lives, his absence was slowly taking shape in our minds and in our hearts.

Curiously, when we got to the checkpoint, the wooden bar was in place and the customs officers were in position. They wanted to know who we were and how we'd entered Kalba without going through the checkpoint.

"Ah, but there was no one here," Alfred told them. "And the thing was open. How were we supposed to know?" The officers continued to interrogate us. They wanted to know what we were doing in Kalba. Alfred and I took turns delivering the sad story.

"So we have come, performed our duty, and now we want to go home," Alfred said, bringing the story to an end. He was a natural with such things. He had a down-to-earth sincerity about him that made people take him at face value. He spoke in a way that was simple, nonthreatening, and believable.

"What is the name of your relation?" the officers wanted to know.

"Mummuni," Alfred said, inventing a name off the top of his head. "He lives not far from the riverbank near the shea nut tree." The entire town was not far from the riverbank, and there were hundreds of shea nut trees.

The officers waved us on. We drove through the checkpoint, satisfied with the performance we'd given. Little did we know that our performance had instead stirred their suspicion. After we'd driven away, the officers went into the village in search of the house that we'd visited.

Dad, in his usual fashion, was settling in comfortably at Bukari's house. The two men had shared a warm chat over a cup of tea and some bread. Bukari had shown Dad his sleeping quarters and asked him to get some rest because they were going to be leaving early in the morning, well before dawn. Bukari then excused himself. He had to go into the village to make a few more arrangements for the early morning crossing.

While Bukari was out, he saw the customs officers knocking on someone's door. He carried on, not thinking much of it until he saw them exit that house and then knock on the door of the next house. He found a little corner in which he could conceal himself, and he watched them go from door to door. After the officers had covered a bit of ground, Bukari went to the first few houses they'd entered.

"What did they want?" he asked his neighbours.

"They wanted to know which big man that vehicle came to drop." Bukari ran quickly back to his house. He wanted to be long gone by the time the customs officers arrived at his door. He woke Dad up and said, "We have to go. We have to leave now." Dad grabbed his bag and his little radio and followed Bukari outside.

Bukari's house was less than a kilometre's walk to the riverbank, but they didn't have time to waste. They hopped onto his motorbike and rode there. Bukari helped my father get into the canoe. He then lifted his motorbike and placed that inside as well. He pushed the canoe into the water, got in, and started to row. He rowed as hard and as fast as he knew how, through the blackness of both the water and the night.

Dad and Bukari were about halfway down the river when the customs officers showed up and started running toward the riverbank. He could see their silhouettes and he could hear their footsteps. He kept rowing, powerfully, steadily. The customs officers were shouting at the top of their lungs.

"Stop, I say, stop! Come back . . . come back!"

Bukari rowed and rowed. The officers, seeing that he wasn't minding them, fired a few warning shots into the air. Bukari looked around. To the uninitiated eye, every section of the riverbank in that area would have seemed identical to any other, but Bukari knew exactly where he was, and so did the customs officers. He buried the blades of the oar and gave three strong drives. One. Two. The officers fired another warning shot. Three. By the finish of the third drive, they had crossed over into Côte d'Ivoire.

There was nothing the customs officers, the military, or any-body else on the Ghana side could do. E. A. Mahama would remain a free man.

GHANA MUST GO

THE BUS RIDE from Accra to Lagos was bumpy and painfully slow, filled with all kinds of unnecessary stops and starts. Our driver had warned us to prepare ourselves for all of it.

"De gendarme be plenty-o," he had told us after the passengers had boarded and taken their seats. "We for stop for dem barrier all."

This made everyone grumble, even though we knew the driver would have no choice in the matter. If we wanted to ever see the light of day from the inside of Nigeria, the bus would have to stop for every single gendarme and the driver would have to make a monetary plea for us to be allowed passage. There were no two ways about it.

Our driver was a corpulent man who looked to be in his early fifties. He was as wide around as a hippopotamus, but his head was very small in comparison with the rest of him, too small. It looked as though it belonged on the body of a more slender man. He had a cheerful disposition, which I thought was unusual for a bus driver.

All the bus drivers I'd ever encountered were ill-tempered and boorish. They had no patience whatsoever. They behaved as though they hated their jobs and were angry that life had consigned them to such a fate, and they were determined to make everybody with whom they came into contact share their misery.

This driver told us to call him Wofa Leonardo. *Wofa* means "uncle" in the Akan language. Uncle Leonardo. He was a skilful moderator. When we first boarded, I'd watched him quell the complaints a lot of the passengers were waging about the service fee we'd been charged in addition to our fare. It was a staggering amount, almost 50 percent of the bus fare.

The seasoned passengers, ones who made that journey regularly, started chattering on about how quickly those fees were increasing. They floated suspicions and accusations. Some of them believed the bus drivers were in cahoots with the gendarmes and that they kept a portion of the fee for themselves. Why else, they argued, would the fee differ so drastically from driver to driver and from journey to journey?

"I' no be every driver him pocket wey money dey," one man said.

"Ah, him size an' him pocket for make de same," someone else remarked. That made everyone laugh. Wofa Leonardo, who'd obviously heard the comment, started laughing too, even though the joke was on him.

"I swear, i' no be for me-o," he insisted, slapping his hands against his big stomach. "I' be for de gendarme."

Whether that was true or not, nobody seemed to care anymore. Wofa Leonardo's unself-conscious response had taken what began as antipathy and turned it into affection. We all continued chuckling. Wofa Leonardo released the emergency brake; he put the bus into gear, and our adventure began.

AFTER DAD FLED GHANA FOR Côte d'Ivoire, he'd spent several months in Bouna, one of the small towns near the Ivorian border. In addition to "the Frenchman," Dad had a couple of sisters who lived there. It was a comfortable place for Dad to land, and since it was just on the other side, not too far from Ghana, my brothers and I were able to visit him frequently.

This proximity turned out to be a real blessing, because it was almost impossible to reach him by telephone. Telecommunications in Africa were horrible, especially between Francophone and Anglophone countries. The place where you were calling might have been only an hour's drive and a twenty-minute boat ride away, but the call would have to be routed first through Europe before being redirected back to Africa.

The postal service worked in much the same way. It was often faster to drive from one West African country to another than it was to send a letter there. If the mail was sent from an Anglophone country to a Francophone country, it would more often than not go to England for processing and then be forwarded to France for further processing before being sent on to its final destination in Africa. Mail from Francophone to Anglophone countries went through the reverse process.

Travel between West African countries was equally as inconvenient. Only two main carriers provided service between countries in that subregion, Air Afrique and Ghana Airways.

Both airlines suffered from terrible mismanagement. Their schedules were routinely unreliable, and their flights were often heavily overbooked. A flight could be delayed for hours or days, if not for weeks. Then again, a flight could take off an hour or two early without anyone bothering to inform the poor passengers, who were still in the midst of checking in, until the plane had already reached its cruising altitude.

Several international carriers that were decidedly more reliable, such as Lufthansa, Pan Am, British Caledonian, and Swissair, also offered service to key locations on the continent. What they did not offer was service between the countries. As with telephone calls and postal mail, you'd have to travel to Europe first and then find your way back to wherever you wanted to be in Africa.

The problem was that it seemed as though there weren't too many places in Africa where people wanted to be. When Africans boarded those flights headed for Europe and North America, return was usually not in their itinerary. They were leaving in search of a better life, one that was free of the undue hardships and fears that had now become pervasive in nearly every country on the continent.

The post-colonial experiment in nationhood was failing miserably. Many African countries were being dominated by their military. Professionals, artisans, educators, and skilled workers were all packing up and leaving. It was the beginning of the phenomenon widely referred to as the brain drain. In a short space of time, the continent lost its most vital human resource, all the people who were desperately needed to drive forward Africa's growth and development.

Ghana was no exception. The country experienced a slow

but relatively steady emigration of its citizens during the era of General Acheampong's administration. As the years passed and the coups continued, those numbers only increased. After the 31st December coup, Ghanaians started leaving en masse. The fortunate ones who'd managed to secure visas from foreign countries fit what they could into suitcases and left the rest behind. Husbands said good-bye to their wives; parents entrusted family members with the care of their children.

Others who were not able to acquire a visa through legitimate means surreptitiously crossed borders under cover of darkness or whatever credible guise they could manufacture. Circumstances had forced our father to become a part of that movement, which found Ghanaians having to abandon the only place they'd ever lived and called home.

Dad's time in Côte d'Ivoire was nomadic. He rotated from relative to relative in Bouna; then he moved to Abidjan, which was then the capital, and stayed with the relatives we had there. Dad remained in Abidjan for several months before he finally decided that Côte d'Ivoire was not where he wanted to live. He migrated to Nigeria, where we also had a number of relatives.

Nigerians and Ghanaians have a lot in common, not least the fact that theirs were among the few English-speaking countries in West Africa. This may well have played a part in Dad's decision to move there. Whatever the case, Nigeria felt more like the home he once knew, a place where he felt he could settle down and begin anew.

Peter, Alfred, and I would occasionally travel to Nigeria to visit Dad. During one of those visits, he spoke of how much he missed us and fantasised aloud about how wonderful it would be if one of us could come to Nigeria to live with him. I told him that I would be willing to do it; I would be willing to move to Nigeria.

As we continued to discuss the possibility, we realised that it might well be the perfect solution for both of us. My two-year obligation to national service had been fulfilled, and I'd been mulling over what to do next. I hadn't reached the stage where I was ready to take a job. What I really wanted was to return to university and complete a postgraduate programme, preferably in history; but I lacked the sponsorship. Education was still free in Ghana, but with Dad gone, I didn't know how I would be able to pay for my living expenses while attending school full-time.

Dad came up with an idea that made Nigeria all the more appealing to me. He suggested that I attend Ahmadu Bello, Nigeria's largest university, which is located in Zaria, a town in Kaduna State, in the northern part of the country. It was too late to apply for that academic year, but there was plenty to do before the next application period. I could tend to the details of my migration, get to know my new surroundings, and re-acquaint myself with Dad, whom recently I'd been able to see only during short visits.

Leaving Ghana wasn't as difficult as I would have imagined. The country had hit rock bottom. With the exception of my siblings and a few friends, there was nothing holding me there. There was no reason to stay, especially not when the prospect of a better life was beckoning.

IT'S 167 KILOMETRES FROM ACCRA to Aflao, the town on our side of the Ghana-Togo border. If the road has been properly maintained, it's a smooth three-hour ride. If the road is in disrepair, which it was when I was emigrating, the drive feels interminable, kilometres and kilometres of potholes.

There was greenery on either side of the road. Every so often when the bus passed through a village, the hawkers would come running up to the passengers' windows in hopes of making a sale. Wofa Leonardo would purposely slow down so that we could lean out of the windows to hand the hawkers our money and collect the bananas, groundnuts, or boiled maize on the cob that we were buying.

Aflao is a commercial centre that thrives on the brisk trade between Ghana and Togo. Every day traders would cross the border into Lome, the town on the Togo side, which was the capital of the country, and buy goods to bring back to Ghana to sell. There was very little that you could buy in Lome that wasn't available for purchase in Aflao, though depending on the shortages Ghana was experiencing, prices could be outrageously expensive. Still, people would be willing to pay those prices to avoid dealing with the hassles that went along with crossing the border.

In 1975, fifteen countries in West Africa came together to establish the Economic Community of West African States (ECOWAS). They signed a treaty to work toward the establishment of a free trade area in the subregion. Various protocols were ratified by the member countries that, among other things, guaranteed free movement of people and goods. Despite these protocols, travel between the ECOWAS countries was hellish, like what we were experiencing travelling in Wofa Leonardo's bus.

One of the realities of the colonisation of Africa has been the arbitrary border demarcations. In almost all of Africa, borderlines distinguishing nation-states have separated ethnic groups and even families. In Ghana, our boundaries with our neighbours Côte d'Ivoire, Burkina Faso, and Togo cut through villages and communities.

There's a story that Salifu, the man who once worked as our watchman in Tamale, told us about a house that sat directly on the border between Ghana and Togo.

"The house was there long before that line was drawn," Salifu said. The people who lived there, the Gali family, had always known what to call themselves. They were Ewes, but this new boundary had brought confusion into their lives because they suddenly found themselves straddling two places and two identities. The front door, living room, eating area, and kitchen were officially on Ghanaian soil. The bedrooms, bathrooms, and back door were all in Togo.

During the day, the Galis considered themselves Ghanaians. Those were the people they met when they stepped over the threshold of their front door. They were schoolmates and business colleagues and church congregants, and the Galis felt they belonged to that land and to those people.

At night, when they passed through the back door to join their neighbours in the common courtyard, the Galis would find themselves in another country. Whenever they started laughing, drinking, and dancing with the neighbours, they'd know for sure that it was their country. Those were the people whose families became like theirs, the people whose dreams informed their own. How could the Galis not belong to that land and to those people?

"You see the problem those British and French made, and then left for us to solve?" Salifu would ask my brothers and me. "What happens when your house is divided?"

If, like the Gali family, you're a member of the Ewe tribe, the line between the two countries is virtually invisible, changing nothing—not landscape, not food, not language. You can comfortably walk, as the Galis did, from kitchen to bathroom and consider both places home. The problem, of course, is that the line isn't invisible; it's a very real border, and people can truly belong to only one side.

If you're not an Ewe and you're not conversant in the indigenous tongue, the border between Ghana and Togo, drawn by England and France, like two children at the beach dragging a stick in the sand, is immediately apparent. You know you're in a foreign country.

When the Togolese are not speaking Ewe or another indigenous tongue, they are speaking French, the country's official language. Motorbikes weren't all that common in Ghana, but in the neighbouring Francophone countries, they appeared to be the main mode of transportation. You'd see a woman riding with her baby strapped to her back or a trader riding pillion while balancing a tray of oranges on her head. Businessmen wearing suits and ties would hop on their motorbikes to go to work. Parents would use the family motorbike to drop their kids off at school; the father would sit in the front, the mother would be at the back, and there could be as many as two or three kids squeezed in between them. Never in Ghana had I seen anything like that.

The culture in the neighbouring Francophone countries of gendarmes extorting bribes with homemade patrol checkpoints had also not crossed over into Ghana.

After transactions are completed with the Ghanaian customs officers in Aflao, there are roughly one hundred metres of no-man's-land to travel before reaching Lome. At Lome, there are Togolese customs officers with whom transactions must also be completed.

The distance between Lome and Aneho, the last town before the Togo-Benin border, is forty-five kilometres. It should have taken our bus a relatively short time to arrive there, but every five kilometres or so we would have to stop for a gendarme. Wofa Leonardo would get down and greet the gendarmes. Their easy smiles and lighthearted conversation made it look more like a meeting of old friends than a bargaining over bribe money.

Once an agreement was reached, Wofa Leonardo would shake the gendarme's hand again, covertly slipping the officer the cash; then he would board the bus and drive away. Wofa Leonardo would try to make up for the time we'd lost with the gendarme by speeding. He would drive as though we were on an open highway, going faster and faster until the scenery became a blur of faces and foliage, but then he would have to stop again, get down, and appease the next gendarme.

We continued in this way until we passed through Aneho, the last town in Togo, and crossed over into Benin. At Hilla Conji, the town that sits on Benin's border with Togo, Wofa

Leonardo let everyone get down for a few minutes so we could stretch our legs and, if we wanted, buy some food.

After we boarded and the bus took off again, it was more of the same, stop after stop after stop for gendarme after gendarme after gendarme. We were relieved when Wofa Leonardo drove through Seme and crossed the border into Badagry. At last, we were in Nigeria.

LIFE IN LAGOS SEEMED TO be coming together for Dad in the year or so since he'd arrived. He was comfortable there. He had family, and he'd made friends. He'd even started sowing the seeds of a new business plan, one for which he had already found a prospective investor. Dad had gone to the Office of the United Nations High Commissioner for Refugees and officially registered as a refugee, so his status in Nigeria was protected.

My presence in Lagos further grounded Dad in his new home. It lightened his mood. He and I went everywhere together. We marvelled at all the differences between Nigeria and Ghana and at how much more buoyant and promising life was in Nigeria. Whereas Ghana was visibly marked by struggle and adversity, Nigeria was beaming with prosperity and promise.

Many of the same factors that had pushed Ghana into a steep economic decline had created a boom in Nigeria. The country was oil-rich, making a windfall on the profits of oil sales. Nigerians were basking in their newfound wealth. They were very colourful people who would not hesitate to show how well they were doing. The affluent sprinkled cash around as though it were water. Every weekend there were hundreds of parties, from outdoorings to weddings to anniversaries to promotions. Any excuse to party was seized, and the service at those celebrations was lavish.

Back then, when it came to wealth and affluence, Ghanaians were not as impressive in their display. This was true even before the coups and their resulting misfortunes. Ghanaians had a certain modesty, a reluctance to show how wealthy they were.

All the cars in Ghana had become rickety. Most of the cars in Nigeria were brand new. Peugeot had established an assembly plant there, and their 504 model had become a badge of the middle class. The country's infrastructure was also well maintained, and everywhere we looked, construction was active. New flyovers and skyscrapers were being built. There were long bridges and overpasses.

The Nigerian shops were full of all the goods we had come to treasure in Ghana. There was tin milk, sardines, corned beef, soap, washing powder, toilet roll. All the things that had been labelled "essential commodities" in Ghana, things that had been smuggled into the country and were being sold for nearly ten times their original price, were stocked in abundance on the shelves of Nigerian shops.

Many of the Ghanaians who had voted with their feet and left the country were now living in Nigeria, and along with them came their talents. There were teachers, doctors, engineers; there were shoemakers, blacksmiths, auto mechanics. The estimated number of Ghanaian immigrants was a little over one million.

It was hard to tell just by looking at someone whether he or she was Ghanaian or Nigerian; the physical features were too similar. Our accents were the defining difference. It became clear whether someone was Ghanaian or Nigerian only when that person opened his mouth to speak.

The Ghanaian immigrants tended to live in clusters, forming their own little replicas of the communities in which they'd once lived. You'd walk into certain neighbourhoods and feel, for an instant, that you were back in a certain section of Ghana. The speech and the smells would all be hauntingly familiar.

Sometimes Dad and I would go to the houses of other Ghanaians to visit. With the door and windows closed to the distinct sounds of Lagos, we could have easily been in Tamale or Kumasi. We would sit and eat *tuo zaafi*, groundnut soup with guinea fowl, or *fufu* with *aponkye nkrakra*, goat light soup.

During those sorts of gatherings there was only ever one topic of conversation, Ghana and what was happening there. People spoke of Ghana lovingly; they spoke of Ghana angrily; they shared stories from back home: stories about events from the past and stories about current events that had been told to them by a visiting friend or relative. They immersed themselves in nostalgia and openly admitted their longing for home.

In some ways, Nigerians prised the Ghanaian immigrants. Schools would advertise that they had "ten Ghanaian teachers employed," in hopes of increasing their enrolment. Auto repair and body shops would do the same, posting signs announcing, "Ghanaian mechanics." The level of expertise and experience that Ghanaians brought was respected and valued.

At the same time, Ghanaians also roused an undercurrent

of bitterness within the Nigerian community. It wasn't a simple xenophobia. It was a deep and complex resentment based in a shared history of the two nations.

During the civil war that occurred from 1967 to 1970, Nigerians had fled to Ghana in much the same way that Ghanaians were now fleeing to Nigeria. After the Aliens Compliance Order was enacted, the Nigerians had all been forced to desert the lives they'd been building in Ghana and return to a country that was still in the midst of conflict. The hostility ran side by side with the hospitality. It was often difficult to tell which was present when the locals called out "Omoghana," which was the word they used to distinguish Ghanaians.

If there were a million Ghanaians living in Nigeria alone, the numbers now living in Europe, North America, Asia, and other places were unimaginable. Everybody knew somebody who had moved abroad. There wasn't a free country in the world that didn't now have a small population of Ghanaians, even the most remote and unlikely places. So many Ghanaians settled in Papua New Guinea, which is called PNG for short, people began to joke that those initials stood for People's New Ghana.

We had formed our own diaspora. That, in large part, was what kept Ghana afloat, via remittances that were sent by the mothers and fathers and sisters and brothers who had gone in search of greener pastures.

Whenever anyone they knew was returning to Ghana for a visit, they'd organise packages of clothing, shoes, and envelopes of dollars or pounds for the traveller to take back to the folks at home. It soon became an important part of the culture, a means of survival for those who'd remained.

For those of us who lived in Nigeria, the most valuable re-mittances we could send to our families were packages of canned food products, soap, washing powder, and toilet roll. These meant far more than any amount of naira, the Nigerian currency, we could shove in an envelope.

ONCE I GOT MY BEARINGS, I started to travel around Nigeria. I wanted to see the country not as a tourist, but as a resident. I had become quite adept at getting around. There were a fair number of motorbikes, which were called *okadas*, far more than you would see in Ghana, though not nearly as many as in the Francophone countries.

The four main modes of transportation were taxis, *damfos*, *moluwes*, and public transport buses that were operated by the metropolitan authority. The taxis were bright yellow, and painted down the entire length of the vehicle were two thick black latitudinal stripes that were about two inches wide. I rarely took taxis because they were much too expensive for my inflexible budget.

The public transport buses were inefficient. They suppos-edly ran on a schedule, but they were hardly ever on time, so nobody stayed and waited for them to arrive. Most people would just hop on the first *damfo* that passed by. *Damfos* were a lot like the *trotros* in Ghana. They were private, unregulated minibuses that carried people from one part of the city to the other.

Moluwes were a fascinating invention. They were truck heads and chassis that had been fitted with the body of a bus. Often the seats had been made of crude metal that had been hand-welded. I'd seen people tear their clothing on the jagged edges of those seats or cut themselves badly enough to draw blood. They were made to take between thirty and forty passengers, but there was also provision for standing room.

The *moluwe* drivers, none of whom were as friendly and sophisticated as Wofa Leonardo, would pack as many people as they could in the standing room area, fitting up to sixty people on a bus that had been designed to hold only thirty. Whenever I went out to explore Lagos, I'd usually take a *damfo* or a *moluwe* and ride around for hours, learning the street names and taking in the scenery.

Dad was busy with the preparations for his new business, a plant in which shea butter would be processed for export. He'd sold the idea to a businessman, who'd commissioned Dad to conduct a feasibility study. Since Dad was occupied with the project, I decided to visit one of our relatives who lived in the northern part of the country in a town called Kano. Ahmadu Bello University, where I had planned to enrol, is also located in the northern part of Nigeria, so I thought it might be good for me to get to know that territory.

Geographically, Ghana and Nigeria are essentially the same. The countries share the same climate, the same rainfall patterns during the same period of time, and the same vegetation. The coastal plains and forested zones are in the southern parts of both countries; the northern parts are savannah, which gradually gives way to a Sahelian zone the farther north you travel.

Another likeness between the two countries is that their Muslim populations are more heavily concentrated in the north. Unlike in Ghana, however, in Nigeria there were deep tensions between Muslims and Christians. While I was in Kano, a major religious riot broke out there, a continuation of the Maitatsine riots that had taken place in 1980. That first wave of the Maitatsine riots, which were centred mainly in Kano, had resulted in more than four thousand deaths.

Malam Mohammed Marwa, who went by the name Mai- tatsine, was the leader of that eponymous sect of Muslims. They were fundamentalists who took issue with the secular influences they felt were destroying the culture and tainting their religion by corrupting the lives of Muslims. They didn't believe bars that served alcohol should be allowed in northern cities. They were against the use of bicycles, radios, televisions, and other such Western conveniences.

Though Marwa, who was a Cameroonian immigrant, had been killed in 1980 during the first wave of the Maitatsine ri- ots, the sect was still in existence, now under the leadership of Musa Makaniki, a former auto mechanic turned prophet. The clashes between the Maitatsine Muslims and the police were brutal. The police were heavy-handed in their attempts to control the uprisings. They would fire into the crowd of Mai- tatsine Muslims after they'd emerged from their Friday prayers at the mosque. The Maitatsines in turn would become more aggressive in their rebellion.

I grew uncomfortable staying in a community that was in the midst of such large-scale violence. I left the north and re- turned to Lagos.

THE HOSTILITY TOWARD GHANAIANS WAS growing and mani-
festing itself in various ways, one of which had a direct impact on me and my future plans. School fees in Nigeria were
nominal and they were the same for all students, regardless of
national origin. There was the feeling among numerous Nigerians that Ghanaians had come to their country and were
taking jobs and enjoying resources that were meant for them,
the Nigerians. Policies and programmes were put in place to
prevent this from continuing. One such policy was the creation of a different fee scale for foreigners. The increase was
steep. Dad was an exile with limited financial means. There
was no way he would be able to afford the tuition for me to do
my postgraduate work at Ahmadu Bello University.

With this recent development, I no longer knew what my
purpose in Nigeria was. I was there to keep Dad company,
yes, but I had also been biding my time, waiting for the application period for the next academic year to arrive. Now I
had no idea what to do with myself.

Dad was also developing a discontentment with his life in
Nigeria. His business plans weren't falling into place as quickly
and as solidly as he had hoped. He was also becoming sensitive
to the fast-spreading xenophobia that had taken root. He
sensed trouble, something he had seen and experienced far too
many times in his life.

Nigeria was a society in which, out of frustration with the
law enforcement or justice systems, people often took it upon
themselves to mete out punishment to purported criminals.
This did not bode well for Ghanaians, who were largely blamed
for every crime that took place in the country, from armed
robbery to petty thievery. At the time, the street punishment

for theft called for the accused to be lynched with a tyre necklace. Many innocent people needlessly lost their lives as a result
of this sort of vigilante justice.

Several times during my one-year stay in Nigeria, while
walking in town, I would hear the cries *"Ole, ole, ole."* Ole is
the Yoruba word for "thief." Usually it would be from a distance, far from my line of vision. Following those cries, I'd
hear shouts and the footsteps of people running and know that
a mob was gathering and a lynching was about to take place.
Whenever this happened, I'd always leave what I was doing
and go somewhere else to seek refuge from the mayhem.
Then one day it happened while I was someplace from which
there was no escape.

I was going to visit my cousin who lived in a place called
Yaba, which is in Surulere, a suburb of Lagos. I had boarded a
moluwe. As usual, it was overcrowded. When I arrived at my
destination, I jumped off. Just as I did, another *moluwe* passed
by. I heard a lot of commotion on that bus, so I looked up.
Right then, somebody jumped out of one of the windows and
started sprinting. He was a young man in his twenties, dressed
in blue jeans and sandals.

The bus came to a stop. You could hear people shouting,
"Ole, ole, ole," from inside. Most of the passengers rushed out
and started running after the young man. The people on the
street tried to block his path. He managed to skirt a lot of them,
but he didn't get far. He was knocked down when a humongous muscled man cut him off and then kicked the young man's
legs out from under him.

People were filtering into the streets, walking toward the
young man, who was now writhing on the ground, pleading

his innocence and begging for mercy. I wanted to turn and leave but decided it would be too conspicuous. If I was the only one walking away from the spectacle, it might cast suspicion on me. I'd heard talk about how people who tried to intervene or run away from the scene were accused of being accomplices and subjected to the same treatment as the accused, so I joined the crowd and slowly walked toward the young man.

The people who arrived started hitting and kicking the young man. He was beaten and beaten until he was a bloody mess. It was barbaric. I knew what was coming next and wanted to scream for them to please stop, but of course I didn't. The young man they were beating was a Ghanaian. I could tell from his accent. If I so much as spoke a word, they would be able to tell that I was a Ghanaian, too. It would have surely been a case of guilt by association.

Somebody appeared with a car tyre and a can of petrol. They pulled the young man to his feet, draped the tyre around his neck, and spilled the entire can of petrol over it. Someone else struck a match and threw it onto the tyre. I will never forget the young man's screams or the smell of his flesh being burnt. I will never forget the mob's cruelty. Even as he burned, they were hurling stones and anything else they could lay their hands on at him.

I prayed that somebody would pick up an extremely large stone, aim well, and hit the young man in a location that would cause instant death. That would have been the merciful thing to do, because the kind of torture he was being put through was inhumane. Soon enough, the screams faded and the young man stopped moving. He was dead.

I'd never witnessed someone being murdered before. It was devastating. A few people from the crowd approached the corpse and removed the contents of its pockets. There were a couple of naira notes and a few coins, nothing significant. Other than that, he had nothing else that could have stood as proof of a crime.

"So what did he do?" someone in the crowd asked as we all started walking away. Nobody knew the young man's crime, and nobody came forward as his accuser. It had all been for nothing.

Dad and I decided to leave Nigeria. He'd wanted to stay in Africa but was realising that everywhere he went on the continent, he would most likely be confronted with the same woes. He chose instead to travel to London, where, under the auspices of his official refugee status, he would be able to settle. Several of his old political allies had sought asylum in the United Kingdom, so he would have a network of friends there. We also had family members in the United Kingdom.

There was one member of our family with whom Dad was especially interested in reconnecting, his son Samuel. When Samuel was nine years old, Dad had allowed the headmaster and headmistress of his school to take him to England with them. They were a middle-aged couple, childless missionaries with whom Dad had become close. They were fond of Samuel and wanted to oversee the remainder of his primary education in London. Dad, who always wanted to ensure the best education for his children, agreed. Once the couple arrived in London, they fell out of touch with Dad, and he never saw his son Samuel again.

London was not an option for me. I still had hopes of com-

pleting a postgraduate degree and did not see how that would
be possible in London. Given the spate of recent immigrants
from Ghana to London and other Western places, it was incon-
ceivable that the British High Commission would grant me a
visa. I was no longer a minor, so I couldn't travel on Dad's visa.
I was a twenty-five-year-old man, a university graduate with
no profession and no domestic obligations. Even if by some
miracle I was granted entry into the United Kingdom, there
was still the issue of school fees and how they would be paid.
My only option seemed to be a return to Ghana, where I would
try to find a way to make things work.

Dad boarded a flight to London. We said our good-byes. It
was an emotional departure. No matter how uncomfortable or
inconvenient the journey, Côte d'Ivoire and Nigeria had been
accessible by road. My father would now be half a continent
and an ocean away. We didn't know when, or if, we would see
each other again.

I boarded a bus headed for Accra. The driver wasn't as warm
and engaging as Wofa Leonardo. He barely spoke the entire
time. The only time he came alive was when he got down to
interact with the gendarmes. As soon as he was done with
those negotiations, the scowl that he'd been wearing returned
to his face. But he carried us safely through the slew of strate-
gically placed gendarmes in Benin and Togo straight to Accra,
where my brothers were waiting to welcome me home.

My father was right when he said that he felt trouble was on
the horizon in Nigeria. Shortly after Dad and I left, Nigeria
enacted its own version of an Aliens Compliance Order. They
gave the immigrants living there, a significant number of whom
were Ghanaian, two weeks to pack up and leave the country.

A lot of people didn't receive their salaries for the work they'd done; children had to be withdrawn from their schools; families were forced to abandon homes they'd either built or bought. The upheaval was traumatic.

In their haste, Ghanaians even started using plastic bags as luggage. It was a specific type of bag made of cheap woven plastic. The bag was boxy, had handles, and was designed with a checkered plaidlike pattern, either in red and white, black and white, or blue and white. Ghanaians referred to this bag as *efiewura sua me*, which translates to English from the Akan language as "help me carry my bag." Nigerians began calling the bags "Ghana Must Go," a name that has persisted until today. Interestingly, the European fashion house Louis Vuitton has recently adopted the distinctive pattern of the "Ghana Must Go" bag and imprinted it on several items in their line of merchandise.

This sudden expulsion of Ghanaians from Nigeria was a grand retribution, payback—whether purposeful or not—for the sudden expulsion of Nigerians from Ghana in 1969.

The Ghanaian government launched an exercise to repatriate its citizens. Vehicles were placed at their disposal, medical teams were mobilised to offer treatment, food and temporary shelters were provided. For many, this return was only a transit stop. Nothing in Ghana had changed. The conditions that had forced those individuals to leave were still present. They stayed in Ghana for only as long as it took to put a little something together to make yet another journey to yet another country. Some managed to get visas to Europe and North America. Others left by car or boat to Côte d'Ivoire, Togo, and Burkina

Faso, and still more went by foot, trudging their way across the Sahara desert to Libya.

Things had come to this: the feeling that life anywhere else, no matter how dangerous it was to get there or how difficult it was to live there, was better than life in Ghana, the home we had all once loved and cherished and had never before dreamt of leaving.

PROVIDENCE

WRITING BECAME MY salvation. That was something I could never have foreseen. For most of my life, words had failed me. I'd been unable to express myself in any meaningful way. Too many of the events I'd experienced had left me speechless, bursting with emotions I could not lay bare. Sometimes I would withdraw; I would travel deeper and deeper into silence until it completely enveloped me.

I had no problem speaking up in defence of myself or in defence of others; the challenge came when I had to find a way to describe my innermost feelings. What do you say, at seven years old, when you find out that your father has been detained? There were no words in my vocabulary for what I felt, so I held everything inside. I was an introspective child who grew to become a reserved young man.

But words had always also fascinated me. I loved to read, and I could spend hours with my nose buried in a book. I marvelled at the words, and at how clearly they painted the pictures their writers wanted me to see. I could envision the characters so precisely that they would begin to feel real to me, like people

I might bump into in town. When I read their dialogue, I could practically hear their voices.

Every time our watchman, Salifu, used to play the guitar and sing for my brothers and me, I would hold every word of every lyric as though it were a precious gem. The words did more than express pain, sorrow, or joy; they pulled me into those emotions so I could feel them for myself. I was in awe of the writers' ability to do that.

It was when I first fell in love that I started to learn how to take what was inside of me and shape it into words. I would write love letters to Alice. I wanted her to know how I felt about her, and I wanted to invite her to share with me my experience of the private world in which I lived. This moved me to put pen to paper and figure out a way to use words to paint a picture of that world.

When I returned from my stay in Nigeria, I started writing again—not love letters, but thoughts, reactions, and ideas. I kept a small notebook, and whenever something struck me, I would write it down. I didn't fancy myself a writer, and the words I jotted in that notebook never took any form. They weren't poems or stories or lyrics. My writing was merely an exercise in self-expression. I wanted to become a better communicator, and that seemed to be the best way for me to go about it.

I did also write letters, but only to my father, who was now living in London. I would walk to the post office and buy an aerogramme. Sometimes I would stare at the light blue paper for hours, wondering what to write to Dad beyond the salutation and few lines of assurance that my brothers and I were doing well. I wanted to give Dad more details, more insight. I wanted to tell him the truth about what was happening in Ghana, how difficult our lives still were, but I also wanted him to laugh, to know that we were finding humour in our adversity. So I wrote and wrote. When I was done, I would fold the aerogramme so it became its own envelope, and I would lick the gummy sides, seal it, and send it off.

Dad always wrote back right away. His handwriting was neat, ordered, and legible. He also responded on aerogrammes. The paper had no lines, but his sentences were all as straight as a ruler, from one side of the aerogramme to the other. The words seemed to flow, as if he'd poured them out at once, without any hesitation. Yet the stories he told were involved and well thought out. He wrote often of the weather in London, wondering if he would ever grow accustomed to the persistent fog. He missed Ghana's sunshine. He wrote of how he spent his days. He was in the constant company of relatives and had reconnected with a circle of old friends who were also living in exile.

In one of the first letters I received, Dad informed me that his search for Samuel, my brother who'd been taken to London by the Thompsons, the missionary couple that ran the school he'd attended, was progressing. Dad had learned of the Thompsons' whereabouts and was preparing to make contact.

"I have every reason to believe," Dad wrote, "I will soon be seeing Adam."

SAMUEL ADAM MAHAMA IS THE third of the four children my mother and my father had together. My father named two of his sons Adam, which is an Anglicised version of his father's name, Adama. He passed on the Christian name he'd been given, Emmanuel, to the elder of the two Adams. The younger of the Adams was given the Christian name Samuel. Nobody paid any mind to either of those Christian names. Both boys were called Adam. There was Big Adam and there was Small Adam.

When they lived in Ghana, Edith and Harold Thompson ran a small residential school in Yendi. By the time Samuel turned four, Mum had transferred guardianship of him to our father, as she had done with Alfred and me, her older boys. Dad enrolled Samuel at the Thompsons' school, which was considered one of the best in that area. Our cousin Michael, who was about six years older than Samuel, also attended the school.

At the time, the Thompsons were probably in their late thirties or early forties, but I couldn't say for sure. They appeared to be ageless. They had the sort of faces that remained fixed and resisted any type of chronological categorisation. They could well have been in their late twenties or early fifties.

There was a conservatism about them that may have been a result of their religious practise, but they also displayed a slight Bohemian streak. They had a penchant for motorbikes and would ride them all throughout Ghana as they went around spreading the word of God.

Samuel and the other children at the school knew how to ride a motorbike long before they learned how to pedal a bicycle. Sometimes, when the Thompsons were not paying attention, the boys would take the motorbike and ride into town even though it was against the rules. They enjoyed the sensation of speed. Nothing could compare with the thrill of feeling the wind rushing against their faces and hearing it blow past their ears.

Dad was close to the Thompsons. He considered them his good friends. They would call on each other socially, drink tea together, and meander through various topics in the course of one conversation. One thing the three of them shared was their love of children. The Thompsons didn't have any biological children, but they considered all of the children at the school theirs and would often speak of them in that way.

"Our youngest, Abednego," Edith Thompson might say in her clipped British accent, "is simply a handful."

In 1969, when the Aliens Compliance Order was put in effect and immigrants were being forced to leave Ghana, Dad used every political contact he still had to exempt the Thompsons from deportation. Even so, the Thompsons could see the direction in which the country was headed. They predicted that things were bound to get worse before they got better. They decided to return to London.

Samuel was one of the best students at the school, and the Thompsons were fond of him, especially Edith. They asked Dad if they could take Samuel along with them to London to complete his primary school years. Dad readily agreed. Ghanaian schools provided top-rate education, but part of the legacy of colonialism was the mentality that institutions abroad, particularly in Europe, were superior to those at home. Why wouldn't Dad want Samuel to have the best?

When speaking of the ease with which he'd made the decision, Dad would often draw a parallel between his own educational experience and the opportunity he felt was being offered to Samuel. When education was made available in the north, the few schools that were established were residential. The northerners refused to send their children to school. They were afraid that if they handed their children over to the white man, they might never see them again.

The decision to send Dad away to school had been made under duress. His father and grandfather shared the villagers' beliefs about the dangers of letting foreigners take their children away. In a country like Ghana, which was at the heart of the transatlantic slave trade, such fears were not baseless. Nevertheless, Dad went away to school and it turned out to be an opportunity that altered the direction of his life.

Perhaps more important is that, much to the relief of his father and grandfather, Dad eventually returned home.

WHEN I CAME BACK FROM Nigeria, it was too late to apply for a postgraduate programme; the deadlines had all passed. I was offered employment at Tamale Secondary School teaching history.

"But why history?" my friend Jones asked me when I'd told him I wanted to get my master's degree in the subject. Jones was a schoolmate from university. He'd also attended Tamale Secondary School with my brothers. "Why do you need two degrees in history? Do you intend to be a university lecturer for the rest of your life?"

I hadn't given much thought to what I wanted to do with the rest of my life, but being a university lecturer didn't sound like such a bad idea. I liked teaching and had been brought up to believe that it was an important and honourable profession. On numerous occasions Dad told us that after the coup, had he not been banned from holding public appointments, he would have happily resumed his career as a teacher.

Jones urged me to consider another subject. He also intended to apply to the university for postgraduate studies and was excited about a new programme that was being offered by the University of Ghana.

"It's called communication studies," he said. "It's becoming one of the most popular schools at the university."

I was wary of choosing a subject of study solely because of its popularity. I had done that when I'd applied to university as an undergraduate. I was grateful that the university didn't grant me admission into business administration, the programme that I had listed as my first choice.

"Are you doing it because it's popular?" I asked Jones. "Or because it's something you like?"

"No," he said. "It just sounds like an interesting programme." He started telling me about courses that were offered in the communication studies programme: print journalism, broadcast journalism, and the history of mass communications. I had to agree; Jones was right, it sounded interesting. I was intrigued. Jones said he was going to the university to pick up a set of application forms. I asked him to pick up a set for me as well.

After that conversation with Jones, I started making my own queries about the programme. I was still passionate about history, but the more I learned about communication studies, the more I felt, for reasons that I wouldn't have been able to articulate at the time, that it was the direction in which I needed to go.

THE THOMPSONS TOLD DAD THAT in order to take Samuel to London with them, they would have to be his legal guardians, and in order to be his legal guardians, they would have to legally adopt him. Dad agreed to sign over his parental rights. To him it was nothing more than a formality, a piece of paper that was required. He would always be Samuel's father. Nobody could change that.

Dad may have been a good businessman, the sort of person who is able to sniff out a successful endeavour and put all the pieces together to make it happen, but he was a much better friend and human being. Making decisions on good faith was his Achilles' heel. He had a pure heart, and he trusted that other people were operating with the same level of sincerity and transparency. That tendency to trust had cost him his rice mill business, and it would ultimately lose him an entire lifetime with one of his sons.

Our mother was opposed to the idea of sending Samuel away with the Thompsons. She had never been outside Ghana. She'd barely travelled beyond the north. London, to her, was like the edge of the world. She didn't want her son there, so far away. She protested and protested, but in those days a woman's words held little weight when measured against a man's. He was the father, the head of the household. His decisions stood.

Whenever Dad pointed out the parallels between this opportunity that the Thompsons were giving Samuel and the opportunity that the district commissioner had given him, he never made mention of the most obvious similarity. Dad's mother had been unwavering in her refusal to let him be taken away. Our mother was no different. She wanted no part in what she saw as the giving away of her child. She refused to meet with the Thompsons to hear their justifications and assurances. She refused to go to court for the formal adoption proceedings. My parents' relationship had already reached its end by the time Samuel was taken to London, but the situation caused a rift between them that Dad was never able to mend.

After Dad had been taken away to school, his mother suffered an anguish that everyone believed eventually led to her death. She cried endlessly. She was inconsolable. She waited and waited for her child to return. Our mother did the same. She cried. She worried. She waited. She kept a picture of Samuel with her. As the years passed, she would look at the picture and wonder where her son was, what he looked like now, and if he would ever come back to her. The hurt never went away. It was a pain that had settled in the very core of her being, a pain so pervasive and biting that we all thought it might kill her.

Samuel was nine years old when he left for London with the Thompsons. For the first couple of years they kept in frequent touch with Dad, though he didn't have much direct interaction with Samuel. Slowly, the correspondence between them dwindled to nothing.

While he was running his rice mill, Dad travelled to London at least once a year for a trade show. Whenever he was there he would contact the Thompsons. Harold Thompson was never anything less than gracious and kind, and he received Dad's calls warmly. He would provide Dad with basic information about Samuel's progress in school, his interests, and how much he had grown; but for one reason or another, the Thompsons were never able or willing to let Dad see Samuel or have any direct interaction with him. There was always some excuse. This was not what they'd agreed on. Samuel was not the Thompsons' son. Or was he? After all, permission had been granted and papers had been signed. There was very little that Dad could do. It soon began to dawn on him that he had lost his son.

I COMPLETED MY APPLICATION FORMS, and the next time I saw Jones in Tamale, I gave them to him. By then I was sure I was making the right choice to study communication. The remarks that I scribbled into my notebook reflected this. I was now consumed by the significance of communication in society, professionally and personally.

Communication is the bridge that joins individuals, that keeps citizens informed of the work their government is doing—or not doing—on their behalf, that connects businesses with clients and customers. Communication plays a vital role in the advancement of all aspects of civilisation.

Jones returned to Accra with our application forms. He was to hand mine over to William, the friend I'd attended university with and also lived with while completing my national service duty. William went to the airport to meet Jones and get my forms from him. While there, he visited and spent time with Tom Dakura, a customs agent whom we had befriended, a man who would soon step into the role of guardian angel in my life. As planned, he submitted them to the university. Somehow, in all the running around he was doing over the next few days, Jones lost his forms. When he went to the university to pick up another set, they told him that he had missed the deadline. They were no longer giving out forms or accepting them for submission.

Jones was extremely upset, but he promised himself that he would apply the following year. Little did he know that life would take him through a series of unexpected twists and turns that would place him on an entirely different path. He never reapplied.

The university accepted my application and invited me to come for an interview at the School of Communication Studies. I was elated. I requested leave from my job at Tamale Secondary School so that I could travel to Accra for the interview.

Life in Ghana was still extremely difficult. Even God seemed not to be on the side of Ghanaians. There had been a drought, and the country was experiencing problems of severe hunger, especially in the northern areas, because of the poor harvest. Additionally, the roads were terrible and transportation was in a bad state. It was difficult to move around from one part of the country to another, especially from north to south. A journey that should have taken anywhere from seven to eight hours often took twenty-four hours, and by the time you arrived you'd be covered from head to toe in a fine film of dust.

The State Transport Corporation (STC) buses were few

and far between. There was one bus a day going to Accra from Tamale, and if you missed it, you were just out of luck. Even if you showed up on time, the number of people who would also be there at the station hoping to travel was staggering. There could be as many as a few hundred people waiting to board a bus that sat only fifty.

Tickets for travel on the STC buses were difficult to come by. The only guaranteed ways of securing a ticket were to either know somebody who worked for the STC or pay a heavy bribe. There were other alternative modes of transportation, though not all desirable.

There were the *watonkyine* buses. They were identical to the *moluwe* buses in Nigeria, a truck head and chassis that had been fitted with the body of a bus. These were old buses that had long been retired and the heads of trucks that had been used and abused. They'd each carried their lifetime's quota of cargo and belonged in a scrap yard, not on the streets. Ingenuity and desperation had now placed those vehicles back on the road, and they were being used to transport people. Passengers would be packed in like sardines, eight people squished beside each other on a seat that should have held no more than five.

These trucks turned buses frequently broke down on the road in the midst of their journeys. That's how they earned the name *watonkyine*, a question in the Akan language that in the case of the buses was meant to be rhetorical. Its English translation is "Have you bought salt?" The implication was that it would take you a long time to get where you were going because the bus was sure to break down, and when it did you would by all means have to cook some food to eat and would need salt.

After the *watonkyine* buses, articulated trucks were the next alternative for travel. Once they had loaded whatever cargo they were carrying, the drivers would also pick up passengers. It was a way for them to make some additional money. They would charge the passengers a fare and permit them to sit in the cab or on top of the cargo.

Another means of travel within the country was by air, especially if you were going from Tamale to Accra. At this time Ghana Airways had stopped operating domestically, so there were no commercial flights available. However, there was an air force plane that made routine duty flights between Tamale and Accra on a fairly regular basis.

Whenever there was an air force flight taking off, the airport would be packed. The plane could take only forty-four passengers, so, as with the STC buses, the majority of people waiting would be left behind.

The day before my interview I woke up very early. I packed a small bag with two changes of clothing, toiletries, and the letter I'd just received from my father, which I intended to read on the way to Accra. The timing of its arrival was perfect, and I viewed it as a good omen. Had my father been in Ghana, I would have called on him for some words of support and encouragement before going to the interview. I didn't call him because the phone lines were unreliable, but here were those words anyway, folded up inside the aerogramme.

I got to the STC yard at four A.M. and queued. I was number forty in the queue, so I felt confident that I would be able to buy a ticket and board the bus, which was a fifty-seater. What I didn't realise was that more than two-thirds of the tickets would not be sold according to the queue but would be given through the back door.

After the ticket office opened, the place became crowded. Those of us in the queue remained there, waiting for our turn. The others who'd arrived walked straight to the back of the ticket office. After a while, the woman in the ticket office started calling for people in the queue. I was surprised when the first person in the queue paid his fare and was given ticket number ten. The second person received ticket number sixteen. The third person in the queue received ticket number twenty-one. After the tenth person in the queue had been served, a woman made an announcement.

"The bus is full," she said. "The tickets are finished."

Often some of the people who'd finagled their tickets through the back door lingered in the STC yard and resold them for three or four times the price. I didn't have enough money to buy a ticket at black market prices. I left the STC yard and quickly made my way to the air force base to see if a plane was scheduled to fly to Accra that morning. I was happy to learn that there was, but dozens of people were already waiting to board the plane. This time, I decided, I wouldn't leave my chances to fate. I saw two soldiers whom I knew and had befriended during my youth. They were nice, friendly men, not at all like the soldiers who'd wreaked havoc in Tamale after the last coup.

I approached the soldiers and explained my situation. I told them that I absolutely had to get to Accra to attend this admissions interview for a postgraduate programme at the university. They promptly ushered me to the office where the booking for the air force plane was done and told the soldier in charge what was going on. He didn't seem the least bit sympathetic. He probably spent his entire day listening to everybody's urgent stories, excuses, and explanations to justify their need to be given priority status.

"The flight is full," he told us. "There is no way he can get a seat." My spirits started to wane. My friend the soldier patted me on the shoulder and said, "Hold on, it's not yet over. In Ghana there are always ways and means." The two soldiers then went around the airport trying to use whatever influence they had to get me on that flight. They weren't successful in their efforts, but they encouraged me to hang around anyway.

"By the time the flight is ready to take off," they told me, "we might have figured a way to put you on board." I prayed that's what would happen.

When the flight was ready to board, the soldier who'd been in the booking office came out holding a manifest. He started calling names. I was envious of each smile that erupted on the faces of the people whose names had been called. My name was not on the list of the forty-four that were called. There is no reason it should have been, but I still half expected that through some miracle, I would hear it.

"Anybody whose name was not called," the soldier sternly told the crowd, "should not come anywhere near the plane."

That warning was not enough to deter those of us whose names had not been called. We were desperate, willing to try any last-minute pleading or trickery to get ourselves on board. As soon as the soldier holding the manifest walked to the plane, we charged behind him. The perseverance paid off for some of the people. They were placed in the jump seat or other reserve seats that were not normally used for civilian passengers. By the time I was able to push and elbow my way to the front, all of those extra seats had been taken.

My spirits were thoroughly smashed. How was I going to get to Accra? I was determined to be in the School of Communication Studies, and I didn't want another academic year to pass me by. I needed to get to that interview. I stood and watched with great sadness as the soldier shut the airplane door. I continued to watch as the plane taxied and took off and ascended into the sky.

There was a part of me that was holding on to the impossible, wishing that the pilots would look down and see me, standing so far below them on the tarmac. I wished that somehow I could telepathically explain to them the predicament I was in, and they would turn around and come back for me alone. I wished and I watched until there was nothing to see but sky and nothing to wish for but luck.

My next option was to catch a *watonkyine*. I rushed over to the stop, which was directly next to the GOIL (Ghana Oil Co.) filling station in the centre of Tamale. When I arrived, I could see that it didn't look promising. There were men curled up on benches, dozing away. My presence roused them from their sleep.

"Where are you going?" one asked. I told him that I needed to get to Accra as soon as possible.

"Oh . . ." He yawned, stretching his arms. "You're late. The Accra *watonkyines* are gone." Knowing how frequently the *watonkyines* broke down, I wondered if they had even reached Yapei. Maybe if I found a way to travel the twenty-six kilometres to Yapei, I could catch one of those *watonkyines*. At least, I reasoned, I wouldn't be stationary. I'd be heading in the right geographical direction.

"Wait," the man said as I started to walk away. "The Bolgatanga *watonkyines* will be arriving soon. If there's space, we can squeeze you in."

I waited. It took about an hour for the next *watonkyine* to arrive. When it stopped, a few of the passengers whose destination was Tamale got down. There was still no space for an additional passenger. The driver said it was not possible. They had been overfull and it had been a relief to everyone on the bus to drop off those passengers in Tamale. He could not add another person. The driver closed the door and drove away.

The men at the stop did not know when another *watonkyine* would come.

"Why don't you go to the police barrier?" one of them suggested. "Sometimes government vehicles going to Accra pass by. Give the policemen a little tip and they will find a way to squeeze you in."

I thanked the man for the advice, though I wasn't sure if I would take it. Nothing seemed to be going my way. I was beginning to believe that maybe it simply wasn't meant to be. I considered going back to the Tamasco campus and just forgetting the whole idea about the School of Communication Studies. As frustrated as I was, I couldn't bring myself to give up that easily, not without trying this last option. I decided to go to the police barrier. If nothing came of it, I would go home, knowing that I'd at least done everything in my power to get to the interview.

I dashed off to the police barrier, which was on the outskirts of Tamale at a place called Lamashegu. I walked up to

the policemen and explained my situation. They were com-
passionate and said that they'd help me if they could.

"But you cannot stand here," one of them firmly warned.

"Go there," the other said, pointing to a tall tree at a distance. "We'll call you if a vehicle comes."

I went and stood by the tree. After watching the police interact with the drivers of the cars that passed by the barrier, I
understood why they didn't want me too near them. I recognised all the gestures of bribery: the affected friendliness, the
small talk about trivial matters, and the hearty good-bye hand-
shake that was used to covertly exchange money from one palm
to another.

Vehicles passed by in spurts, overcrowded *watonkyines*, private cars, and trucks. I stared at every passenger in those vehicles, thinking what I wouldn't give to exchange places with
him or her. I'd been standing by the tree for more than an
hour when one of the police officers called out to me.

"Hey, my friend," he yelled. "Come, come. This vehicle is
going to Accra."

It was a Ministry of Agriculture cargo truck loaded with
jute sacks. Each sack contained about one hundred kilos of
maize. I ran toward the truck, stopping automatically at the
passenger's side of the cab. I looked inside and it was full. There
was enough space in there for three people, but I counted five.

"Okay, climb up," the driver said. "Jump on top."

Me? Jump on top? I'd never ridden in an open truck before,
seated on cargo, maize no less. But what choice did I have? I
climbed up and joined the other stray passengers the driver
had picked up along his journey.

The truck was overloaded. The cargo had been stacked

taller than the sides of the truck bed. There was nothing to prevent those of us who were sitting on the sacks from falling off. It was a game of balance, of holding on tight to a sack and allowing your body to yield to all the bumps and the turns. Thankfully, the truck was so weighted down by everything it was carrying that it could not travel at any appreciable speed, despite the driver's constant attempts to accelerate.

I opened up my bag and took out the aerogramme from my father but realised it was probably not the best place to read it, so I put it back. I thought about the ironies of our lives. I thought about Jones and how excited he had been to apply to the School of Communication Studies. I remembered that first conversation we had about it and how reluctant I'd been to consider a subject of study other than history.

I thought, too, about Dad's house in Tamale at Agric Ridge. It was a beautiful home and he'd been so proud of it. Back then he was a wealthy businessman. Our family owned six cars. We boys were never in want of anything. We had record players, bicycles, and scores of friends. We went to discos regularly and wore the latest fashions.

Now Dad was living in exile in London, a city that he'd told me in his letters could not be any more different from Tamale. He spent his time desperately searching for his son Samuel.

"Life is like a cycle," Dad used to tell us. "Everything goes around and comes around again. One day you're up, but the next day you might be down."

I realised, sitting carefully atop those sacks of maize, listening to the whistle of the truck's wheels as they drove along the poorly surfaced road, that what Dad said was very true.

It was almost dawn when we arrived at Kintampo, where I

spotted an STC bus that was loading up to go to Kumasi. Even though I'd paid the truck driver for passage to Accra, I asked him to let me down. I ran to catch the bus. There were no tickets available, but a ticketed passenger had suddenly decided not to travel, so he sold me his ticket. I paid extra for it, but it wasn't as high as it would have been had I bought it through the black market. I boarded the bus and melted into my seat. The road from Kintampo to Kumasi was much better. It was smooth and sound, and it felt like heaven compared with the ride I'd endured atop those sacks of maize. We made it to Kumasi in good time.

When we arrived, the buses for Accra were loading. Because Kumasi and Accra are Ghana's largest cities, it is a well-travelled route. The tickets had been sold out and there was no room on any of the buses, not a single available seat.

Fortunately I ran into a friend who knew one of the drivers of the buses. I waited off to the side while he went and told the driver about my situation. I prayed the driver would find some solution. I'd made it this far against all odds. That meant something, didn't it?

My friend waved me over to the bus. He started to introduce me to the driver, but as soon as I saw the man's face he needed no introduction.

"Wofa Leonardo!" I said, excited at the coincidence of seeing the man who had driven the bus that had carried me from Accra to Lagos.

"Seat no dey," Wofa Leonardo said, looking down the aisle of the bus as if he were quickly recounting the seats to make sure each one was, indeed, full.

"Make you sit down here," he said, pointing to the stairwell by the door. It wasn't a seat, but it also wasn't a sack of maize. I dropped my bag and sat sideways on the top step so I was facing the front windscreen. When we got to Nkawkaw, an hour's drive from Kumasi, a passenger got down and Wofa Leonardo let me take over the now-empty seat.

We arrived in Accra at midmorning. There wasn't enough time before my appointment for me to go to the house where my brothers were staying to shower and change, so I headed off in the direction of the university.

When I got to Achimota, I knocked on the door of one of the bungalows and begged the woman who answered to give me a bucket of water. I told her about the interview, where I'd come from, and what I'd gone through to make it there on time. I only needed to brush my teeth, wash my face, and clean up a little so I looked presentable. She let me in. I washed the dust off myself; I ironed my shirt and trousers and put on the change of clothes. I thanked the woman, grabbed my bag, and looked for a taxi to take me the rest of the way to the university.

"Your name has already been called," the secretary at the School of Communication Studies told me when I went to check in. "You've missed your turn."

I gave her my explanation, describing every leg of my journey so she'd understand that my presence there was only by God's grace. The secretary had no discernable reaction, one way or the other, to my story. She asked me to have a seat and wait a moment while she went to check if the interviewers would still see me. When she returned, she told me they would allow me to be interviewed, but I would be placed at the bottom of the appointments list. I'd have to wait until everyone else had been interviewed, then I could go in. I told her I did not mind; I would wait.

I sat down, not believing I was there, at the School of Communication Studies. I had actually made it. I felt as though I'd successfully completed an obstacle course. Once the rush of adrenaline had slowed and the stress of it all started to slip away, I took Dad's letter from my bag, tore it open, and started to read.

Dad was now convinced that the Thompsons were deliberately withholding his messages from Samuel. He believed if Samuel knew his father was trying to reach him, he would phone him back. Why would the Thompsons not want him to see his son? What could they possibly gain from keeping them apart? Samuel wasn't the small boy who'd left Ghana. He was in his early twenties. Samuel deserved to know his father and to know that it had never been Dad's intention for him to be permanently kept away from Ghana or from his family. Dad said he would not give up; he would never stop trying until he'd reached Samuel.

"Tell your mother," Dad wrote, "that it will not be much longer. I will find your brother. And God willing, we will all one day be together again back home."

TOVARISCH

DURING MY UNDERGRADUATE years when I belonged to a socialist cell, the other members and I used the word *tovarisch* to address one another. In the Russian language, it means "comrade." We all had views that were left of centre and we believed thoroughly in socialist ideology. We felt the majority of the problems in Ghana, and in most countries experiencing social or political turmoil, stemmed from class struggle, the friction that was caused by one class's attempt to subjugate other classes and quash their efforts to resist that oppression. In our estimation, the Union of Soviet Socialist Republics (USSR) was the best model for the sort of society that all countries should aim to become, one that supported the equality of its citizens and ensured them access to the basic services and necessities for a productive and dignified life.

In 1986, when I boarded an Aeroflot plane headed for the Soviet Union, I was no longer an active member of any socialist cells or organisations, but I still held those beliefs. I was one of five people in Ghana who had been chosen to attend the Institute of Social Sciences in Moscow to complete a postgraduate programme in social psychology.

Because of the emotional and financial support I'd received from my stepmother, Joyce, and my friend Tom Dakura, I had recently completed my postgraduate degree in communication studies. The programme was exhilarating and informative, everything I'd hoped it would be. It was the perfect complement to the undergraduate degree I'd received in history because I learned how the events in our collective memory are shaped and documented. In the course of my communication studies programme, we'd briefly studied social psychology and I'd found it interesting, so I looked forward to having it as the central focus of my next degree.

All five of us who'd been chosen for the programme were apprehensive about flying with Aeroflot. We'd heard rumours that the airline had a bad safety record and its planes had been involved in numerous crashes over the years. We all sat, frightened, with our seat belts fastened as tightly as possible while we waited for the plane to take off.

I've always had a passion for aviation but had flown only domestically. The length of our flight was worrying. I tried to calm my nerves by envisioning myself already in Moscow, where we would be based, walking through the streets greeting other like-minded socialists.

"Tovarisch," we would say to one another while shaking hands. Of course, I had no idea what the streets of Moscow looked like. I based my imaginings on the Western streets I'd seen on television shows and in films. Everything I knew about Russia was historical or philosophical. I had no practical knowledge and no visual references. The flight attendants were the first Russian people I'd ever met.

"Pozhalovat," they'd said, smiling, to each of us as we'd

entered the aircraft. I had no clue what that meant. The only word of Russian I knew was tovarisch, and I hesitated to say it because I wasn't sure if it was an appropriate response.

This would be my first trip outside of Africa. Actually, I'd never travelled outside of the West African subregion. I had also never been away from my family for any significant length of time. The plane landed in Malta to refuel. We stayed in the terminal during the two-hour layover. I stood at a window, straining to see beyond the airplanes parked on the long stretch of tarmac, hoping to catch even the slightest glimpse of the country's landscape.

We landed at Sheremetyevo International Airport in Moscow.

"Pozhalovat," said the woman who'd been sent to meet us and escort us through the customs and immigration process. "Welcome."

With the exception of the four other students in my group, everybody we saw at the airport was white. There were scores and scores of white people. They were all friendly and welcoming, offering greetings we did not understand. I had been in the minority before in many ways and circumstances, but never racially. It was startling at first not to see anyone with features that I recognised or found familiar.

In the correspondence the school had sent us, we'd been instructed to bring clothing that was appropriate for cold weather. They'd warned us that the winter season had started early that year and it was expected to be one of the coldest winters ever. I had packed a few pullovers and a jacket that I promptly slipped on as soon as we exited the plane.

During the harmattan season, when Alfred and I went to visit our mother in Damongo or our grandparents in Busunu, the temperatures could drop to as low as 20 or 18 degrees Celsius. We would sometimes have to build a fire to stay warm. I thought I knew the definition of cold. When we left the airport with our escort to get into the van, I found out what cold really was. The temperature was in the single digits on the positive side of the Celsius scale. It was bone-crushing cold. The icy air blew through my clothes and stung my skin. Within minutes my lips were chapped, my eyes were watering, and my nose was running. I wondered how people could live in such a climate, and I wondered if I would be able to make it through an entire winter.

Our escort and driver had anticipated the reaction that five African boys who'd never been in winter would have to the weather in Russia. They had put on the heat in the van so it was nice and warm when we got in. Everything thawed immediately except my fingers, which were numb. I tried to warm them by rubbing my hands together. I was so preoccupied with this that I didn't pay attention to my surroundings as the van exited the airport. By the time I thought to look out of the window, we were already travelling on a highway. There were dual carriage roads in Ghana, but I'd never seen a highway as large as the one we were on. It had six lanes going in one direction and six lanes going in the opposite direction.

When we turned off the highway, the van drove along a series of winding country roads that were all well paved with asphalt. The other boys and I stared out of the van's windows, taking everything in. The cars on the roads were unfamiliar to us. I'd never heard of a Volga or a Tatra or a Lada. They were utilitarian, not as sleek as the Western cars that were imported to Ghana.

We were taken to a villa about an hour's drive outside of Moscow. It was a grand and impressive structure. We were told that we would stay there for a short while until the school was prepared to receive us. By the time we arrived, it was dark. There was fresh snow on the ground, and the instant I got out of the van, I reached down and grabbed a handful of the white powder. I'd heard about snow. I'd read about snow. I'd seen it in films and on television, but I'd never seen it in real life. I looked at the clump in my hand. The reflection of the lights from the villa on the flakes made them look like a cluster of fragile crystals.

That first night, we were fed a dinner of steak and potatoes with vegetables. We were told that we could watch TV, so we settled ourselves on the sofa and turned on the set. All of the stations broadcasted in Russian. We watched the images and tried to guess the story lines of the shows. When we grew tired of doing this, we went upstairs to our rooms and retired to bed.

The next morning, a staff member from the school came to the villa and conducted an orientation. We were given litera- ture that included information on the history of the Soviet Union, the history of Russia, and the history of Moscow. We were also given a Russian primer that contained all the ques- tions, answers, and phrases we would need to know to get by until we became fully immersed in the language. I noticed tovarisch wasn't among the words listed in the primer.

A medical team came to give us an examination. They con- ducted a routine physical with each of us and then drew blood.

We were told that we were being tested for malaria, typhoid, yellow fever, and HIV-AIDS, which was still a relatively new disease with a heavy stigma.

When they'd informed us that we would be staying at the villa while the school got things in order for us, we assumed it would be for a day or two. Little did we know that we would be sequestered in that house for two whole weeks. While we were waiting to begin our courses, the administration was waiting for the results of our medical tests, specifically the HIV-AIDS test, before allowing us into the general population.

There was another group of Ghanaian students staying in a villa that was not too far from ours. We'd seen them at the airport in Accra and had even flown to Russia on the same plane with them. They had also been brought to Russia to attend the Institute of Social Sciences, but they were enrolled in a different programme, so our groups were kept separate. We heard that one of the boys from the other group was sent back to Ghana because he had tested positive for HIV.

During our stay at the villa, the boys from my group took the opportunity to get to know one another. We were each from a different part of Ghana. Nii was from the Greater Accra Region. Osei was from the Brong-Ahafo Region. Longi was from the Upper West Region. Mensah was from the Eastern Region, and I was from the Northern Region.

We played table tennis and billiards and taught ourselves to ski. Since we weren't able to understand anything on TV, we spent our evenings practising the Russian terms that were in our primer.

Kak tebya zovut? What is your name?

Menya zovut John. My name is John.

Kak dela? How are you?

Spasibo horosho. A u vas? I am fine. And you?

Ya iz Ghana. I am from Ghana.

The phrase that we used most in the beginning months of our stay was *Ya ne ponimayu.* I do not understand.

AFTER ALL OF US IN my group had received our medical clearance, we were discharged from the villa and taken to the school. In the two weeks we had been in the Soviet Union, we hadn't been allowed to leave the grounds of the villa. We were all excited that we would finally be able to see Moscow, and what a sight it was. We were amazed at the trams and how they used the roads. They would even stop at traffic lights, just like cars. I had been diligently reading the literature we'd been given about the state and the city, but nothing in those pages prepared me for the beauty and intricacy of the architecture.

Driving through Moscow was like stepping into the history books I'd read during my undergraduate years. The buildings looked ancient, as though they were remnants of civilisations long gone. You could detect the influences of other cultures in the columns, the arches, the domes, and the gables.

I was especially taken by the Russian Orthodox churches, all of which were built in a classical style, with a cross that was affixed to the domed top. I later learned that because socialism discouraged organised religion, those churches did not have active congregations worshipping in them. They were all empty, but the state maintained them as museums and organised tours for visitors and locals to showcase Russian history and culture.

There was a small park in front of the Institute of Social Sciences that was well manicured and serene, with several benches situated throughout. The trees in the park had tall trunks and their branches spread so high up that if you stood on a bench and stretched your arms toward them, you'd barely be able to graze a leaf with your fingertips. In Ghana, the only places you could find trees like that were in the forests. The trees in the villages and urban areas had branches that were low enough to climb without any propping.

The school building was massive. It occupied an entire city block and was several storeys high. It was rectangular in shape and had a courtyard in the middle. One wing of the structure served as a dormitory. Our lecture halls were in another wing. In yet another wing were the administrative offices and a caf- eteria. There were also recreational facilities: a sports gym, table tennis, basketball courts, and badminton courts. The building had a post office, a small grocery, a café, a hair salon, a barbershop, and a clothing shop. It was astounding: a city within a city, with everything a person could possibly need.

After having been kept in that villa for two weeks, we were eager to start taking classes and interacting with other stu- dents. We were provided with a translator, a beautiful young woman named Natalya who spoke English well and helped us to understand both the language and the culture.

The academic day began at nine A.M., right after breakfast, and went until two P.M. Our first class of the day was phi- losophy. It was taught by Mr. Gudoshnik, a sixty-some- year-old man who wore crumpled wool sweaters, had a full head of wild, wiry white hair, and brought to mind Albert Einstein.

"Dobroe utro," he said that first day. Good morning. He told us he was happy to welcome us to his class on philosophy, but unfortunately, he wasn't sure what to teach us.

"We have a curriculum," Mr. Gudoshnik assured us, "in which we have various topics, but right now we ourselves are questioning the whole basis of our philosophy." The entire class fell silent. I asked Natalya to repeat what she had just translated because I was sure I had misheard. When she did, I was disappointed. I had been anticipating in-depth explanations and conversations on dialectical materialism, anarchism, and Berdyaev's brand of existentialism. If Mr. Gudoshnik wasn't going to be teaching us those schools of thought, then what would he be teaching us?

"I suppose what we will have to do in this course is learn from each other," Gudoshnik continued, as if reading my mind. "Which of you has studied philosophy before?" As soon as the translation came out of Natalya's mouth, I raised my hand. I had studied aspects of philosophy in my undergraduate history courses, and I had read philosophy widely on my own, especially when I had borrowing privileges from the personal library of Mr. Wentum.

Mr. Gudoshnik asked me to talk a bit about the philosophy I'd studied. I gave a brief rundown. He seemed surprised by how much I knew about Russian philosophers. He pulled out a sheet of paper and started to read, item by item, what had once been the curriculum of his class. He suggested that instead of him teaching us those topics and the different schools of thought as unassailable pillars, he wanted simply to present them and for us to discuss them in a modern context and a questioning manner. That class, and the events that were tak-

ing place in the Soviet Union, challenged my idealised view of
socialism.

IN 1985, THE YEAR BEFORE I travelled to Russia to study at the
Institute of Social Sciences, Mikhail Gorbachev came into
power as the general secretary of the Communist Party of the
Soviet Union. The Soviet Union that Mr. Gorbachev inherited
was on the verge of economic collapse. Alcohol abuse was rampant, and it directly affected the productivity of the workforce.
Industrial and agricultural output was in decline. The Soviet
Union was in the midst of a conflict in Afghanistan that was
regarded in the Western world as its version of a Vietnam War.

Mr. Gorbachev set the rejuvenation of economic growth as
his immediate priority. He decreased the number of shops that
sold liquor and made it less accessible by banning its sale after
two P.M. Those actions had a noticeable impact on productivity. The overall morale of workers began to lift. This im-
provement was all but overshadowed in early 1986 when there
was a nuclear spill in Ukraine at the Chernobyl nuclear power
plant. The accident was the worst of its kind in history, and
the damage was widespread. The explosions and fires polluted
the air in most of the Soviet Union and parts of Europe with
radioactive materials.

The overall death toll from the Chernobyl accident was in
the hundreds of thousands. There were people who died as a
direct result of the explosions and fires and people who died
as a result of the cancers attributed to their exposure to the
radioactive substances leaked into the environment. Hundreds

of thousands of people had to be resettled. The cleanup placed a tremendous financial strain on the Soviet Union's already ailing economy. It was a disastrous situation.

The Soviet government had long been accused by the international community of being overly secretive. They refused to reveal even the most rudimentary information about everything from aircraft disasters to their space programme. The Chernobyl accident brought these accusations to the fore. It took several days for the Kremlin, the seat of government, to acknowledge what had happened at Chernobyl, and weeks for Mr. Gorbachev to issue a public statement. The Western media called it a cover-up. In order to negate this perception, Mr. Gorbachev made the unprecedented move of giving the international community access to all the information pertaining to the nuclear accident and to all the officials in charge of the plant and the cleanup efforts.

The accident at the Chernobyl nuclear power plant exposed a lot of the weaknesses and inefficiencies of the Soviet administration, and it paved the way to Mr. Gorbachev's introduction of the policy of *perestroika*, or restructuring, as the word is officially defined. It was a controversial policy that met with a tremendous amount of criticism and resistance, but Mr. Gorbachev persisted. As part of this restructuring, the three primary arms of the state authority—Gosplan, Gossnab, and Gosbank—were reformed. Gosplan was the state planning committee; Gossnab was the state committee for material technical supply; and Gosbank was the state bank.

ONE OF THE THINGS I had been looking forward to leaving behind in Ghana was the practice of queuing. We had to queue
for everything from transportation to toilet roll. I was shocked
to discover that queuing was a part of daily life in Russia as
well. There was a perpetual shortage of supplies there. It was
common to see long queues in front of government shops. We
had to queue for meat at the butcher shop. We had to queue
for bread at the bakery. We even had to queue for alcohol.

I began to explore Moscow and would often use the public
transit system to go to other parts of the city. The metro in
Moscow was designed like a compass. There were lines that ran
from north to south and lines that ran from east to west, north-
east to southwest, and northwest to southeast. There was another line that followed a circular route and intersected with all
the other lines. The trains were painted red and white and were
on time, all the time. The stations were spacious and clean, and
each one had unique artwork and architecture inside.

Longi and I had befriended a young lady named Maria. She
was a Russian of German origin, and one of her life's goals was
to travel to Germany. Soviet citizens were not permitted to
leave the Union without permission from the government. This
was a sore point with Maria, who didn't take kindly to her
movements being monitored or restricted by the government.

Maria had completed a polytechnic programme, but she
hadn't started working yet. She was waiting for the government to assign her to a post. That was something she didn't
take kindly to, either.

"Why must they dictate where I should work?" she asked.

She felt that the entire socialist system was flawed. She
thought it limited people's ability to develop their potential.

Maria and I would get into long discussions about the positives and negatives of socialism. We had differing opinions on the subject, but I respected her point of view and took her complaints seriously, because whereas I had only read and talked about socialism, she had lived the reality of it her whole life.

It wasn't just Maria who expressed bitterness at the system. A lot of the young people I met also felt it was rotten. They spoke of how the people at the top, in leadership, enjoyed all of the privileges and how the regular people suffered. They were frustrated and felt that something had to eventually give. They couldn't go on like that. The way they spoke of the Soviet Union made it sound more like a society on the verge of a revolution, not a society that had been created as a result of a revolution.

On the weekends Maria would pick up Longi and me, and we would walk with her to the Aeroport metro station, down the road from our school, and hop on a train to wherever she was taking us that day. She showed us some of the landmarks in Moscow; we toured several museums; we even went to the Kremlin. She also took us to visit her friends and relatives. That's how Longi and I learned how to drink vodka Russian style.

Alcohol was served at most dinners, celebrations, and other social gatherings, and vodka was the preferred spirit. It was normally served in shot glasses. The host or hostess would fill up the glass, and the only time you were supposed to drink was after someone had proposed a toast. The more people toasted, the more you were able to drink. We'd toast just about anything, from perestroika to a babushka's bottom, so we could drink and drink until we were overly toasted.

One weekend, Maria took us to the Pushkin Museum of Fine Arts. It was named after Aleksander Pushkin, a poet of black lineage who is considered the father of the Russian language. Unlike the National Pushkin Museum in St. Petersburg, which I never, unfortunately, had a chance to visit, this museum was filled with European artwork and, other than its name, contained nothing at all that was dedicated to the memory of Pushkin's life or his work. I had read about Pushkin before travelling to Russia and thought his racial background was unique, but while living in Moscow, I noticed that there were a fair number of black people in Russia. A lot of them were students, but some were native to Russia and had family histories that resembled Pushkin's.

There were occasional reports about African students who'd been harassed or beaten by racist Russians. The Russians I met and interacted with never expressed any hostility, and in the two years I was there I had only one encounter that could be classified as racist.

Maria, Longi, and I were hanging out at the park in front of the school. We were engaged in one of our usual conversations about politics when three young men in their late teens or early twenties came walking by. They looked at us sitting in the park chatting away. Each of them made a remark in Russian that was directed to Maria. My knowledge of the language had expanded beyond the phrases that were in the primer we'd been given, but I wasn't proficient enough to be able to translate what the boys said.

Anger resides in tone, not just words, so when Maria responded to their remarks I could tell she was furious. The boys had already walked past us when she said what she had to say, but her words made them stop in their tracks, then turn around. They entered the park and started walking toward Maria as though this time they were going to direct more than words at her. Longi and I quickly stood up and grabbed Maria and pulled her with us out of the park. She tried to pull away from us. She seemed determined to confront the boys, but we wouldn't let her go. One of the boys had a pocketknife, which he took out as he got closer to us. Maria must have seen the knife too because she stopped resisting our attempts to tug at her arms and voluntarily joined Longi and me as we hurried into the school building.

"What did they say to you?" I asked once we were inside. Initially she wouldn't tell us.

"Maria, what did they say?" Longi pleaded.

She told us they had called her a whore and said they hoped she was enjoying having sex with her black monkeys. Longi and I were stunned. Monkeys? Neither he nor I asked Maria what she'd said to them by way of a response.

MIKHAIL GORBACHEV'S POLICY OF *perestroika* included an attempt to infuse socialism with elements of democracy, especially in the economic and governmental systems. The term that was coined for this process was *demokratizatsiya*. There was only one political party in the Soviet Union, the Communist Party. Though that would remain the same, Gorbachev proposed that the Union begin holding multicandidate elections. He also proposed the appointment of nonparty members to government positions. This, it was argued, would decrease the amount of corruption in the Communist Party and the abuses of power that took place in the Central Committee.

Previously, there had been no consequences for state-run enterprises that did not operate effectively. Perestroika changed that. Mr. Gorbachev removed their state subsidies and announced that these enterprises would now be self-financing, and in order to do that, they would have to make sure they turned a profit. If they failed to do so, they would be declared bankrupt and forced to stop operations.

Before perestroika, the materials the state-run enterprises utilised had been allocated with coupons. It was similar to the chit system that had been in place in Ghana and had created the culture of *kalabule*. Under perestroika, the enterprises would start functioning in an open market. They would use the income from their profits to purchase their own producer goods.

Since the 1930s, Gosbank had been the only financial institution in the Soviet Union. The policy of perestroika did away with that monopoly and allowed the establishment of new banks, ones that would also operate on a profit-and-loss basis. If the enterprises were unable to fully finance their purchases of producer goods with their profits, they could go to a bank and secure a loan.

These were radical shifts in the system under which the Soviet Union had been functioning since its formation. Some argued that it was moving the Union toward capitalism, which was antithetical to socialism. Others argued that the changes were necessary. We discussed and debated the different sides of these arguments in Mr. Gudoshnik's class. I was energised by the conversations we had in that class and by how far apart

302 MY FIRST COUP D'ETAT

the Soviet Union I'd idealised was from the Soviet Union I'd encountered.

It was an interesting, and perfect, time for me to have landed in Moscow. Had I not been living and going to school in the Soviet Union, I might very well have been disillusioned by perestroika and demokratizatsiya and the changes that came as a result. Being there, I saw firsthand how in practical terms the socialism by which the Soviet Union was being governed did not automatically guarantee that people's lives were either productive or dignified. This adjusted understanding of socialism began to move me away from a devotion to any one ideology or archetype. It, along with the discussions in Mr. Gudoshnik's class, encouraged me to use my own judgment, to formulate my own political stance.

Many politicians and historians use the collapse of the Soviet Union as a marker for the end of the Cold War. I believe that by the time Mr. Gorbachev and U.S. president Ronald Reagan came together in Reykjavík for talks on the issue of weapons reduction and subsequently signed the Intermediate-Range Nuclear Forces Treaty in Geneva the following year, the Cold War was effectively coming to an end.

When I received my degree in 1988 from the Institute of Social Sciences, Mr. Gorbachev was taking a further step toward transforming the Soviet Union by introducing the policy of *glasnost*, or openness, which promoted transparency, abolished censorship, and offered freedom of information to citizens about the government's activities.

Just as the Soviet Union had changed significantly during the two years I'd spent there, I had also changed. I no longer believed in absolutes. Since their inception, younger nations like Ghana had in some fashion been emulating or replicating the political models of the two superpowers, the United States and the Soviet Union. I now realised that even they didn't have the answers. They were still trying, to borrow a phrase from the preamble of the United States Constitution, "to form a more perfect union." Ghana was no different, and for me or anybody else to expect it to achieve that perfection after just thirty-one years of independence was to deny it the right to grow and learn on its own terms, based on its own potential and needs. Dr. Kwame Nkrumah said, "The best way to learn to become an independent sovereign state is to be an independent sovereign state."

Positive changes were already taking place in Ghana. In the letters my brothers wrote to me, they would tell me about how much better Ghana had gotten, how many of the difficulties we'd once faced had become a thing of the past. Ghana had recently entered into an economic recovery programme with the International Monetary Fund and the World Bank. Food was readily available. Agricultural output had picked up again. Provisions were carried in the shops and markets. People didn't have to hoard or buy their essential commodities on the black market.

The lawlessness that existed after the last coup had been halted. The country remained under military rule, but agitations to return it to a multiparty democracy had started. At that stage, they were merely weak grumblings, but in time they would increase in volume. It was enough, right then, that citizens had started to feel that things were indeed getting better. The country was moving closer and closer to becoming a more perfect Ghana.

CODA: RETURN OF HOPE . . .
ANAA?

THE AIR IN Accra can be thick and moist. When my
Aeroflot flight landed at Kotoka International Airport and
I stepped out of the air-conditioned cabin onto the portable
steps, I could almost see the water vapour. When we entered
the arrivals hall, it was clean and orderly. What I noticed right
away was that the number of soldiers stationed at the airport
was far less than it had been before I'd left for the Soviet Union.
The presence of the few soldiers who were there was not fore-
boding; in fact, it was barely noticeable.

My brothers met me at the airport and we drove home.
They were now living in a house in the Tesano neighbourhood of Accra. While driving there, I did see some armoured
tanks in vantage locations, but I also saw how the drivers and
passengers in the cars that passed by them seemed to do so
without the caution and fear that was once ever-present whenever we encountered a military vehicle.

It's sometimes difficult to gain a sense of how much and
how fast a place is changing while you're still there. Because I
had been away for two years, it was as if I were seeing Accra
with new eyes. Construction was taking place in nearly every

area of the city we drove through. Most of the roads had either been fixed or were in the midst of being fixed. The general mood on the streets appeared to be lighter. People walked with an ease and self-possession I hadn't witnessed in years.

The day after my arrival, I woke up thinking not of my future but of my past. I was so young when that first coup d'etat had taken place, only seven years old. There was still much about that time I did not understand and had never permitted myself to think about.

After eating breakfast with my brothers, I got into a taxi and asked the driver to take me to Kanda, which is the neighbourhood we lived in at the time of the coup. I knew exactly where the house was. It had been pointed out to me several times by different people at various times throughout my youth. I would always look away, as though the very sight of it would transport me back to that day when my dorm auntie took me there to look for my father.

I remember every minute of that day and how slowly each one ticked by. When my dorm auntie and I got to the house and were confronted by a platoon of soldiers, time seemed to stop completely. For years I believed that a part of me, the little boy who did not know where his father was or if he would ever see him again, was arrested in that time and at that place.

Experience and education had armed me with context, reasoning, and words, all the tools I would need to finally sort through the events and the emotions of that day. I had returned to Ghana with a renewed feeling of excitement and expectation. There were wonderful things on the horizon for the country and for me. I could feel it, but in order for me to benefit fully from them, I knew that I had to go back to my beginnings.

When we got to the house in Kanda, I could barely bring myself to get down from the taxi. I told the driver I wouldn't be long and asked him to wait for me. The street was peaceful, not the kind of place where you would envision a military tank or an armed soldier, but in my mind's eye I could see both situated directly in front of our old house.

My memories from our years in that house were still clear. I could remember how inseparable my brothers and I were and how our father used to dote on us. When he came home in the evenings, we would vie for his attention as he was taking off his shoes, talking to my stepmother, and trying to settle in from a long day at work.

As I stood, staring at the house and thinking about those years, a group of boys emerged from the house next door and started playing football. They were small boys; the oldest among them couldn't have been any more than six. It brought to mind my brothers and me and the games we would play outside in our yard. This was before I was sent to boarding school, when our afternoons and weekends were consumed by football and idle conversation. I watched for a few moments as the boys kicked the ball around, thinking how easily that scene could have come from my past. How easily those small boys who lived in that sedate house on that cosy street could have been us, my brothers and me, before our lives were interrupted.

A strange calm fell over me as I got back into the taxi. I had expected my visit to the house in Kanda to somehow release me from the clutches of that coup and its aftermath, but I realised that I was wrong to ever believe that any part of my life had been held hostage by that event. When I studied history during my undergraduate years, I came to understand that everything exists as a continuation of something else. That first coup d'etat was an indelible part of my history, linked to all that had happened before and all that had happened afterward. Trying to erase it from my life would be akin to pulling at a loose thread on an intricately woven piece of clothing; the entire thing would unravel.

MY FATHER WANTED DESPERATELY TO return to Ghana. He was tired of living in London. It wasn't that he disliked his life there. He had created a comfortable situation for himself, one that was anchored by people whom he held dear. Several of my siblings had relocated to London, including my younger brother Eben, who was born there and held a British passport. Along with Eben, Ibrahim, Howa, and Inusah, all part of the younger crop of Mahama children, were also in London with Dad.

Taking refuge in a country is not the same as wilfully relocating there. Perhaps if Dad has chosen to immigrate to the United Kingdom, he would have been content to call it home. For years, he had occupied himself with the search for Samuel, his son who had been taken to London nearly two decades before. That had defined his days, given his presence in the city a purpose. He still hadn't been able to make contact with Samuel, and though Dad hadn't given up hope, he didn't know what else to do. The burden of loss had become too much for him to bear. He wanted to come home.

With Dad's blessings, I wrote a letter on his behalf to the

government requesting a letter of safe passage. This is a document often granted to people who have had to seek asylum or safe haven in other places for fear of their safety in their native countries. In many cases, a letter of safe passage is granted by an administration that has assumed power from a more repressive or dictatorial regime. Dad's case was unique in that the administration from which we were seeking the letter of safe passage was the same one from which he had fled. What had changed were the circumstances under which this administration was now operating. They were no longer a new government; there was no threat of reprisal from members or affiliates of the former government from which they had seized power. The country was moving toward economic and social stability.

In the letter I wrote, I explained that Dad had been living in exile for eight years. He was advancing in age and had no intention of participating in politics upon his return. He merely wanted to be with his family. He didn't want to spend the remainder of his years in a foreign country. I sent the letter off, and we waited to find out what the reply would be.

MY VISIT TO THE HOUSE in Kanda gave birth to a powerful nostalgia. It had placed me in such proximity to Dramani, a name and a boy from long ago that I thought had been displaced, supplanted by another identity. I suddenly had the urge to reacquaint myself with him, to travel backward through my years in Accra.

I went to Achimota, the boarding school where I'd received my primary education. Although Achimota is only a few kilometres from the University of Ghana campus, after I had graduated from the primary school, I never returned, except for the stop I'd once made in the residential area that bears the same name on the way to my interview for the School of Communication Studies postgraduate programme to beg kindness from a stranger.

While walking around the campus of Achimota, I could almost see myself entering and exiting the different buildings. I remembered the lonesomeness of the first couple of years, how I felt untethered, like a balloon someone has lost hold of, drifting out of the grasp of the hands that had once held me. The pain of that separation taught me independence and self-reliance. I learned how to speak up for myself, how to stand my ground.

It was at Achimota that I fell in love with history and with literature. It was at Achimota that I developed an awareness of what politics was and the force with which it could alter an individual's path. Brick by brick, lesson by lesson, the foundation was being laid. The seeds of the life that I was destined to live were already being sown.

From Achimota, I went to the house at Ringway Estates, where my family moved after my father was released from detention. It sits at the top of a hill that in my youth seemed as steep as a mountain. It amused me to now see that it was not even all that large a hill. It was more of an incline.

My brothers and I owned a bicycle that had been broken for a while. I don't remember what exactly was wrong with it, but one of the older boys in the neighbourhood owned a spanner wrench and he was able to fix it. We could ride, but the bike had no brakes. Somebody came up with the idea of riding it down the hill. It was exactly the sort of thrill that young boys live for.

At the bottom of the hill was a busy junction. Just before the junction, on the right side, was a narrow side street. On the left side was a row of hedges that trimmed the yards of the last three houses on our street. The person whose turn it was to ride the bike would walk it up the hill to the very top, right in front of our house. The rest of the group would wait near the bottom of the hill, at the corner of the side street. We would ride the bike down the hill and then make a sharp right turn onto the side street, which was flat, and stay on until we were going slowly enough to place our feet on the road and come to a stop. The next person in the queue would take the bike, walk it up the hill, and have his turn.

When my turn came, I started pedalling as soon as I got to the top and sat on the bike. I pedalled too hard and too fast. The bike was flying. My brothers and our friends who were standing on the corner noticed the speed with which I was racing toward them.

"Dramani," Alfred screamed, "slow down!"

"I can't!" I screamed back. What began as thrill had now become fear. "I can't!"

I saw the side street on my right but was afraid to make that sharp turn because I knew I would fall and I didn't want to get hurt.

"Stop, Dramani!" Peter screamed as I approached the corner where they were standing. "Stop!"

"I don't know how!" I told him. In front of me was the junction. On both sides of the road, there were passenger cars, *trotros*, and articulated trucks travelling at top speed. There was no way I could make it through to the other side without being hit by one of them. All the boys were screaming now, telling me what to do.

"Turn, Dramani! Turn, turn, turn!"

I knew I had to make a decision quickly or else I would be dead. As I came toward the final house on my left, I turned the handlebars and closed my eyes. The bike went into the hedges. I flew off the seat headfirst and also landed in the hedges. The tiny branches and the sharp edges of the leaves scratched all the exposed skin on my body. Most of my injuries were superficial; only a few of the cuts actually bled. Our bicycle, however, was ruined. The front tyre was twisted and some of the spokes were broken. The resilience and determination of children being what it is, within days I was asking when we could get another bike and start riding again.

ANAA IS A WORD IN the Akan language that means "Is that not so?" It can also be translated as "Or?" It is used after a declarative statement, and it is often, though not always, spoken rhetorically. It's an invitation for doubt, for a contradictory opinion. *It's going to rain today . . . anaa?*

I think that following every decision we make is a whispered "*Anaa?*" There is always a hint of doubt, the question of whether what we have said so confidently, whether to ourselves or to others, is really right. Sometimes the answers to that question prompt us to formulate new opinions, make alternative decisions.

My father's certainty that it was time for him to return to

Ghana was followed by *"Anaa?"* Within a couple of months of my sending the letter to the government, we received a reply. They granted him a letter of safe passage. In the letter was an assurance that if my father returned to Ghana, he would not be arrested, molested, harassed, or hindered by any public official. Following that was the request that upon his arrival he report to a particular government office to formally notify them of his presence.

It was this request that made Dad nervous and fed his doubt. In the past when he'd complied with a request to report himself somewhere or other, ostensibly for his "own safety," he had been arrested. He'd left Ghana to avoid another such request, and we soon discovered that it had been the right course of action. All of his colleagues who'd complied with that request had been detained. No amount of assurance could make Dad trust a military government enough to walk into a police station or government office and place himself at their mercy. In the end, Dad opted to remain in London until such time as Ghana had transitioned back to constitutional rule.

In 1992, Ghana adopted a new constitution and entered into an era of democracy and constitutional governance. It was at this time that Dad started making solid plans to return.

I'd often wondered what Dad's return would be like, how it would feel for him to come back to a country he'd been forced to leave at a moment's notice, with nothing more than a hastily packed bag and a handheld radio. Even though he'd understood all the circumstances of his exile, Dad felt that it would be short-term, a few years at most. Thirteen years passed before he finally set foot on Ghanaian soil again.

It took even longer for Dad to find Samuel. In 1996, the

Thompsons reluctantly told Samuel that his biological father was looking for him. I suspect the reason they finally did this was that they knew Dad was battling prostate cancer and recognised the importance of allowing Samuel, who by then was a grown man with a family of his own, to reconnect with his father before it was too late.

The irony of the whole situation was that during the time Dad was in London searching for Samuel, the two of them lived only fifteen kilometres from each other. Samuel lived in West Norwood, just across the Thames River from Dad, who lived in Hackney. What are the chances that they'd passed each other by numerous times on the same crowded street or been on the tube, seated in separate cars of the same train?

In 1997 Mum travelled to London; I joined here there so the two of us could also be reunited with Samuel. It was the first time she'd ever been outside of Ghana. When Samuel walked into the room, he was holding an enormous bouquet of flowers. Mum couldn't have cared less about them. All she wanted was to hold her son, to cup his face with her hands and stare into his eyes, which is exactly what she did. Afterward, she pulled him into a tight embrace, as though to make up for all the years he'd been out of reach, and the two of them began to weep. They stayed that way for what seemed like an eternity, locked in each other's arms, weeping. The entire scene felt surreal, like something out of a film, but the longer I watched, the truer and more tangible their emotions became, and I couldn't help being overcome by the reality of the moment. I also began to weep.

Soon enough, Samuel was familiar with nearly all of his Mahama siblings, and he started visiting us in Ghana, reclaiming his rightful place in the country and in our lives. We have all, at various times, tried to talk Samuel into coming back to Ghana and making it his permanent home. He spends a good deal of time in Ghana, but having lived in London for the majority of his life, Samuel is uncertain about repatriating. I understand his hesitation.

When I first came back to Ghana after my time in the Soviet Union, despite my own conviction that the country was headed in the right direction, my head was filled with whispers of *"Anaa?"* There were times when I wondered whether we were progressing or regressing. Watching other countries in the West African subregion succumb to dictatorships, political turmoil, and civil war, I sometimes feared that Ghana would follow. Thankfully it has not, and never will.

All the decisions I have made in my life were regularly plagued with doubt. It can be challenging to sustain that feeling of hope or the belief that things will turn out for the best. Again and again, I have felt like that boy Dramani, on the bicycle going downhill fast, without any brakes and not knowing which way to turn. What I have learned from Dramani and his experiences—my experiences—is that the possibility of danger lurks at the edge of all of life's decisions. So too does the potential for the most exhilarating ride of your life . . . *Anaa?*

ACKNOWLEDGEMENTS

Without the assistance, encouragement, and goodwill of various individuals, this book might never have been completed. It is my privilege to be able to acknowledge their input and express my gratitude.

Thank you to:

Cindy Spiegel, my new friend, for assuring me that there was something worthwhile in those initial pages she read and for believing in the project enough to help me find the perfect person to represent it.

Emma Sweeney, my agent, for taking a chance on a new and unlikely author and for handling me, and the project, with such care and commitment.

Catherine E. McKinley, who renewed my faith in that old adage about the kindness of strangers when, having heard about the proposal and sample stories, volunteered to pass the pages on to her own editor, who she felt might be drawn to the work.

Nancy Miller, who thankfully is also now my editor. Nancy was not just drawn to the work; she was deeply invested in its success, so she, along with all the other wonderful people at Bloomsbury, offered it a home.

Both legendary Kenyan author Ngũgĩ wa Thiong'o and Commonwealth Prize winner, Sierra Leonean–born Aminatta Forna, for blessing this, my first literary offering, by providing an advance quote of praise, to which I can only pray that I and the book will live up.

U.S. National Book Award winner Andrew Solomon, for also providing a gracious advance quote. Andrew was also quite generous with his referrals and other such literary resources. I will always remember the fantastic dinner party Andrew hosted for me in his Manhattan home that set the ball rolling.

My siblings, with whom I have had so much fun and mischief and who are relatively easy travelling companions on this life's journey. I am grateful to them for teaching me how to stand taller, stronger, and more united than ever during the most challenging years. I would especially like to thank my brothers Alfred and Peter for allowing me to call on them to ask questions, to fill in some blanks in my memory, and to make certain clarifications. Most of all, I'd like them to know how moved I was that they often altered their plans and sacrificed their time in order to meet the demands of the gruelling writing schedule for what they now refer to as "our book."

Samuel Mahama, my brother, who was taken from the family to the United Kingdom at the age of nine and did not return to us for nearly three decades. He has been extremely supportive throughout. Samuel's presence and encouragement during these months of retelling our beginnings, not only as Mahamas but as Ghanaians, serves as a reminder to me that the circle will not be broken. Wherever we are, we are still one: past, present, future. Thank you for that.

My wife, Lordina, for understanding how important this book is to me.

To my children and the next generation of Mahamas. I hope you not only enjoy this book but that it also contributes to your knowledge and understanding of the family from which you are descended.

Uncle Saaka Adams, the Woribili Wura, who provided invaluable information about my grandfathers and grandmothers, my great-grandfathers and great-grandmothers, as well as about my father's very early years. He received call after call from me with good cheer and was always eager to help. His descriptions of the impact that life under the colonial government had on villages in the north were particularly useful.

Shafik Mahama, Lewis Mahama, and Korama Danquah, who proved themselves to be diligent research assistants in matters pertaining to publication. They were thorough and pleasant. This book has benefitted, and I am sure will continue to benefit, from their hard work. Thank you so much, guys.

Ayitey "Iron Boy," Osman Abdul-Razak, Inspector James Mahama, Pak-Wo Shum, and Kwesi Amoafo-Yeboah for their unwavering support, without which I could not have completed this book.

Joe Mara, William Ntow Boahene, Sulley Gariba, George Abradu-Otoo (Bobby Moore), my secondary school and university friends, whom I called upon to help me exercise my memory and gain the necessary strength and insight to recall and share the narratives of our youthful shenanigans.

Tom Dakura, aka Tom-Tom, whose support for me over the years has been invaluable.

These have been the best and most dedicated friends I could ever have wished for. I feel so blessed to have them in my life.

There were many individuals, too numerous to mention in these pages, whose assistance, day in and day out, made this book possible. To them, I would like to say thank you for everything.

Last but not least, I would like to express my gratitude to my friend Meri Nana-Ama Danquah, a warm and delightful person blessed with boundless energy and enthusiasm. She has been utterly inspirational, supportive, and instrumental in bringing this book together. It has been my privilege to collaborate with her.

Nana-Ama's belief in me as a writer has driven me onwards and kept me focussed at times when things seemed bleak. I have come to realise that it is not enough simply to want to write a book; it is not enough simply to be determined to write a book; it requires you to leave a part of yourself, a small part of your very soul within the pages, and without question, she has managed to help me do that.

I thank Nana-Ama for providing the clarity and direction that was at times needed to keep things on track. I especially thank her for bringing me closer to my siblings during this process, rekindling that spontaneity and carefree laughter we enjoyed so easily in our youth and adolescence.

Nana-Ama has been both adviser and critic whilst demonstrating saintly amounts of patience, coupled with sufficient amounts of coercion. She is a special talent, whose contributions made it possible for me to complete this book.

ABOUT THE AUTHOR

JOHN DRAMANI MAHAMA is a writer, historian, journalist, former member of Parliament and minister of state, and sitting vice president of the Republic of Ghana. This is his first book. He lives in Accra with his family and is currently at work on his second book.

A NOTE ON THE ORNAMENT

The Adinkra symbol *dwennimmen*, or ram's horns, signifies the coupling of strength with humility. Though the ram will fight fiercely against any adversary, it also has the wisdom to know how and when to submit, even for slaughter, when defeated. The symbol emphasises that even the strong must know when to be humble.